Gold Glove Baseball

American Baseball Coaches Association

Charlie Greene
EDITOR

Human Kinetics

Library of Congress Cataloging-in-Publication Data

Gold glove baseball / American Baseball Coaches Association ; Charlie
Greene, editor.
p. cm.
Includes index.
ISBN-13: 978-0-7360-6263-3 (soft cover)
ISBN-10: 0-7360-6263-7 (soft cover)
1. Baseball--Defense. 2. Baseball--Training. I. Greene,
Charlie.
II. American Baseball Coaches Association.
GV869.5.G65 2006
796.357'24--dc22

2006027899

ISBN-10: 0-7360-6263-7
ISBN-13: 978-0-7360-6263-3

Developmental Editor: Cynthia McEntire; **Assistant Editor:** Laura Koritz , Cory Weber; **Copyeditor:** John Wentworth; **Proofreader:** Kathy Bennett; **Indexer:** Dan Connolly; **Permission Manager:** Carly Breeding; **Graphic Designer:** Robert Reuther; **Graphic Artist:** Tara Welsch; **Photo Managers:** Dan Wendt, Laura Fitch; **Cover Designer:** Keith Blomberg; **Photographer (cover):** © Rawlings; **Art Manager:** Kelly Hendren; **Illustrator:** Keri Evans; **Printer:** United Graphics

Human Kinetics books are available at special discounts for bulk purchase. Special editions or book excerpts can also be created to specification. For details, contact the Special Sales Manager at Human Kinetics.

Printed in the United States of America 10 9 8 7 6 5 4 3 2 1

Human Kinetics
Web site: www.HumanKinetics.com

United States: Human Kinetics
P.O. Box 5076
Champaign, IL 61825-5076
800-747-4457
e-mail: humank@hkusa.com

Canada: Human Kinetics
475 Devonshire Road Unit 100
Windsor, ON N8Y 2L5
800-465-7301 (in Canada only)
e-mail: orders@hkcanada.com

Europe: Human Kinetics
107 Bradford Road
Stanningley
Leeds LS28 6AT, United Kingdom
+44 (0) 113 255 5665
e-mail: hk@hkeurope.com

Australia: Human Kinetics
57A Price Avenue
Lower Mitcham, South Australia 5062
08 8372 0999
e-mail: liaw@hkaustralia.com

New Zealand: Human Kinetics
Division of Sports Distributors NZ Ltd.
P.O. Box 300 226 Albany
North Shore City
Auckland
0064 9 448 1207
e-mail: info@humankinetics.co.nz

Gold Glove Baseball

Contents

Preface

Things could be worse. Suppose your errors were counted and published every day, like a baseball player's.

—Anonymous

Fielding a baseball. No other task in the sport is expected to be performed error-free, chance after chance, by all participants.

Hitters get the glory, but need to succeed only 30 percent of the time to earn praise. Fail to drive in a run with men in scoring position? No problem; you'll get 'em next time. But mishandle a ground ball to allow a run to score, and be ready for the boo birds and the bench.

The significance placed on perfect fielding is even more apparent in big games. Bill Buckner's error in the 1986 World Series, for example, was rated the fourth most memorable play in the Fall Classic in the past 30 years. More recently, the eighth inning throwing miscue by a North Carolina second baseman, a fielding error that allowed Oregon State to score the deciding run in the 2006 College World Series, is recalled by more people than any of the key hits that ignited the Beavers' brilliant comeback.

Rare is it for a team to combine both a tremendous hitting lineup and a great array of glove men. One notable exception was the 1976 Cincinnati "Big Red Machine" that led the Major Leagues in nine major offensive categories and also led the league in fielding average that season.

While watching all-time hitters like Hank Aaron and Tony Gwynn is always a thrill, the swing is fleeting. Bat meets ball at such speeds that with the naked eye we're left to appreciate the result more than the execution. Conversely, watching a smooth fielder deftly play his position game after game, inning after inning, pitch after pitch helps us to truly appreciate a skilled craftsman at work. The seemingly effortless way in which a Willie Mays manned the center field position; the imposing backstop presence and bullet-firing intimidation of a Johnny Bench; the jaw-dropping range and flair of an Ozzie Smith at short; the amazing artistry and on-the-money arm of a Roberto Clemente in right; all are examples of fielding at its finest.

Perennial Gold Glove third baseman Brooks Robinson once commented that while a player's bat might speak loudest at contract time, in many games the glove has the last word. And yet, although we know the value of such fielding excellence and scorn errors every time they occur, very little quality instruction and information has been published on the proper execution of defensive skills and tactics. *Gold Glove Baseball* now fills that void as the sport's most complete and detailed book ever focused exclusively on defensive play.

All the fundamentals are covered and much, much more. Like the unforgettable fielder, the book handles all the basics flawlessly, but adds special insights and nuances to reveal how any given position or situation should be played in its very finest form. Each chapter topic exposes the contributor's remarkable expertise to provide the reader a greater understanding of what is needed to achieve such a high performance level in the field.

It's no coincidence that the best fielders and fielding teams also tend to be the smartest players and clubs on the ball diamond. *Gold Glove Baseball* is a unique opportunity to raise your fielding I.Q. and keep Es to zero in your box scores. It's the off-field equivalent to a play you have to make.

Photo Credits

Page 3 © SportsChrome USA

Pages 21, 247 (Coach Piraro) Photos courtesy of San Jose State University

Pages 43, 48, 248 (Coach Smith) Photos courtesy of Baylor Athletic Media Relations

Pages 119, 249 (Coach Weinstein) Photos courtesy of Jerry Weinstein

Pages 141, 246 (Coach Maloney) Photos courtesy of the University of Michigan

Pages 192, 195, 245 (Coach Knutson) Photos courtesy of the University of Washington

Page 243 (Coach Greene) Photo courtesy of Charlie Greene

Page 243 (Coach Bennett) Photo courtesy of Bob Bennett

Page 244 (Coach Flaherty) Photo courtesy of Ed Flaherty

Page 244 (Coach Johnson) Photo courtesy of USA Baseball

Page 245 (Coach Land) Photo courtesy of Carroll Land

Page 246 (Coach Maack) Photo courtesy of Mike Maack

Page 247 (Coach Penders) Photo courtesy of Jim Penders

Page 248 (Coach Stricklin) Photo courtesy of Kent State University

Key to Diagrams

X	Player, base runner
C	Coach
——→	Running path, player movement
·······→	Throw
- - -→	Roll (ball on ground)
RH	Right-handed hitter
LH	Left-handed hitter
①	Pitcher
②	Catcher
③	First baseman
④	Second baseman
⑤	Third baseman
⑥	Shortstop
⑦	Left fielder
⑧	Center fielder
⑨	Right fielder

1

Fielding Techniques

Davey Johnson

Most baseball games are decided not by home runs or offensive prowess but by steady and consistent defensive play. Combined with strong pitching, sound defense is the foundation on which championship teams are built.

Gold Glovers aren't born but are made by committing to practice and employing solid defensive fundamentals. There are no shortcuts to success. Most fans admire the so-called naturals, not realizing these players—Ted Williams, Stan Musial, Roberto Clemente, and Albert Pujols, to name a few—spent unlimited hours honing their skill and outworking their competition. Ted Williams worked to become the greatest hitter who ever lived, and his one regret was that he "didn't work harder."

Never was the need for hard work more apparent to me than in the spring of 1966 when, at the age of 23, I attended my second big league training camp. The Baltimore Orioles roster was filled with stars such as Frank Robinson, Brooks Robinson, and Luis Aparicio. Brooks was a five-time Gold Glove–winning third baseman at the time, and Luis had won about 10 Gold Gloves at shortstop.

But more awe-striking than the Hall of Famers' achievements and reputations was the way they worked at their craft. Here was Brooks Robinson fielding ground balls for over 20 hard minutes and sweating profusely under the hot sun. When I asked Brooks why he was taking so many ground balls when he'd already won so many Gold Gloves, he replied, "That's why I've won all those awards."

Also that spring, Luis was constantly urging me to play catch with him and to get involved in pepper games. About halfway through spring training, this young infielder finally understood that the way to be an outstanding defensive player was to work very hard. That's when I started taking more ground balls than anyone on the team. I was no match for Brooks or Luis, but by the end of my playing career, I had won three Gold Gloves.

The 1966 Baltimore Orioles team won the American League pennant and beat the Los Angeles Dodgers, with future Hall of Fame pitchers Sandy Koufax and Don Drysdale, in four straight games to win the World Series.

The lesson that I fortunately learned early in my career—that success is earned only through hard and smart work—is one that all baseball players should remember. Good defense wins ball games, and to play good defense, you must work at it constantly. Field lots of ground balls and fly balls, make lots of throws to all bases, and never miss infield practice.

Getting a Glove

Players should always have at least two gloves available. Having a back-up glove shows good planning and allows the fielder to use a mitt of his choice rather than a borrowed one. Familiarity with a glove helps maintain confidence. A favorite glove or "gamer" should be used in games only. A second glove is to be used and broken in during practices and throwing drills. Brooks Robinson used the same glove for more than 20 years, but only in game action.

Shaving cream can be used to maintain gloves and prolong their best condition. It contains a very light oil and is readily available in most clubhouses and locker rooms. Some players tie a ball up in the pocket and let it sit overnight. A favorite glove should be more cherished and better cared for than a favorite bat because a player spends more time with the glove.

Taking a Stance

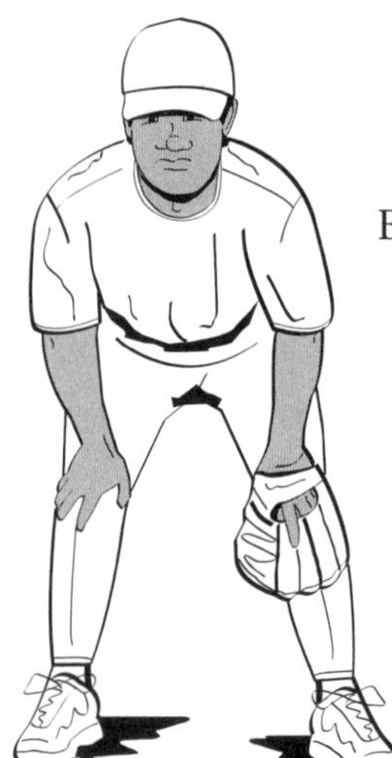

Figure 1.1 The most common defensive stance for infielders and outfielders: feet shoulder-width apart, knees slightly bent, hands resting on knees.

Each player on the field, with the exception of the pitcher and catcher, has basically the same type of stance. The most common stance for infielders and outfielders is to place the feet about shoulder-width apart, with knees slightly bent, and the glove and throwing hand resting lightly on the knees with the fingers pointing down (figure 1.1). When the ball approaches home plate, a player's weight shifts to the balls of his feet, which enables him to react quickly toward the direction in which the ball is hit. Paul Blair, a Gold Glove centerfielder for the great Oriole teams, used this stance while playing very shallow. It was almost impossible to hit a ball over his head because he had great anticipation and always got a quick jump on the ball. This split-second of preparation for movement in any direction is critical for getting that necessary first step to field the baseball.

Brooks Robinson's Stance

A second stance that is also common with third basemen, first basemen, and corner outfielders is called a "walk-into" or "walk-up" stance. The third baseman takes one forward step with his right foot as the pitch is on its way. The left foot should touch the ground at the exact moment the ball reaches home plate. This enables the third baseman to get a quick jump on a slow roller, bunt, or ball hit to his left. This approach was made popular by former Baltimore Orioles third baseman Brooks Robinson, who won 16 Gold Gloves. He kept his hands at chest level, and when the pitch was being delivered to home plate he would extend them as he stepped forward with his right foot. This provided him with great range, particularly going to his left. On hard-hit balls to his right he would often have to dive, make the catch, and make the long throw to first.

The walk-into stance requires a third baseman to be closer to the third-base line because of the difficulty in moving to the right. Shortstop Mark Belanger of the Orioles also used the walk-up move, although his stance was more of a stand-up jump in the direction his great instincts told him to go. He had the best hands at his position and was a major part of one of baseball's greatest infields ever. Left fielders can also use this stance. In contrast, first basemen should start forward with their left foot and bring their right foot forward as the bat meets the ball (figure 1.2). This starting point gives the first baseman greater range to his right. Right fielders can do likewise.

Hall of Fame infielder Brooks Robinson made the walk-into stance popular.

(continued)

Brooks Robinson's Stance *(continued)*

Figure 1.2 Walk-into stance: *(a)* first baseman steps forward with his left foot on the pitch; *(b)* as the bat meets the ball, he brings his right foot forward.

At any position in the field it's important that a fielder move in anticipation of a ball being hit in his direction. A body in motion tends to stay in motion.

Anticipating the Play

Middle infielders have the luxury of knowing what pitch is being thrown to the batter. They can also see the catcher's location, which significantly improves their ability to get the best jump on the ball and also makes it easier to determine who will cover second base in a steal or hit-and-run situation. Failure of a defensive player to make a forward move on every batter's swing is a sign of indifference. If players are alert, they will always take a step in the direction a ball has been hit, whether it's fair or foul.

Keith Hernandez, who played for the St. Louis Cardinals and New York Mets, was one of the finest fielding first basemen in the history of the game. He was so good at holding runners on first base and fielding bunts that they changed the rules to prohibit Keith from having one foot in foul territory while holding a runner. Anticipation was his greatest asset. Seldom in the history of baseball has a first baseman been able to field a bunt on the first-base line like Keith and throw the runner out at third. Keith's anticipation skills were so good that he routinely made plays on sacrifice bunts to get the lead runner at second or third base. His unique ability to assess a situation made him arguably the best-fielding first baseman in baseball history.

Every player, on every pitch, should anticipate the ball being hit in his direction. Any time he doesn't, he needs to be reminded by a coach or teammate. Anticipation is the key. A fielder has to want the ball.

The second baseman, shortstop, and center fielder all generally use stance number one. Any stance that leaves the player in a position to charge the ball or quickly move to his right, left, or back is beneficial. Because the shortstop, second baseman, and center fielder get most of the action, they need to position so that no matter which direction the ball is hit they can get a great jump. No matter what stance a player chooses to use, he should repeat that stance in practice hundreds of times. During a ballgame, fielders must be prepared to react to well over 100 pitches, any or all of which can be hit in their direction.

Positioning the Glove

It's more important for infielders than outfielders to have proper glove position because outfielders have much more time to get into position to make a play. Infielders must always be ready for a ball hit sharply at them. To be in proper position for a line drive or ground ball, the glove needs to be in line with the eyes as the ball is entering the glove. This enables the fielder to follow the ball directly into the glove. Some players prefer to have their throwing hand palm down above the glove (figure 1.3*a*), and others prefer it to be palm up to the side of the ball entering the glove (figure 1.3*b*). Using both hands is extremely important in fielding a ground ball because the

Figure 1.3 Glove- and throwing-hand position when fielding a ground ball: *(a)* throwing hand is palm down above the glove; *(b)* throwing hand is palm up to the side of the glove.

ball might take an irregular hop. The golden rule when fielding a ground ball is that it's always easier to raise the glove up to catch the ball than it is to drop the glove down. The further out in front of the body and the closer to the ground that the player can position his glove before fielding a ground ball, the better. To attain maximum extension of the glove between the player and the ball, the player should widen his feet on the approach and bend his knees.

Glove positioning for the first and third baseman must be immediate because the ball reaches them so quickly. They must try to get in front of the ball or at least knock it down, because balls that evade them have a good chance of turning into extra-base hits.

Ground balls to a right-handed first baseman with a runner on first and fewer than two outs require two different methods for throwing to second base. If the ball is hit straight at him or to his right, he turns clockwise and completes the throw to second. If the ball is hit to his left, he follows his glove and turns counterclockwise to complete the throw. It's common for first basemen to develop the bad habit of backhanding balls even when they're hit straight at them. Fielders should take nothing for granted. They should always try to get in front of the ball.

When an infielder is preparing to catch a ball thrown to him, he should extend both his glove and his throwing hand in the handshake position, with thumbs up (figure 1.4*a*). This way he's able to switch quickly to fingers

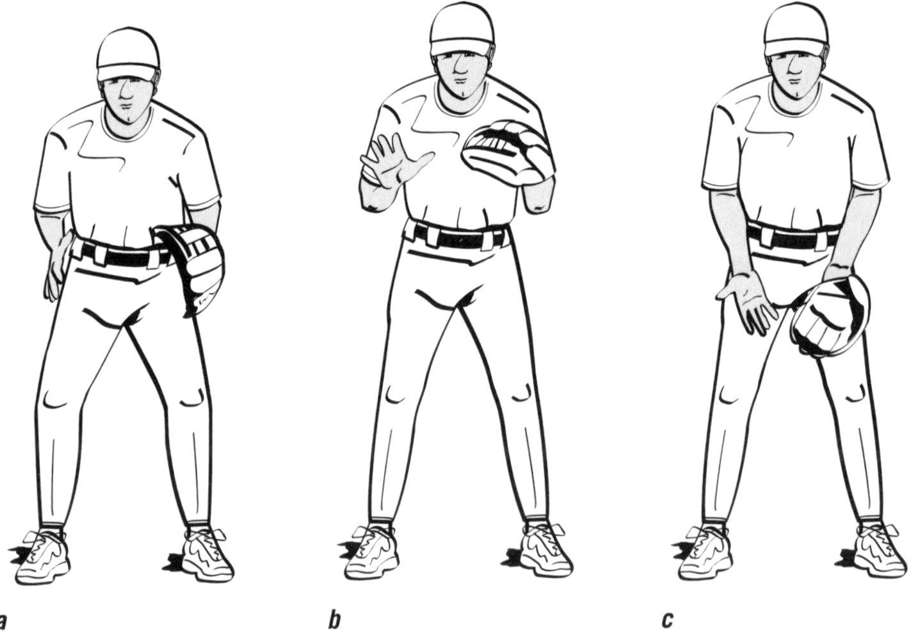

Figure 1.4 Infielder preparing to catch a throw: *(a)* handshake position, thumbs up; *(b)* fingers up to catch a high throw; *(c)* fingers down to catch a low throw.

up or fingers down, depending on the location of the throw (figure 1.4*b* and *c*). If he gets ready to catch the ball with his fingers already pointing up, he would need to turn his hand 180 degrees to catch a low throw. He needs to be ready to go up or down with equal speed.

Moving the Feet

Footwork is extremely important in fielding a ground ball and preparing to throw. After securing the ball, the first rule in footwork is to step toward the target base or the receiving player when throwing. Balance and footwork go hand in hand when practicing fielding. Most errors are caused by bad footwork that causes bad balance that causes a bad throw.

For a ball hit at a fielder, the speed of the ball dictates the speed of movement needed to get the player into position to field and then to throw. Always try to position the ball toward the center of the body. When the ball is hit to a fielder's left, he acquires optimal range by making a crossover step with the right foot. Many fielders take a small step with the left foot before the crossover step to gain extra quickness. Ideally, a fielder wants the left leg extended to give the greatest amount of reach when making the catch (figure 1.5*a*). When a ball is hit to a player's right (backhand), he crosses over with his left leg, moves toward the ball, and extends his left leg when making the catch (figure 1.5*b*). After making the catch, he plants his right foot. With his weight on his right side, he strides toward the intended base with his left foot and completes the throw.

Figure 1.5 Fielding a ball: *(a)* ball hit to fielder's left; *(b)* ball hit to fielder's right.

On a slow roller or a ball that has stopped, the throwing hand should field the ball underneath. To attain the most extension, a right-handed thrower will field the ball with his weight on his right foot (figure 1.6). Conversely, a left-hander will field the ball with his weight on his left foot.

Figure 1.6 When fielding a slow-rolling ball, the right-handed fielder scoops up the ball with his throwing hand; his weight should be on his right foot.

Fundamentally sound stances, glove positioning, and footwork will develop the more a player practices fielding ground balls correctly. Through constant practice, a fielder can learn to position himself to get more long hops, which are by far the easiest to catch. Short hops are the next easiest. All fielders should learn to eliminate the dreaded in-between hop.

On balls hit toward a fielder and slightly to his right, if time permits, he should slightly overrun the ball to the right so he can field the ball while in a position to catch, step, and throw directly toward the target. This maneuver is called rounding or circling the ball.

Catching low throws in the dirt is similar to fielding a ground ball. The only difference is that the fielder doesn't usually have to prepare to throw to another base. Ideally, the fielder wants a long hop that makes it easier to catch and tag the runner. Equally as important as making the play, the fielder must make sure the ball doesn't get by him and allow base runners to advance. There often won't be enough time to move up or back to ensure a long hop to make the tag, so the fielder must catch a short hop and immediately apply the tag.

Throwing the Ball

Obviously, throwing well is key to having a great defense. A shortstop who perfects his throw to first or a right fielder who can pinpoint a throw to the plate are team assets every bit as important as the big sticks with the bat. One vital component of an accurate throw is a proper grip on the baseball (figure 1.7). Hall of Fame shortstop Luis Aparicio, who had one of the greatest throwing arms in baseball history, confided he spent many hours of practice in catching a baseball with two hands and taking the ball quickly out of his glove. His moves became automatic, so that by the time he was in a throwing position, he always had the ball gripped properly across the seams. Luis threw for 15 minutes before every game. He preached gripping the ball across the seams, stepping toward the intended target, and throwing the ball overhand while maintaining balance. This is great advice for any fielder.

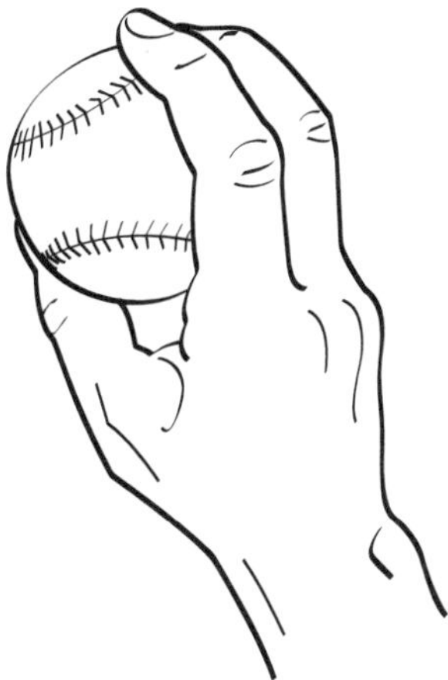

Figure 1.7 Proper grip for an overhand throw.

When a fielder is close to a base, instead of throwing overhand he'll usually toss an easy-to-catch underhand flip. The arm action for the underhand flip resembles a bowling motion. The tosser extends his hand toward the receiver and steps toward him (figure 1.8*a*). The fingers of the throwing hand should end up pointing to the receiver's chest, palm up. The underhand flip is most commonly used by middle infielders on the double play and by first basemen feeding the pitcher covering first base.

The backhand flip extends the hand toward the receiver as the thumb turns downward (figure 1.8*b*). The backhand flip is most commonly used by a right-handed second baseman when he is throwing to the shortstop covering second. When making the toss, the right-handed thrower steps toward second with his right foot.

Sidearm throws (figure 1.8*c*) are usually used at short distances to allow fielders to get rid of the ball quickly. If possible, the thrower should sidestep toward the receiver while making the toss.

A rundown toss provides for a safe exchange of the ball. The fielder holds the ball high and releases it with a push action in front of the body, as if throwing a dart. He should take care not to throw the ball too hard at this proximity to the receiver.

Figure 1.8 Flipping the ball: *(a)* underhand flip; *(b)* backhand flip; *(c)* sidearm.

Fielding Balls in the Outfield

Willie Mays made the basket catch on a fly ball famous, but unless you're Willie Mays this is not the correct way to catch a fly ball. The correct way to catch a ball, any ball, is with two hands. When catching a fly ball, the outfielder extends his glove upward between his eyes and the ball, with the throwing hand about 6 inches from the glove (figure 1.9). As the ball hits the pocket, he secures it with his throwing hand to make sure it doesn't pop out. Then he grips the ball across the seams and withdraws it from the glove for the throw.

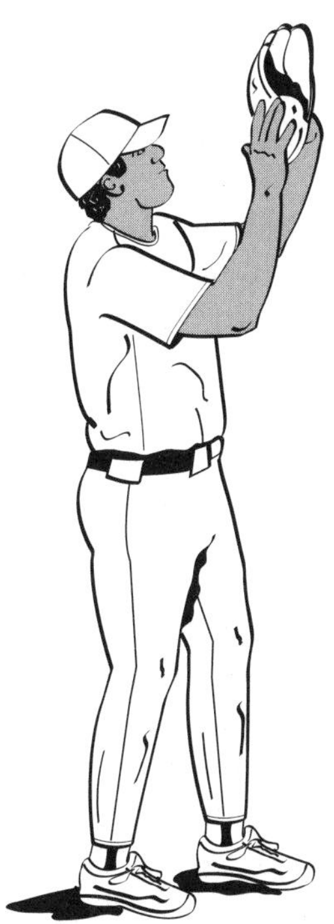

Figure 1.9 Catching a fly ball.

There are two good reasons to use two hands to catch a baseball. First, you're less likely to drop it. Second, with your throwing hand close to the ball, you can more quickly retrieve the ball from your glove and execute a strong and accurate throw. No matter how little time it takes to bring the glove-hand with the ball back to the throwing hand, it still takes more time than it takes when you use a two-handed catch. One-handed catches can lead to dropped balls, poor or late throws, and lost games!

Along with practicing the proper technique for catching fly balls, outfielders must also work diligently on perfecting their approach to the ball. It takes some experience to be able to judge how hard a ball has been hit, and even the best of players occasionally misplay a ball because of high winds. A proper approach to a fly ball makes a successful catch much more likely. When a ball is hit up in the air, the fielder needs to know the direction of the wind and always position on the downwind side of the ball. It's much easier to catch a ball coming at you than one being carried away from you by the wind.

Whenever possible, try to play the ball in front of you, and try to get in front of the ball as quickly as possible. The more quickly you can attain the proper position for catching a fly ball, the easier it is to make necessary last-second adjustments. If the ball is approaching the wall, get to the wall as quickly as you can so that you can make the play while moving *away* from the wall rather than toward it. Sometimes it's necessary to crash into the wall to catch a deep fly, but obviously you want to avoid doing so if you can. A catch while crashing into the wall might look spectacular, but it's far better to avoid the wall and stay in the ballgame. When chasing a long fly, know the width and the feel of the warning track so that you know without looking that you're approaching the wall.

On ground balls hit through the infield, outfielders aggressively charge the ball because the quicker they play the ball, the less time the runner has to advance. Arm strength in an outfielder is important, but runners most often advance when an outfielder doesn't get to the ball quickly enough.

Fielding a ground ball in the outfield is about the same as fielding it in the infield, but misplaying a grounder in the outfield often has even worse consequences. A runner about to stop at third will keep running home if he sees a misplayed ball in the outfield.

Throwing quickly and accurately to the correct base is always important, perhaps especially after a hard-driven ball that has fallen in for a hit. A good throw might catch a runner who has misjudged the pace of the ball and is trying, for instance, to stretch a single into a double.

On this note, all infielders and outfielders should make a point of knowing the speed of opposing hitters and base runners. This knowledge is very important in the fielding of a ground ball, whether in the infield or the outfield. In some situations, such as a slower hit ball that barely gets by an infielder, if the batter is speedy on the base paths, the outfielder knows that he must charge the ball and make a good quick throw to prevent the runner from reaching second base. With a slower runner, the outfielder knows he has enough time to focus on perfect execution before making a good throw to the infield.

One of the trickier aspects of playing the outfield is perfecting the use of the cutoff or relay man. You see way too many overthrown cutoff men in high school and even in college baseball. Missing the cutoff man often leads to an extra run in an inning, and in a close contest, that run might make all the difference. The only time I can forgive a missed cutoff is in the bottom of the ninth with the winning run about to score. Otherwise, there's no excuse for an experienced outfielder to overthrow his cutoff man.

Drilling for Success

Before performing drills, players need to warm up properly. A few minutes of running followed by some calisthenics is enough to get the blood flowing. Stretching releases tightness from the muscles and joints and reduces the risk of injury during drills.

I also recommend at least a few minutes of long catch to loosen up players' arms and to help develop their throwing skills. After players warm up with a partner of similar arm strength at the usual 60- to 90-foot distance, have them extend the distance to 200 to 300 feet. Make sure players use proper execution as they go for longer throws.

Use the progression method (part to whole) in teaching fundamental skills. Start with the basic movements of a skill and repeat them until they're familiar. Don't use a ball until the movements are clearly understood. For example, when teaching the pivot at second base, first have the fielder start at the base and execute the footwork. Second, have him approach the bag and then execute the pivot. Third, place a ball in his glove and have him make the pivot and throw the ball to a screen placed about halfway to first base. Fourth, have him approach the base, make the pivot, and throw into the net. After these four progressions, he's ready for an underhand flip, catch, and pivot. Go for an overhand throw next, and proceed to a full-speed infield drill performed at gamelike intensity. The progression method can be used to teach many skills, including fielding ground balls and throwing.

Infielder Drills

Infield practice is like dancing—if you want to be a good dancer you have to keep going to the dance. Infield practice should include the following:

- Outfielders throwing to second base, third base, and home plate.
- Outfielders fielding sure doubles and throwing to the relay man, who in turn throws to third or home. On the last throw from an outfielder to home plate, the catcher can initiate a series of gamelike throws around the infield to the bases, prior to the first fungo to third base (takes very little time): 2-5-4-3-2 double play, 2-3-6-3-2 double play, 2-6-4-3-2 double play, 2-4-6-3-2 double play, 2-6-2 delayed steal, 2-4-2 delayed steal, 2-3-2 catcher fielding a bunt, 2-6-3-2 catcher fielding a bunt, 2-5-2 catcher fielding a bunt. Finish with the first fungo hit to third base.
- Infielders making two throws to first, two throws to second (double play), a long throw to first, and finishing with a play at the plate.
- Catchers making two throws to each base and fielding bunts with a throw to each base.

Pivot Drill

The pivot drill allows for several repetitions in a short time. The footwork around second base provides some of the most graceful movements in the game. Done properly, the movements are poetry in motion. This drill also helps condition players.

Position half your infielders at shortstop and the other half at second base. Each group is about 15 feet from the base. A coach rolls a ball to the shortstop, who flips it to the second baseman, who makes a pivot and throws to a coach standing about three quarters of the way to first base (figure 1.10*a*). The shortstop then proceeds to the back of the second-base line, and the second baseman goes to the back of the shortstop line. Balls are continually rolled to the shortstop at a rapid pace. The drill is fun for all players and forces them to concentrate. After a few minutes, the process is reversed—the second baseman fields the ground ball and throws to the pivoting shortstop (figure 1.10*b*). Competition can include counting the number of consecutive plays without an error or timing how long it takes to complete a set number of repetitions.

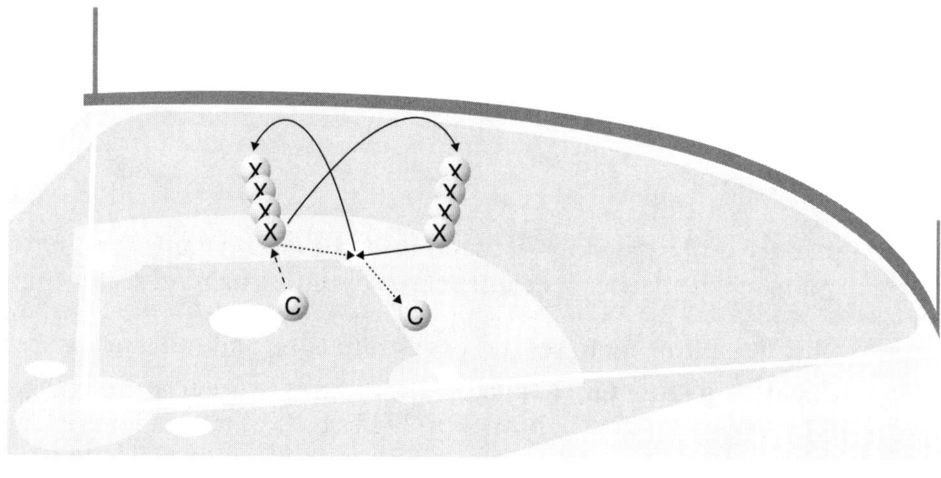

a

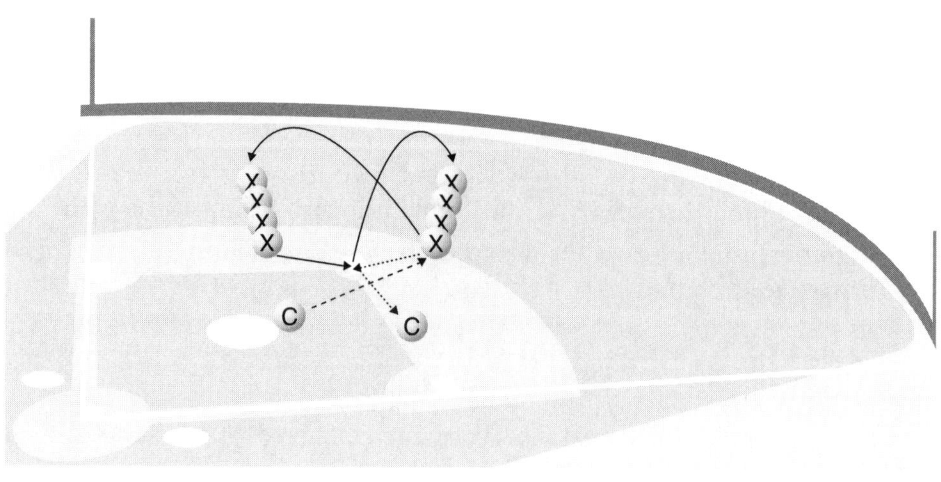

b

Figure 1.10 Pivot drill: *(a)* 6-4-3 double play; *(b)* 4-6-3 double play.

This drill provides a great opportunity for middle infielders to practice the straight underhand toss while stepping toward the base. It also gives the second baseman a chance to work on the backhand flip, which is generally used on balls hit close to the baseline between first and second base. Fielders should step with the right foot to second base and extend the hand toward the shortstop, turning the thumb down.

Diving Left and Right

This drill helps reduce wear and tear on the body when a player dives for the ball.

The fielder starts in a kneeling position with both knees on the ground and the back straight. Balls can be hit to either side of him. He dives right or left to make the catch with the glove-thumb down for the backhand and up for extension to the glove side. This drill should be run on grass or indoors on a tumbling mat to absorb the shock and allow for more repetitions.

Pepper

The pepper drill, which has been lost in many ballparks, is a great way to develop quick reactions. Two to five players participate. One player is the hitter, and the rest are fielders. The hitter hits grounders to all fielders, who field the ball as if in a game and throw it back to the hitter. Pepper trains players to field all kinds of hops and to throw accurately. The hitter can practice his bat control while hitting grounders to all fielders. Pepper is a fun activity and develops good hands; it might be the most effective way to practice fielding short and in-between hops.

Pitcher Fielding Drills

In their fielding drills, pitchers work on becoming the fifth infielder.

Covering First Base

A pitcher's fielding practice usually begins with grounders hit to a first baseman, who then flips the ball to the pitcher covering first. Also be sure to hit some grounders to the right of the first baseman to be fielded by the second baseman. This play results in a longer throw to the pitcher covering first base, making it more difficult for the pitcher to catch the ball and touch the base. Pitchers should learn to catch the ball and tag first base without running near the baseline.

Fielding Bunts

Fielding bunts down the first-base line while communicating with the catcher and first baseman requires many repetitions. Fielding bunts down the third-base line presents similar challenges on bunts back to the pitcher.

The pitcher should never call for the ball but should always assume the play is his unless he's called off by another player. This is an important drill because it enables the catcher, first baseman, and third baseman to gauge the pitcher's range and athletic ability. The pitcher avoids calling for the ball because doing so might keep him from hearing another player calling him off. By repeating this drill many times, the pitcher learns to throw to the proper base.

Fielding Comebackers

Comebackers (balls hit right back at the mound) help pitchers develop solid fielding techniques and accurate throws to the proper base. Comebackers occur frequently in games, so this drill is extremely valuable in developing the total pitcher. Step-and-throw techniques required on a throw to second to start a double play are important for all pitchers to learn and perfect. Throwing to a base or to home plate after fielding a ball is much different from throwing a pitch. The pitcher must know beforehand if he's throwing to the shortstop or to the second baseman. He must make an accurate throw to start a successful double play. In this drill, throws can also be made to first, third, and home.

Outfielder Drills

Outfielders are often neglected when it comes to drilling defensive skills. Many coaches devote most of their precious practice time to pitchers, catchers, and infielders. Often, a pitcher is assigned to hit fly balls to outfielders, and the hope is that the fielders will become proficient after catching enough. This is probably not the best use of your outfielders' practice time. There are better ways to improve outfield play.

Football Pass (Coach Throws)

The football pass drill teaches fielders to adjust their routes to different types of fly balls.

Line fielders up at the foul line. Each player has a ball. The coach stands between left and center field. The fielder jogs toward the coach, flips him the ball, and starts to sprint. The coach leads him by throwing the ball over his left or right shoulder or directly over his head (figure 1.11). The next player in line starts his jog toward the coach as the preceding flip occurs, flips him the ball, and likewise responds to one of the three types of football passes. Players form another line in center field and repeat the same procedure going the other way. Repeat the cycle as needed. This drill is a lot of fun and is also good for conditioning.

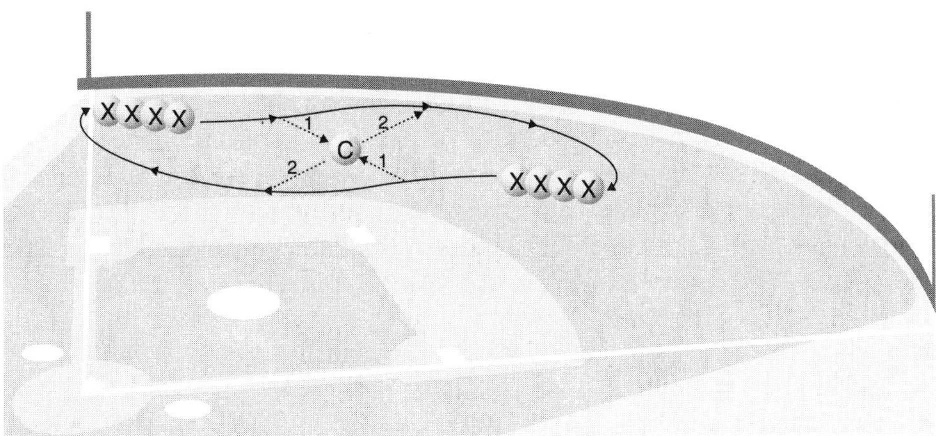

Figure 1.11 Football pass (coach throws).

Football Pass (Player Throws)

This variation of the previous drill helps players better understand the football pass drill. This drill is the same as the football pass with the coach's throw but involves players throwing to each other.

Start with the squad split into two groups of five or six players each, one group near a foul pole and one group in center field. To accommodate additional players, two other groups can line up closer to the infield the same distance apart. The front player in each group starts without a ball and runs a route toward the outfield group or to the foul line. All other players will have a ball and throw a football-type pass to the first player in line (figure 1.12). When the ball is released, that player now becomes a "receiver" and runs toward his opposite group. All groups start at the same time, and coaches keep track of consecutive completions. The competition provides full intensity and loads of fun. It's great for the end of practice because players leave on an upbeat note.

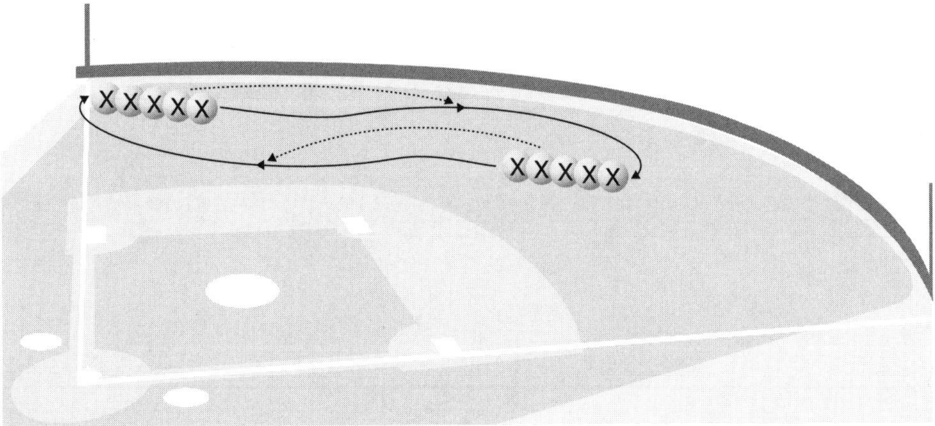

Figure 1.12 Football pass (player throws).

Long Hop

The long-hop drill simulates fielding a line drive on one hop.

Begin with four or more outfielders, two at each end, positioned about 175 feet apart. Players throw one-hoppers to each other. The throw serves as a line drive for the next fielder in line, who catches the ball and returns another line drive. Use a crow hop to add more power to the throw. A few throws each day will pay off in the long run.

Fungo

Fungo hitting creates a gamelike sound when the bat meets the ball. When hitting balls to outfielders, make sure that catches are accompanied by an actual throw with proper throwing technique. Bad habits are formed when players catch the ball without making a throw.

2

Fielder Positioning

Sam Piraro

Proper prepitch positioning is vital to any team's defensive package. The name of the game is to secure 27 outs as quickly as possible. Having the ability, expertise, or good fortune to place fielders in the right spots is crucial to the success of any team.

One of the main duties of a coach is to instill great pride in his players' defensive efforts. Sound alignment certainly falls under this umbrella. The coaching staff must provide proper instruction and detailed reports to players. No detail is too small. Each step is important when placing a defensive player in position to make a play.

Using the Five Factors of Positioning

When putting together a defensive game plan, a top priority is figuring out how to position fielders to cover each hitter. When positioning players, always consider five factors:

1. **Hitter's reputation.** Every hitter has hitting tendencies that inform pitchers on how to pitch him. Although good hitters adjust to different pitching patterns, the majority of hitters follow their own inherent inclinations and perform on a consistent basis. Factors such as a hitter's power, foot speed, bunting ability, two-strike tendencies, and propensity to pull the ball play heavily into any prepitch alignment.

2. **Pitcher's repertoire.** The nature of the pitches thrown is a huge consideration when forming an alignment. The primary factor in this regard is pitch velocity. A pitcher who throws 90+ mph can override the hitter's

reputation as the most significant variable. Other key items that define a pitcher include the kind of off-speed pitches he has at his disposal. How do these pitches tend to move as they approach the plate? Do they sink? Do they tail? Will the ball's movement promote a pull mode for the hitters that calls for the shortstop to shift to the six hole?

3. **Pitching pattern.** When attacking hitters, the pitcher's ability to use location can take the sting out of a hitter's swing. Exposing a flaw in the opponent can create tremendous anxiety throughout a lineup. When reviewing hitters before a game or series, it's common to discuss location patterns against certain players. Game plans revolve around pitching strategy; all fielders should adjust to the pitches being made. Each defender has the responsibility to make the proper adjustments in his alignment. All information should be considered when making any positioning adjustment. Pitchers and fielders must always be on the same page. Pitching to the defense is a sound strategy against most opponents. Obviously, the pitcher's command, control, and consistency determine the success or staying power of this plan.

4. **Pitch type.** At all but the introductory levels of baseball, it's common for all four infielders to know the type of pitch being thrown to a hitter. Usually the shortstop and second baseman verbally relay the pitch to the corner infielders after picking it up from the catcher. This information allows for a slight, discreet movement that can make for a better jump or create a better angle for the defender. Although anticipation or getting a jump on the ball is geared more to pitch location than to pitch type, fielders need to be alert to the catcher's last-second switch to his receiving position.

5. **Pitch count.** Most good hitters make adjustments in their approach according to the pitch count. Thus, defensive players must play every pitch and know the count in every situation. When the count favors the hitter (1-0, 2-0, 3-0, 2-1, 3-1), expect the batter to look for a pitch he can drive or pull. The bat head will accelerate through the hitting area with a little more quickness and sometimes a little more recklessness. This type of contact results more times than not in the hitter pulling the ball. Defensive players should anticipate and adjust to the count unless a hitter is known to hit the ball where it's pitched.

With two strikes, the hitter is more apt to shorten his swing and try to adjust his scope of contact to the middle and off-field. Once again, the defense must adjust before the pitch. An outfielder can adjust about two or three times as many steps as an infielder. He keys on the shortstop's movement.

Scouting Hitters

Where do coaches and players gather the background information they need to make wise positioning decisions? Any worthwhile scouting report contains data to assist in this process. Depending on the level of baseball, you might play the same opponent several times, which will help to ensure the reliability of your information. Plus, scouting reports can be traded with another team; if you need information on an unfamiliar opponent that the team you are exchanging with has played, and if they're preparing to play a previous opponent of yours, offer to trade reports.

To help with defensive positioning, a scouting report should include details about each hitter's scope of contact to the outfield and infield, his ability to go with the pitch location, his ability to drive the ball with power, his ability to drive the ball to the opposite field, and his speed, because infielders should try to keep fast hitters and base runners on their glove side.

Many hitters will pull on the ground and hit the ball straight away or in the air to the opposite field. Other hitters are dead pull, and still others are considered opposite-field hitters. The opponent who creates problems and is the most difficult to defend is the one who can hit the ball consistently where it is pitched. This type of hitter keeps fielders honest and prevents the defense from cheating or overplaying holes or gaps. A good scouting report will indicate and identify this type of hitter.

The accumulated data should be studied and reviewed until the plan is totally comprehended. A scouting report can be extremely beneficial when organizing a defensive spray chart or defensive scheme against a hitter. Each player must take responsibility for knowing each opposing hitter's tendencies.

Figure 2.1 shows a defensive alignment against a dead pull right-handed hitter. In this particular coverage, the defense is allowed to plug the left side of the infield, daring the hitter to use the middle of the field. The outfield has taken away both the left-center and right-center field gaps. The left fielder is poised to handle any contact toward the line. The weak spot in this defense is down the right-field line. This type of shift is designed to take away the contact lanes this type of hitter has continually used.

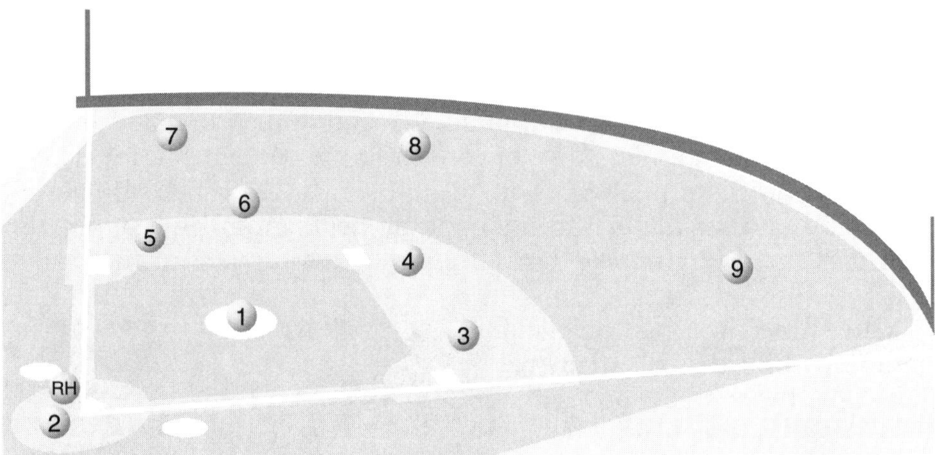

Figure 2.1 Alignment versus dead pull right-handed hitter.

In figure 2.2, the defense is positioned for a left-handed hitter who pulls on the ground but is straight away or slightly opposite in the air. The infield is in good position to take away most contact to the right side of the infield.

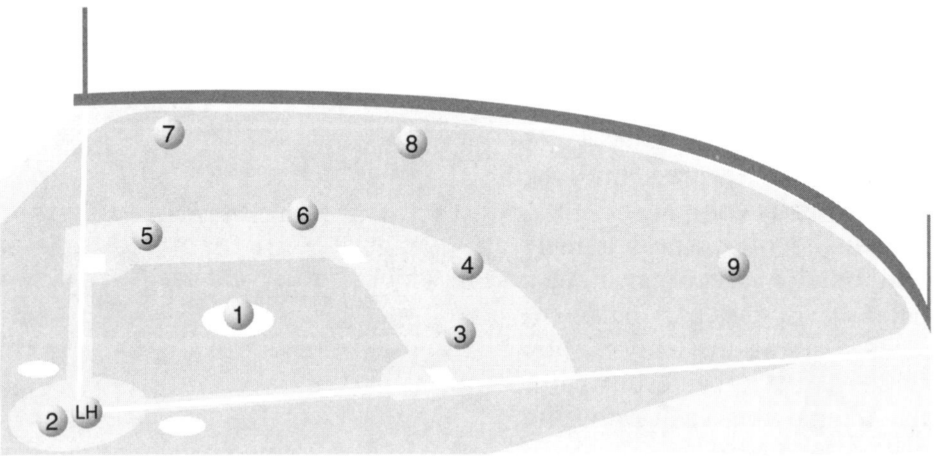

Figure 2.2 Alignment versus left-handed hitter who pulls on the ground and hits straight away or slightly opposite in the air.

The six hole is exposed because the shortstop is shaded to the middle of the field. The outfield is set up to cover most balls in the air that are straight away. The right fielder is covering the gap in right center. The weakness of the alignment is down the right-field line. Remember that most balls toward the lines are doubles, anyway. Try to envision each foul line as an extra defensive player.

Savvy coaches and fielders take all these factors into account. It's very impressive to watch a Major League game and observe subtle movements that reflect these tactics. Each club employs advance scouts who study each opponent and formulate spray charts that relate to each opposing player. The best positioning schemes result from careful scouting, closely observed batting practice, and actual competition against an opponent.

Playing Straight-Up Defense

Many times, you won't have sufficient information about an opponent to make confident positioning decisions. In these cases, at least for the first at-bat, you might wish to play the opponent straight up. This is the standard manner for positioning fielders and is sometimes called the Abner Doubleday defense (figure 2.3). The approach here is to try to place fielders in the best position to defend the field, avoiding large gaps or holes in the alignment. Note that for outfield alignment, second base is a point of reference to help establish a normal starting position.

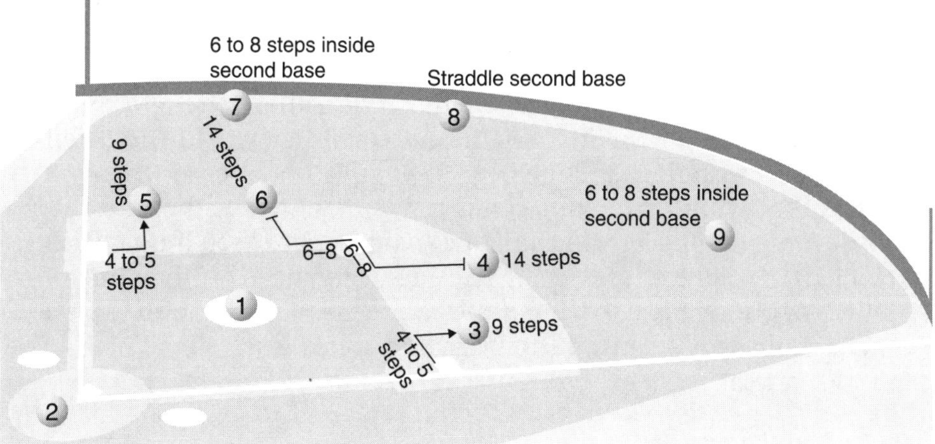

Figure 2.3 Straight-up alignment—also called the Doubleday defense.

Left fielder: Place left foot about six to eight steps to the right of second base.

Right fielder: Place right foot about six to eight steps to the left of second base.

Center fielder: Both feet straddle second base.

Shortstop: Using second base as a marker, walk off six to eight large steps toward third and then walk off 14 large steps toward left field. This will provide a basic gauge for a straight-up position.

Third baseman: Using third base as a marker, walk off four to five large steps toward second and then walk off nine large steps toward left field.

Second baseman: Use the same formula as applied at shortstop.

First baseman: Use the same formula as applied at third base.

Markers are open to adjustment. However, they are excellent starting points to establish comfort, ability, and efficiency when trying to develop the soundest formations possible.

Positioning the Infield for Specific Situations

Obviously, the team that has a deep, quality pitching staff will have a pretty good start to denying opponent's runs. However, defensive performance in key situations also plays a huge role in neutralizing an opponent.

Many different situations occur during a ball game. Each scenario requires a certain defensive adjustment from the standard infield and outfield alignments. In tailoring your tactics to these circumstances, consider the score, inning, game situation, opponent's style, hitter's strength, runner's and hitter's speed, pitcher's strength and consistency, and the defense's strengths and weaknesses. Be willing to gamble on defense when you're ahead and the winning or tying run is not represented by the batter at the plate. Be more careful early in the game—you want to keep the game close. In challenging game situations, make sure everyone is on the same page. Scout the opposing team to learn if they are aggressive or station to station. Evaluate your own defense's strengths and weaknesses. Remember—you can't hide a weak fielder.

Runner at First Base

When holding a runner on first base, the first baseman must line up in a position that will allow him to tag out the runner on an attempted pickoff throw from the pitcher, prevent the runner from blocking his access to a

Critical Situations

To compete for a championship or to have a winning season, a team must be able to stop their opponents from scoring in crucial situations. The times I consider most critical in determining the outcome of a contest are the first inning, any at-bat after a score by your squad, and the eighth and ninth innings.

poor throw from the pitcher, and allow him to release to a defensive position once the pitcher has committed to throwing home.

A first baseman who throws right handed normally places his right foot on the inside corner of first base that's closest to second base. Note that the defender must be in fair territory when assuming this position. His left foot is pointed to the pitcher and is about 6 inches in front of the right foot. The distance between his two feet is 16 to 18 inches. The knees should be flexed, and he should present a definitive target with his glove, providing a focal point for the pitcher. The bottom line is that the first baseman should assume a low, athletic position that allows him the option of a quick tag and rapid movement toward a poor throw.

A left-handed first baseman has a slightly different stance in his prepitch position. He also aligns his right foot near the inside corner that is closest to second base. His heel is in contact with the inside portion of the bag, and his toe points directly to the pitcher. The heel of his left foot is on the first-base line, about 10 to 12 inches in front of the base. The distance between his two feet is about 16 to 18 inches. This foundation allows for the best athletic position for the first baseman to move quickly in any direction. Knees are flexed, and the target is clearly presented to the pitcher. The low position is very important for the quick tag and emergency reaction.

On occasion, it's necessary and tactically sound to play behind the runner at first base. For example, it would be prudent to play behind the runner at first when runners are on first and second, when the bases are loaded, when the runner on first is slow and a left-handed hitter is at the plate, and when there are two outs and a full count to the hitter. Specific situations dictate defensive positioning strategies. The score of the game is always at the top of this list, but many other factors come into play as well.

When playing behind the runner, the first baseman should assume a position directly behind the runner. He should pressure the runner with his presence and execute several bluffs to prevent the runner from extending his lead. Once the runner recognizes the threat and decides to stay close to the base, the first baseman can retreat to a normal back position. By the time the pitcher releases the pitch, the defender should be in an area that allows him to comfortably range.

Double Plays

The execution of the double play (figure 2.4) is one of the most significant defensive elements in the game of baseball. The double play is a fundamental that is practiced and rehearsed every day in practice.

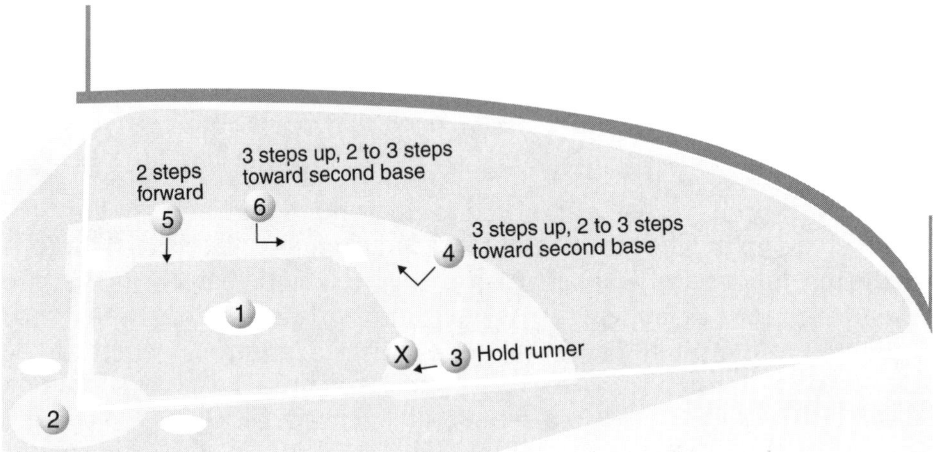

Figure 2.4 Positioning for the double play with runner on first base.

For the double play to work consistently, a positioning adjustment in the infield, especially at shortstop and second base, must occur before the pitch. The second baseman and shortstop form the hub of the double play. They must both sacrifice precious ground so either one of them can get to second base in a timely fashion. How much ground should be sacrificed? Start by looking at a common situation in which a runner is on first with fewer than two outs. In this situation, the following tasks apply:

First baseman: Hold the runner at first base.

Second baseman: Shorten normal positioning by moving forward three steps and moving two or three steps toward second base.

Shortstop: Shorten normal positioning by moving forward three steps and moving two or three steps toward second base.

Third baseman: Shorten normal positioning by moving forward two steps.

Note that a coach should never be predictable in every situation that occurs during a game. As mentioned earlier, the key element in basic positioning depends on the hitter's reputation. If the double play is in order but the alignment calls for a defender to cover more ground, then positioning for the hitter takes precedent over double-play positioning.

Here's another situation in which the score of the game determines positioning. If your team has a healthy lead in the late innings, getting outs is the priority. It's not necessary to surrender real estate just to execute the double play. You don't want ground balls that would have been outs to scoot through the infield just because the fielders weren't playing a little deeper in the middle of the infield. Again, don't become predictable in every situation.

Common sense also applies when dealing with the inning-ending force-out option at second base and the cover man in defending the steal of second base. Again, all of the key factors in prepitch positioning, along with situations such as the score and stage of the game, will heavily influence how to align the defense. Keep in mind that game experience and practice of game situations will greatly benefit infielders. They'll become more comfortable and confident with their decision making. Be sure to give players feedback in these scenarios as they develop during practice and game competition.

Sacrifice Bunts

Properly defending the sacrifice bunt requires a lot of practice and repetition. Prepitch positioning is crucial, and timing and communication are vital in determining who's going to make the play and to which base the ball will be thrown.

As in the double-play alignment, bunt coverage requires fielders to compromise field position. Infielders must place themselves in areas that give them the best opportunity to field a bunted ball and make a play, either at a lead base or to get the sure out at first base. Normally, all bunt coverage is conservative early in the game. Bottom line? *Always* get an out in a sacrifice situation. As the game develops and enters the later innings, more sophisticated movements will occur to foil the advancement of runners into scoring position.

In figure 2.5, normal bunt coverage is in effect with a runner on first base. Note that bunting has been diagnosed as the high-percentage play in this situation. Here's a rundown on the infielders' prepitch defensive positioning:

First baseman: Hold runner at first base.

Second baseman: Cheat slightly toward first base so you can get there in plenty of time, if needed. Also create a backup lane if the first baseman is taking the throw at first and protect against a push bunt or hit and run in your area. Clog up the four hole.

Shortstop: Align in double-play position. Don't take yourself out of the play by vacating too soon. Protect against the slash, a slug bunt, or the hit and run.

Third baseman: Stand on the grass with an angle established to go from outside to in (from the line to the mound).

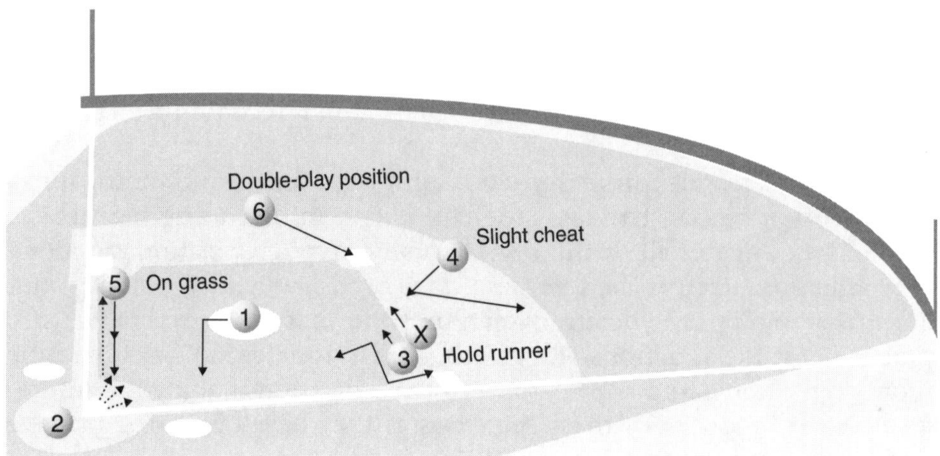

Figure 2.5 Alignment to defend a sacrifice bunt with a runner on first base only.

When defending a sacrifice bunt with runners at first and second base, defenders have three options to secure outs. The defense has a force play at all three bases. As in the alignment shown in figure 2.5, the prepitch fielding position is established because the bunt is in order. The infielders are surrendering their normal double-play positions to prepare for the bunt. Prepitch preparation includes knowing the speed of all runners as well as the athletic ability and arm strength of the defensive people involved.

Figure 2.6 shows the starting prepitch positioning of the infielders. Note that the coverage is designed to ensure an out will always be recorded even if there's no play at the lead base.

First baseman: Play on the grass, defending outside to in. Protect against a push bunt to your right because the pitcher will break to the third-base line. Start wider than normal.

Second baseman: Assume the same positioning as before. Slightly cheat toward first base while plugging up the push lane or hit-and-run option. You must be able to get to first base when the ball is bunted.

Shortstop: Assume the same positioning as before. Apply pressure to the runner at second base to keep him close. Start in double-play position and don't vacate too soon.

Third baseman: Stand up on the grass and keep an eye on the runner at second base. Don't put yourself out of position so that the runner can steal third behind you. Pre-positioning is crucial in this situation.

There are several other types of bunt coverage. The emphasis here is to explain the basic starting points and responsibilities of the defenders. Continued practice and repetition will create a comfort zone for prepitch positioning. Taking shortcuts is not an option. Precise alignment allows for successful execution.

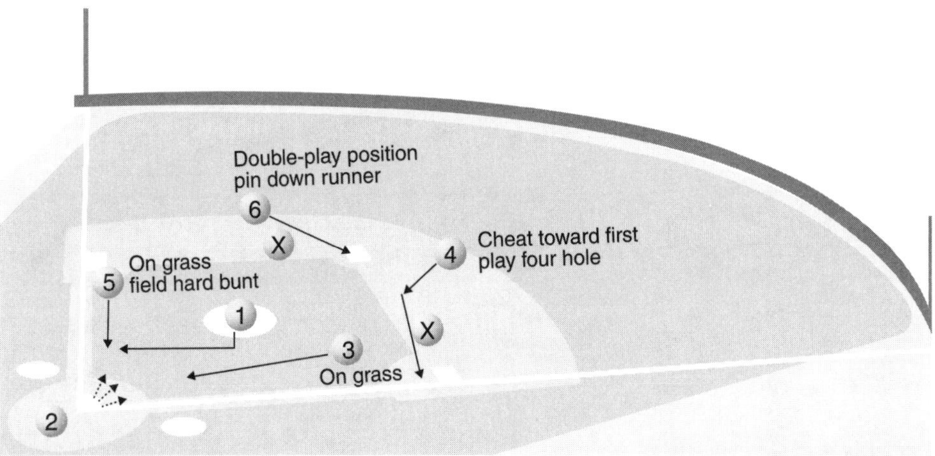

Figure 2.6 Alignment to defend a sacrifice bunt with runners on first and second.

Runner at Third Base

Holding a runner on third base is not like holding a runner on first base. When holding a runner, the first baseman starts at the base and moves to his fielding position when he's certain the pitcher is going to the plate. In contrast, the third baseman starts in his fielding position and only occasionally must field a pickoff attempt from the pitcher. The pitcher can throw to first base at will, but pickoff throws to third base are rare.

One of the most important tactical decisions a coach can make involves where to position the infield with a runner at third and fewer than two outs. A multitude of considerations go into this decision, including the inning, the score, the number of outs, the type of pitcher on the mound, the hitter, the pitch count, the speed of the runner at third base, whether the defensive team is home or visitor, the type of infield surface, and the infielders' arm strengths.

Play the Infield In

Bringing the infield in early in the game is a great risk for the defense because even average or minimal contact by the batter can beat the defense, possibly opening the door to a big inning (three or more runs). When you give up a big inning to an opponent, you place yourself in a vulnerable position. If you have a pitcher with overpowering stuff, the decision to move the infield in is much easier to make in early innings.

A third baseman who is assuming the in position takes four to five steps from the base, positioning just on the edge of the infield grass (figure 2.7). This alignment will prevent a ball from hitting the lip of the infield prior to the third baseman fielding the ball. The third baseman is vulnerable to the high chopper over his head or any hard contact to his right or left. No doubt the third baseman's range is greatly compromised. If the third base-

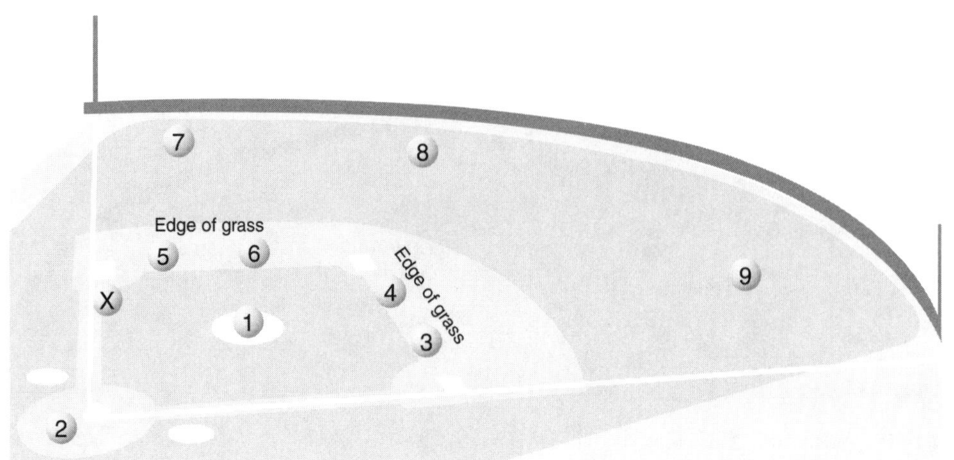

Figure 2.7 Infielders in with runner at third base.

man senses a suicide squeeze, he may alter his positioning by moving one or two steps closer to the bag to hold the runner tighter to third base.

The shortstop uses his normal starting prepitch position. He adjusts depending on the five factors of positioning. The shortstop's in position is on the edge of the infield grass, or even with second and third base if playing on artificial turf. Be flexible with this positioning. A slow runner at third base will allow the shortstop to maintain a little more depth and range. Also consider the shortstop's arm strength and best range side. Does he cover more range to his left or right?

The second baseman uses the same formula as the shortstop. Consider all factors that go into positioning. The first baseman uses the same formula as the third baseman. If a squeeze play is anticipated, especially the safety squeeze, the first baseman should cheat in a little more toward home plate and be prepared to charge the hitter at the first sign of a bunt.

Playing the infield in should be viewed as a desperate measure to be used late in the game when one run may win or tie the game. This alignment also creates an adjustment for the outfield. Because the infield is in, any short fly ball or pop-up will be nearly impossible for the infielder to run down. Because of that possibility, the outfielders will most likely alter their prepitch positioning by coming in five to seven steps, which makes them vulnerable to a deep drive that might have been a routine catch before the adjustment.

The percentages are against you when you compromise that much real estate. It's the responsibility of the coaching staff to take into account all the necessary criteria when deciding to play the infield in.

Play Halfway

The halfway position (figure 2.8) applies to the second baseman and shortstop. This defensive alignment gives them the opportunity to retreat seven

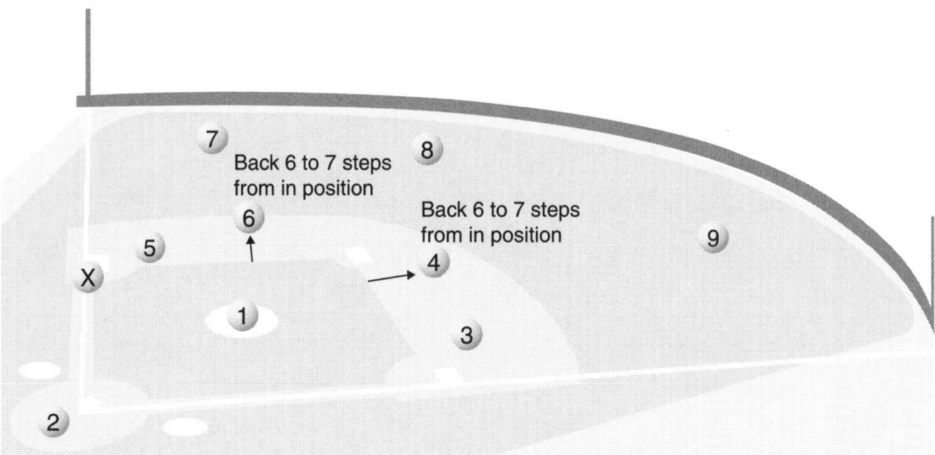

Figure 2.8 Second baseman and shortstop in the halfway position with runner at third base.

or eight steps from the in position. It provides options that don't require infielders to play all the way in. The obvious advantages include added range and reaction time. Infielders will probably still get beat on hard contact to their left or right, but they'll have a better angle on a normal ground ball.

The halfway alignment can also cause problems for both the runner at third base and the third-base coach. When ground contact is made, the runner at third might be indecisive about going home. It's not unusual for the runner to stay at third on a batted ball to either the second baseman or shortstop even when instructed by the coach to go on ground contact.

The halfway position can also provide options for a double play because any hard contact to the second baseman or shortstop permits the chance to turn the twin killing. If the ball is hit softer and is played aggressively, the run can still be cut off at the plate. The speed of the runners involved will dictate whether a throw home is the best strategy.

Guard the Line

One of the most discussed and controversial defensive tactics in baseball involves guarding the foul lines. Many coaches religiously and consistently apply this tactic. They are unwavering in their commitment to this prepitch alignment. On the other hand, as many or more coaches feel this strategy is overrated and contributes more to losses than to victories. Baseball is a game entrenched in statistics and percentages. The beauty of the game lies not only in the odds that everybody thinks they know but also in the instincts and gut feelings coaches or managers employ in every game.

Two basic techniques are used to guard the line. The first positioning strategy is called protecting the line (figure 2.9). This alignment calls for either the first or third baseman to position about 2 or 3 feet off the line,

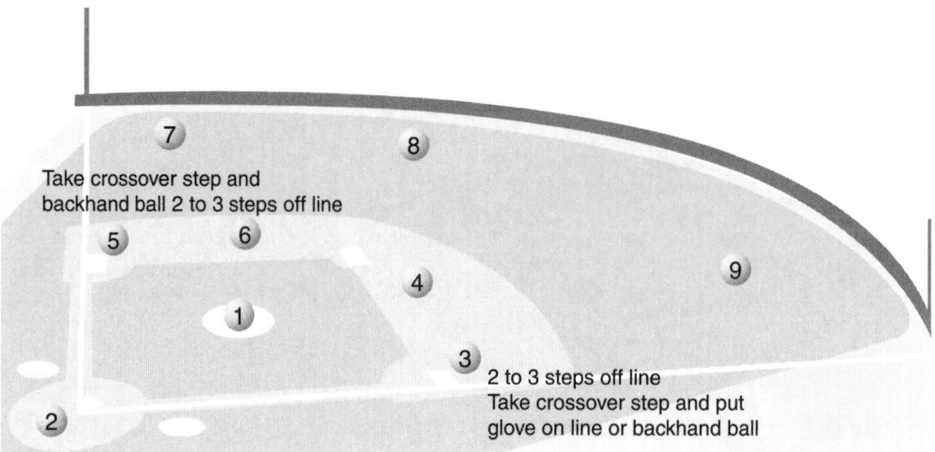

Figure 2.9 Protecting the line.

which allows him to take a crossover step and either backhand the ball or place the glove hand on the line. A hard line drive could get inside him, but he's in good position to field most balls.

The second technique for guarding the line is hugging the line (figure 2.10). In this case, the third baseman's right foot or the first baseman's left foot is in contact with the foul line. It is virtually impossible for a ground ball to get by the defensive player on the line side. Obviously, any decent contacts to the left of the third baseman or to the right of the first baseman will likely get through the infield.

Most coaches defend the foul lines in the eighth or ninth inning, when the tying or go-ahead run is at first base, or when the tying or go-ahead run is at bat.

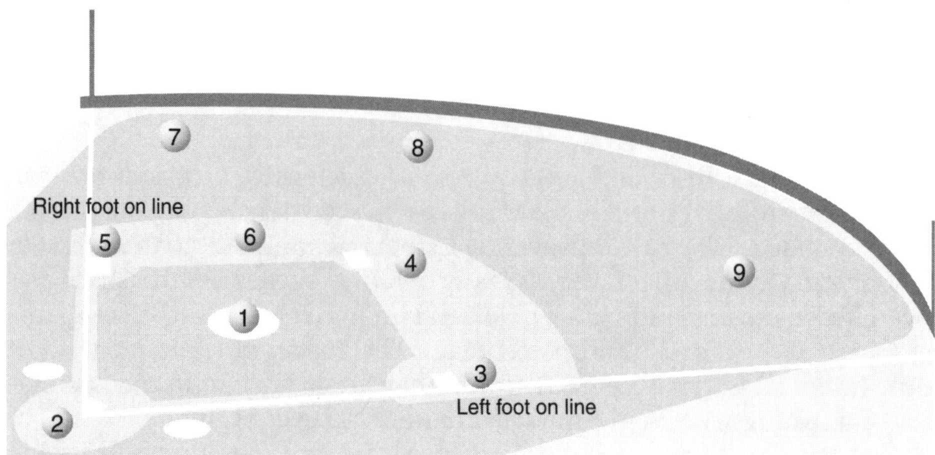

Figure 2.10 Hugging the line.

The number of outs plays a huge role in determining prepitch positioning. Many coaches are reluctant to surrender a leadoff double to start an inning. Others are more concerned with the two-out double. Still other coaches will keep their normal double-play position in order no matter how many outs there are. The idea of missing a chance to convert a double play would keep some managers up all night long!

There's no one best strategy when making crucial decisions regarding playing the line late in the game. The odds are that more contact will take place in the holes rather than down the lines. However, always consider the five factors of positioning (page 19). This allows a coach to be unpredictable and to use all of the data at his disposal. If a coach believes a team will need three singles to score a run, it's understandable that he'd want to guard the line against the extra-base hit. If he feels the contact will find its way to the normal alignments, he must position his players based on that criteria. That's the beauty of the game.

Play a Five-Man Infield

In certain situations late in a game, the visiting team has few options remaining. The scenario usually involves the home team having the winning run at third base with fewer than two outs. The visiting team realizes that the percentages are highly against them.

One of the tactics commonly used in this situation is the five-man infield (figure 2.11), a strategy that forces one of the following changes in the normal defense:

- Bring one of the outfielders in to be a fifth infielder. Some teams bring in the best athlete from the outfield or, in other cases, the slowest outfielder. This fielder positions in the middle of the diamond, just in front of second base on the grass.

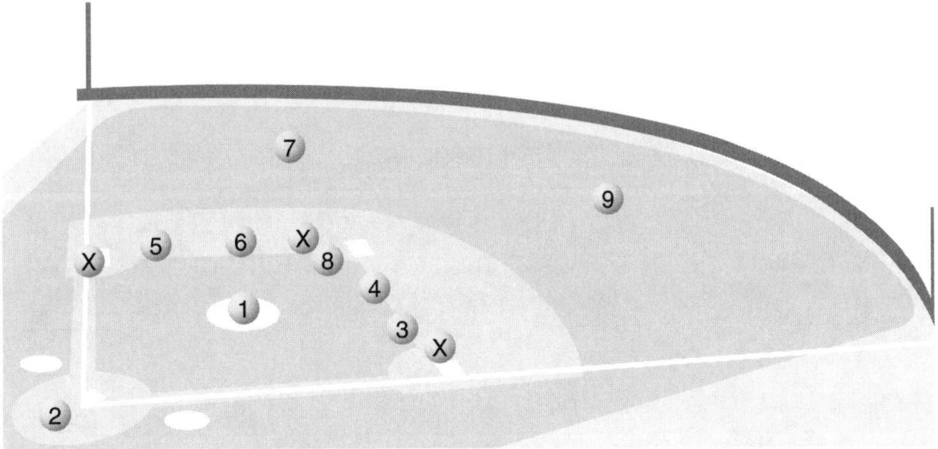

Figure 2.11 Five-man infield.

- Bring in an extra infielder from the bench and replace an outfielder. Again, this player will usually position in the middle of the diamond, just in front of second base on the grass.

The two remaining outfielders split the outfield in half. Their depth is shallow because any deep fly ball will score the runner at third. They try to catch any line drive or short ball hit into the air. How they position prepitch depends on the five factors of positioning.

Sometimes the unfamiliarity of the five-man infield confuses a hitter and he'll alter his swing or chase a bad pitch. The five infielders might also put pressure on the hitter and disrupt his concentration.

Appeal Plays

The execution of the appeal play is not to be taken for granted. It's not unusual to see a defensive team appeal a missed base during the course of a game. Not infrequently, an appeal is voided by an umpire because of improper defensive positioning.

After an umpire has given the defensive team permission to appeal, all defenders must make sure they're in fair territory before the pitcher throws to the appropriate base. Assuming an appeal is being made at first base, both the second baseman and right fielder place themselves in proper backup positions in anticipation of a poor throw. They must not leave fair territory until the pitcher has thrown the ball to the first baseman. Once the ball leaves the pitcher's hand, the defense is allowed to cross over into foul territory. Many attempted appeals are denied because of improper preappeal positioning.

The situation in figure 2.12 pertains to the fielders as they anticipate an appeal to first base. Keep in mind that there are runners on second and

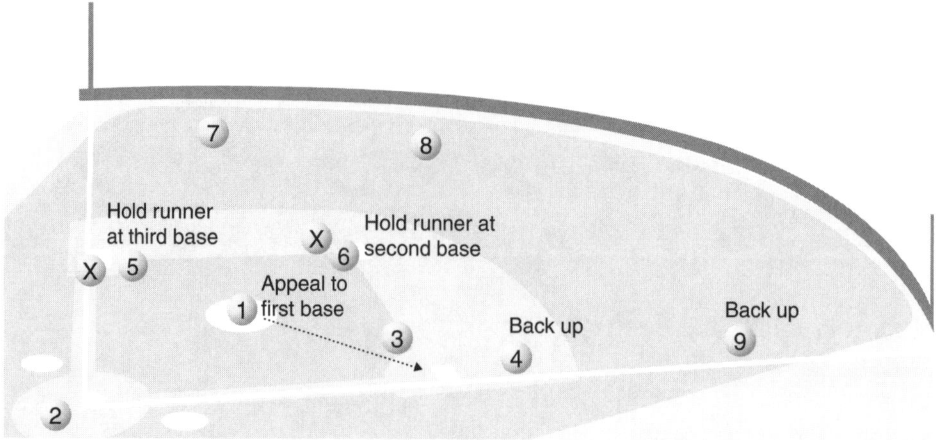

Figure 2.12 Appeal play at first base with runners on second and third.

third. Also note that the third baseman is holding the runner at third and the shortstop is holding the runner at second.

Intentional Walks

The catcher has guidelines and restrictions when a batter is being intentionally walked. If these are not followed, a balk, wild pitch, or a hit could result. After receiving instructions to intentionally walk a hitter, the catcher relays the message to the defense, which creates adjustments in defensive prepitch alignments. Once the defense is in position, the catcher notifies the pitcher of the intentional walk. Assuming that the catcher is right-handed and that a right-handed hitter is up, the following fundamentals apply to the catcher's prepitch position:

- He aligns with his left foot behind the outside corner of the plate and his right foot about 18 inches from his left foot. His right arm extends at a 90-degree angle.
- He cannot shift to his final position until the pitcher releases the ball. If he leaves prematurely, a catcher's balk can be called, and all runners will advance one base. Once the pitcher releases the ball to the target, the catcher can shuffle his feet to receive the pitch, which is typically thrown at about three-quarter speed.
- He maintains his normal depth in relationship to home plate and the batter's box. His stance should be straight up with his knees slightly flexed. He presents his glove to the pitcher with his right arm extended to 90 degrees. As always, he should anticipate an erratic pitch.

Positioning the Outfield for Specific Situations

Don't underestimate the number of tactics related to outfield play, especially late in the game. Various game situations will dictate appropriate prepitch positioning. Usually, the coaching staff assigns someone in the dugout the responsibility of setting up the proper alignment. Waving a towel is an effective way to get the outfielders' attention.

Outfield position strategies are similar to the infielders guarding the line. Consider where the tying run or go-ahead run is, whether you're playing at home or away, the inning, and the five factors of positioning.

No-Doubles Defense

In some situations, outfielders will assume a no-doubles defense (figure 2.13), in which they position about 12 to 15 steps deeper than usual, depending

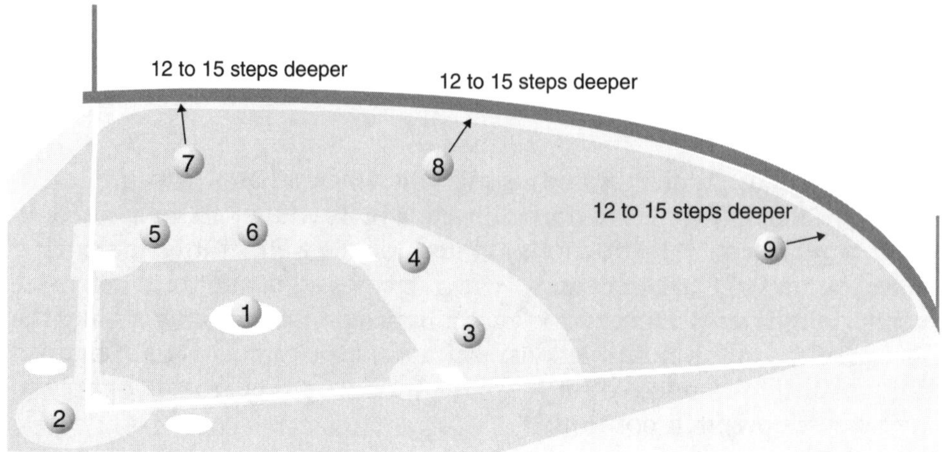

Figure 2.13 No-doubles defense.

on the hitter and the speed of the base runners. Retreating into this defense allows outfielders to close off the gaps and create better angles on deep balls. The idea is to keep the ball in front of them to prevent the runner at first from scoring or to keep the batter from getting to second base. In general, teams won't use the no-doubles defense until very late in the game, although some coaches will try it much earlier in the right circumstances.

Cheat Defense

The cheat defense (figure 2.14), in which all outfielders move up six to eight steps, is employed when an important run is at second base. The off

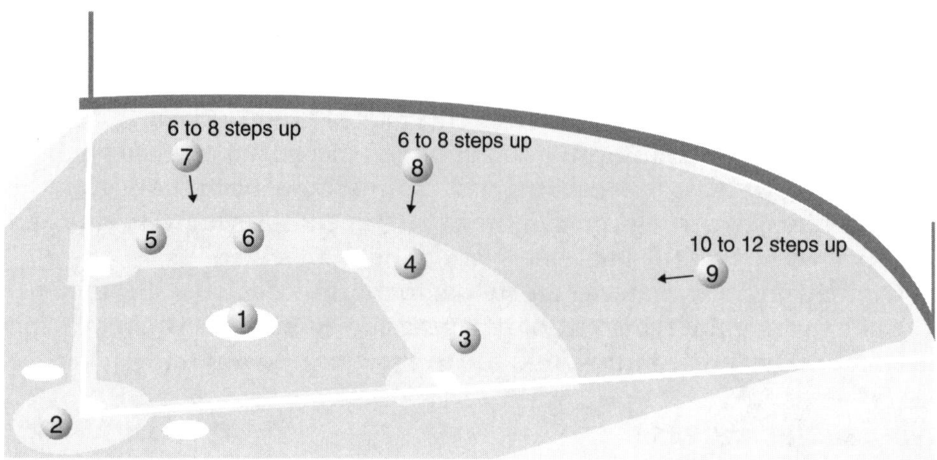

Figure 2.14 Cheat defense.

outfielder (the right fielder for a right-handed hitter) usually moves up an additional two or three steps. In this defense, outfielders assume a prepitch position that brings them closer to home plate. As is true of the no-doubles alignment, each coach has his favorite time to use the cheat defense, but most coaches won't use it until late in the game.

The objective of the cheat defense is to allow outfielders to charge a ground ball and get to it as quickly as possible, which also shortens the throw to home plate. The obvious danger of the cheat defense is that it compromises gap coverage. As always, several factors affect how the outfielders will position. The strongest arms can maintain a more normal depth. The speed of the runner at second base is also a key consideration.

Off-Field Defense

It's common to see a right fielder playing shallow against a right-handed hitter and a left fielder playing shallow against a left-handed hitter. This adjustment is based on the assumption that the majority of hitters lack power to the opposite field. How far up the outfielders come will of course depend on the strengths and tendencies of specific hitters.

In the off-field defense, using the normal position as a starting point, the off outfielder moves toward the plate six to nine steps (figure 2.15). From this position, on a sharp single to right, the right fielder might be able to throw out the batter running to first base. He also has a better chance of preventing a runner at first from advancing to third. The off-field defense is often employed in the National League when the pitcher comes to bat.

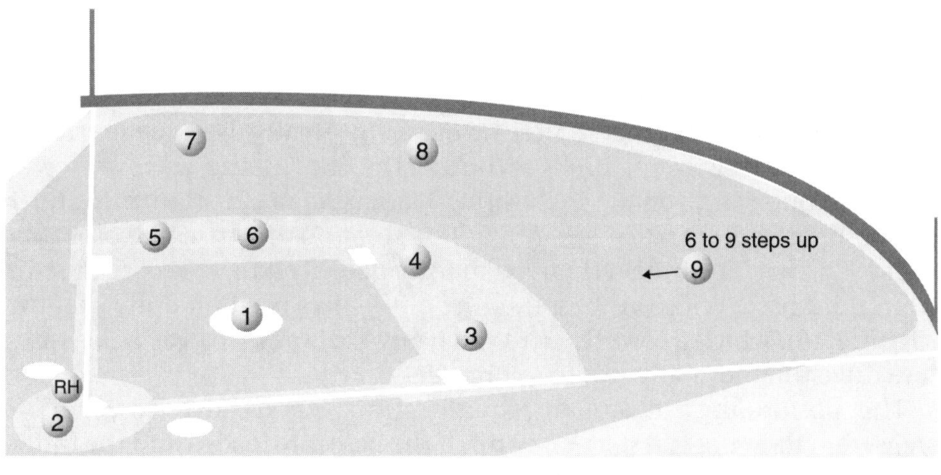

a

(continued)

Figure 2.15 *(a)* Defending the off-field versus a right-handed hitter.

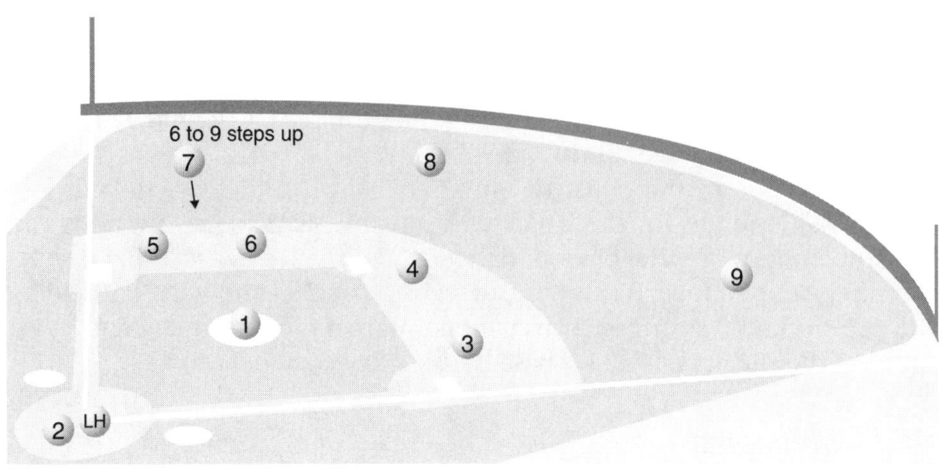

b

Figure 2.15 *(continued) (b)* Defending the off-field versus a left-handed hitter.

Infield In

In nearly every game, a situation will develop that forces a coach to bring the infield in. This positioning not only compromises the range of the infielders but also leaves them vulnerable to pop flies or short fly balls that they could normally run down. To help in this situation, many coaches bring their outfielders in to put them in a better position to catch a shallow fly ball. When making this alignment adjustment, the outfielders must consider many factors that will alter their depth. It's a simple decision to move in against a hitter who lacks power, but how can that same positioning work against a hitter who has power?

The normal number of steps in for the outfielder in the infield-in adjustment is five to seven. The off outfielder might add three to five more steps. Once again, although some coaches feel the need to employ them earlier under certain circumstances, these tactics are normally used late in games. Imagine that the winning run is at third in the final inning, there are fewer than two outs, and you are the visiting team. Such a situation falls under the heading of desperate measures. In this scenario, the bases are probably walked loaded. The infield is pulled in. Any deep fly ball will score the run from third base. With this in mind, the outfielders position quite shallow (figure 2.16), which allows them to catch any shallow fly ball as well as any line drive that normally would fall in safely.

This positioning adjustment requires outfielders to advance 25 to 30 steps from their normal starting point. If the bases are loaded and the hitter strikes a ground ball through the infield, it's important that the defense not give up. It's possible to turn a double play in this situation. The outfielder will charge the ball and throw to second for the force out, and the infielder

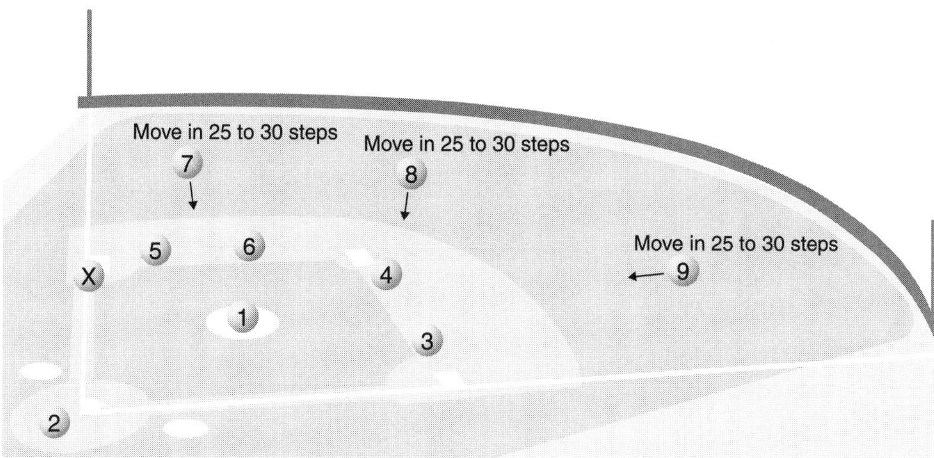

Figure 2.16 Winning run at third base, fewer than two outs, final inning, visiting team in field.

attempts to turn the twin killing with a throw to first base. Some runners will let up and not run full speed in this situation, making the double play more likely.

Scouting reports, statistics, and percentages always play a major role in determining the best situational defensive tactics. But once fielders are in position, they must also be able to execute. A fundamentally sound defensive club will consistently put themselves in position to win.

3

Pitching Strategy

Steve Smith

The development of a complete pitcher involves the contribution of several factors, some more basic than others. Over the course of my career, I've found it useful to organize the primary factors into a pyramid arrangement, as shown in figure 3.1. This set of variables and their hierarchical arrangement serve as a framework for an effective development program for pitchers.

At the foundation of the pyramid are arm care and strength and conditioning, in short, the physical health and fitness of the pitcher. At the next tier come the mechanics of the delivery, obviously closely related to a pitcher's health but also to his performance. As you move up the pyramid, the factors become more technical and often require more time to develop.

The factors involved in the mental side of pitching are among the most advanced and thus appear at the top of the pyramid.

Inner Game of Pitching

Coaches of pitchers often ask themselves two questions: Why do some pitchers with less stuff outperform those with more velocity and a wider array of pitches? And why do some pitchers with great physical talent and skills struggle to perform well consistently?

Clearly, the mental side of pitching has much to do with an athlete's success on the mound. The mind can either help a pitcher perform better than his physical abilities would seem to allow or, conversely, cause him to perform worse.

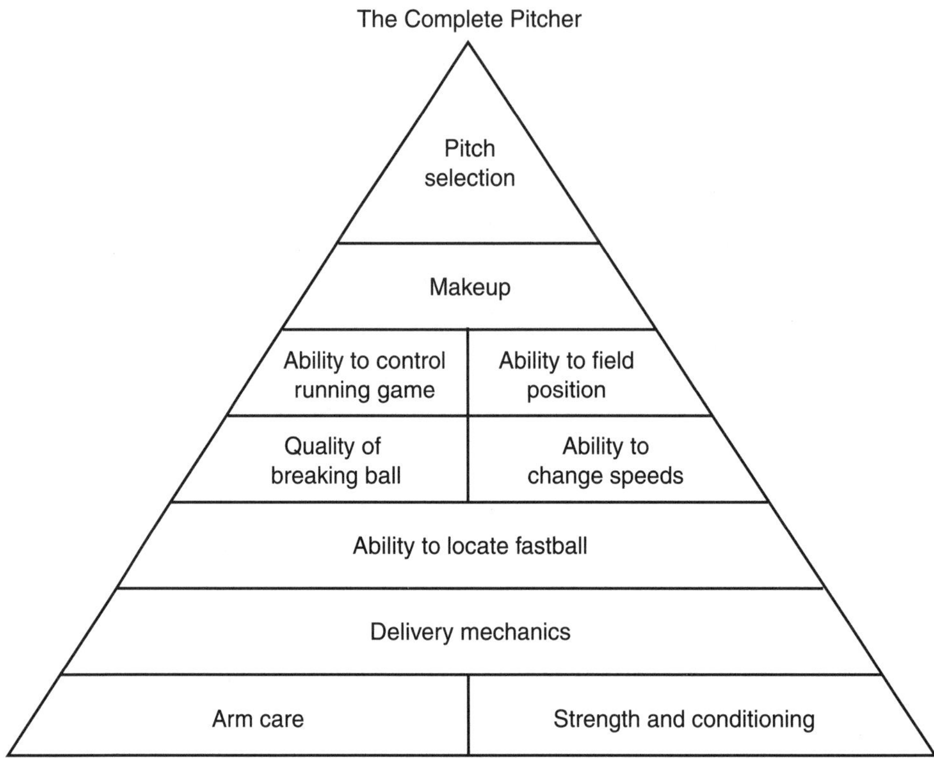

Figure 3.1 Factors that contribute to the development of a complete pitcher.

What is involved in the mental side of pitching? What are the mental skills or attributes that a successful pitcher masters? In the broadest terms, the successful pitcher wins both the inner game and the outer game. The inner game is the game played inside the pitcher's mind—what he's thinking, where his attention is focused, how hard he's concentrating, how quickly he recognizes and responds tactically to ever-changing situations, and whether he reacts positively or negatively when beset by adversity. All of these are issues for pitchers to address with an inner game. The best pitchers have a very effective inner game.

During the course of a contest, a pitcher encounters constant challenges that can throw him off track mentally. Fielders commit crucial errors. Umpires miss the call on close pitches. The condition of the mound goes from bad to worse. Opposing fans and players might try a variety of tactics to get inside the pitcher's head. The mistakes of the pitcher himself and the unfortunate rolls of the ball that occur in any game also compete for the pitcher's attention.

Winning the inner game is about maintaining focus and keeping composure. Before the pitcher can even begin to play the outer game, he must first win the inner game. Coaches typically describe pitchers who excel in this area as having a good makeup. Such pitchers share three characteristics that put them in a position to win the inner game: command, composure, and confidence.

Command means the pitcher is in control of himself and in command of the game despite the competing distractions around him. Pitchers who exhibit command are able to make sound decisions and execute them when the heat is on. They have a presence on the mound that puts their teammates at ease.

To teach command, create situations that put pressure on the pitcher during bullpen sessions and intrasquad games. For example, use a scripted bullpen plan and grade the bullpen based on whether the pitcher locates the pitch successfully or not. In intrasquad games, begin the inning with the bases loaded or have each hitter start with a 2-1 count. These types of situations create gamelike challenges for the pitcher and force him to practice not only the physical execution of the pitch but also the mental approach necessary for success.

A pitcher who maintains *composure* is able to respond to situations as opposed to reacting to them. He maintains focus on the present without dwelling on the past or the future. Examples abound of pitchers who in moments of frustration or anger lose their composure and injure themselves by hitting the dugout wall. More common are those pitchers who lose their internal composure, become consumed with the misfortune of the past or their fear of the future, and can't stay focused on the present.

Pitchers who win the inner game have a strong belief in themselves. Their *confidence* is not built on or shaken by the actions or opinions of others. It's not diminished by a few bad outings. Performances, good and bad, are looked at objectively and as part of a process. Truly confident pitchers look at all experiences as part of learning and don't focus on whether an inning or an outing was good or bad.

Possibly the single biggest key to developing command, composure, and confidence and displaying them in competition is preparation. Current Boston Red Sox pitcher Curt Schilling is a veteran Major League pitcher who has a well-established reputation for the extent to which he prepares himself mentally for each start. He reviews a variety of informational sources—scouting reports, stats, and so on—including video on opposing hitters and their tendencies.

This type of preparation allows a pitcher to visualize each hitter he will face and actually to play the game in his mind before he plays it on the field. It allows him to anticipate situations he'll likely face during the game which, in turn, allows him to respond to those situations with command, composure, and confidence. Whether the pitcher is pitching in the Major Leagues or the Little Leagues, his success in the inner game can be significantly improved by preparing well.

Most of the available instructional materials about pitching concern the physical side of the craft. Without question, proper physical conditioning, pitch mechanics, grips, pickoff moves, fielding techniques, and so on are critical to a hurler's success. But a key ingredient to successful pitching—including fielding the position—involves factors that are less tangible.

Several sources pertaining to the mental side of baseball (or other sports) are worth reading; each of these books has helped form my approach to working with pitchers. They include *The Mental Game of Baseball* by Harvey Dorfman, *The Inner Game of Tennis* by W. Timothy Gallwey, *Heads-Up Baseball* by Ken Rivizza and Tom Hansen, and *The Mind Gym* by Gary Mack.

Outer Game of Pitching

The outer game is the contest played on the field, the game we all can witness. Winning the outer game from a mental perspective is about making sound decisions in a variety of situations. These decisions range from selecting the proper pitch to throw to a particular hitter, to which pick sequence, if any, to use with the runners on base, to what type of tempo to set between pitches.

Winning the inner game is paramount to a pitcher's winning the outer game. While winning the inner game requires command, composure, and confidence, winning the outer game requires applying knowledge and understanding in two areas: game management and pitch selection.

Pitchers have a tremendous opportunity as well as a responsibility to control much of what takes place in a baseball game. Fulfilling this responsibility requires skills and abilities that go beyond the pitcher's physical talents. Effective game management is much more of a mental and emotional challenge than a physical one. It requires understanding that the game is 27 outs played 1 out at a time. It is grasping that it's sometimes preferable to allow a single run in exchange for an out. It is having the temperament to make sound decisions before, during, and after the pitch is thrown in the heat of competition. A pitcher who excels at game management will be able to consistently avoid big innings; control the tempo of the game; and analyze, visualize, and execute.

Avoid Big Innings

By definition, a big inning is one in which the offensive team scores 3 or more runs in an inning. At all levels of baseball, you find a high correlation between big innings and the outcome of the game. In short, the team that's able to put together a big inning wins about 75 to 80 percent of its games. Conversely, a team that avoids allowing a big inning usually wins about 75 to 80 percent of its games.

Going a step further, a high percentage of big innings occur when the pitcher walks a batter, the pitcher hits a batter, or someone makes an error in the inning. Few big innings occur because of hits alone. Thus, all pitchers should understand that their chances of winning a game significantly improve if they avoid the big inning by eliminating walks and hit batters.

Many pitchers get themselves into trouble by being too fine and not pitching to contact. In an attempt to avoid allowing even a single run, they put batters on base via walks and ultimately give up the big inning that costs them the game. Clearly, pitchers can't control the defensive errors made by fielders, but they should work hard not to magnify the impact of those errors by following them with a walk or a hit batter. Recognizing the need to disallow a big inning is an important first mental step in winning the outer game.

Control the Tempo

A second important part of game management for the pitcher is the extent to which he controls the pace of the game. He needs to do so in a way that gains an advantage. In most cases, pitchers should try to work quickly because this helps keep the defense more alert.

Pitchers who take a lot of time between pitches by always leaving the dirt to take the throw back from the catcher make it more difficult for position players to remain focused. This delay also gives opposing hitters plenty of time to adjust and prepare mentally for the next pitch. When a pitcher is making quality pitches and keeping the hitter off-balance, he should keep the pace moving and not give the hitter time to make adjustments.

Analyze, Visualize, and Execute

Conversely, when a pitcher is struggling for command, he might be able to clear his mind and refocus on the present by slowing the pace. The most important pitch in the game is the next one, not a pitch that has already occurred. This is often a difficult lesson for players to learn. A pitcher particularly can't afford to dwell on past mistakes because doing so inhibits his ability to perform in the present. Slowing the pace when struggling affords the pitcher extra time to make necessary adjustments, analyze the situation, and visualize his next pitch before the actual execution.

Running Game Control

Controlling an opponent's running game is a significant factor in the outcome of many games. Bases advanced by a team via the stolen base or wild pitch are what many coaches call *free bases*. Other free bases include bases reached via walks, hit batters, and errors.

The team that records the most free bases in a game usually scores the most runs and wins the game. Moreover, the inability to control the opponent's running game can be quite demoralizing to the entire team.

The physical abilities of the pitcher and catcher are very important in controlling the running game and reducing free bases, but the pitcher's mental approach is equally significant. One of the ways in which a pitcher begins to control the running game mentally is to classify the base runners. By classifying runners, the pitcher can formulate a strategy appropriate for the runners on base. Base runners can be placed in three general categories: runners, count runners, and nonrunners. Before each game, the pitcher should be able to put each of the opposing team's players into one of these three categories. The information necessary to classify the runners can be obtained through scouting reports or by looking at the opponent's stat sheet. Once he has classified the opposing team's runners, the pitcher can implement a good strategy for the runners who reach base.

Runners

Runners look to steal a base at any time during the game. These are the players on the opposing team who generally have a high number of stolen bases and a high number of attempts. They usually hit at the top or bottom of the order. Runners are, by nature, very aggressive. They run early in the count; they like to time the pitcher; they prefer to be moving or leaning in their primary lead rather than be stationary; and they usually try to guess when the pitcher will try for a pickoff.

With runners on base, the pitcher needs to vary his rhythm and counts both when he pitches and when he picks. He might pitch off a 1, 2, or 3 count. He might at times hold the ball until the batter asks for time. The pitcher should reserve his best move for the runners. Given the tendency for runners to guess, the pitcher should repeat picks two or three times consecutively. The pitcher should also use his quickest delivery to the plate, whether it's a true slide step or a quick lift. Most runners won't try to steal when a pitcher is using a slide step. A pitchout is also an appropriate strategy to use with runners.

Count Runners

Count runners have the quickness and foot speed to steal a base but usually try to pick a breaking ball count (0-1, 1-2, 2-2) on which to run. They also might be used in hit-and-run or run-and-hit situations (2-0, 2-1, 3-1, 3-2).

Given that count runners try to pick breaking ball counts to run on, pitchers should recognize these situations and always precede the delivery of an off-speed pitch with at least one pick. Using a slide step in breaking ball counts is also a deterrent. A pick might not result in a successful tag, but it will create uncertainty in the mind of the runner and hinder his ability to get a good jump, giving the catcher a better opportunity to throw him out.

Nonrunners

Nonrunners rarely attempt to steal a base. Their best opportunity to run might be in a delayed steal situation if the catcher is going to his knees and the middle infielders aren't doing a good job of covering second base.

The pitcher should not be distracted in any way when a nonrunner is on base. His complete focus should be on the hitter, leaving the responsibility for the runner in the hands of the catcher and middle infielders should a delayed steal be attempted. Too often pitchers use some of their best moves or go to their slide-step delivery with a nonrunner on base. This not only reduces the pitcher's effectiveness against the hitter in the box but also tips off the runners on the opposing team.

Pitch Selection

It's difficult to underestimate the importance of pitch selection as it relates to winning games. Whether coaches choose to make these decisions or leave them to the pitcher and catcher, these basic principles should guide the pitch-selection process:

- Think ahead, taking into account the entire lineup.
- Don't let the best hitters beat you.
- Think like a hitter.
- Be aware of your own strengths and weaknesses as well as those of the batter.

Always choose pitches with the entire lineup in mind. The pitcher, catcher, and coach should always know where they are in the opposition's lineup and, most important, who's on deck.

You usually find a significant difference between the type of hitter at the top or bottom of the order from the type of hitter in the middle of the order. Typically, the best on-base percentage guys are at the top of the order. They're usually the best runners and often are not the guys who can hit the ball out of the park. Many are the type of hitter inclined to take pitches, especially when ahead in the count.

Bottom-of-the-order hitters are usually there for a reason—they don't hit as well as the guys who bat ahead of them. Pitchers often create their own problems by pitching to the guys in the top or bottom of the order in the same way they pitch to the guys in the middle of the order. This leads to increased walks, high pitch counts, and a pitcher forced to face the middle of the order with runners on base.

Good hitters will get their hits. The key is to limit the number of opportunities these hitters have with runners on base and to keep them from hitting the ball out of the park. Force the top and bottom of the order to hit to get on base. Be aggressive with pitch selection and don't shy away from forcing contact. When possible, avoid giving in to the opponent's best hitters. Force them to get on base by hitting borderline strikes and, if necessary, pitch around them entirely.

The best pitchers can almost get inside an opposing batter's head. The pitcher looks for any physical cues that might tip off what pitch the hitter is anticipating. The ability to guess what the hitter expects and then to counter that expectation with an unexpected pitch is critical to achieving a high level of success on the mound.

Last, it's extremely important for a pitcher to know both his own strengths and weaknesses and those of the batters he faces. He should know his best pitch and to what location he throws it best. Generally, a pitcher's pitch selection should reflect his strengths rather than the hitter's weaknesses.

While previous history versus hitters and scouting reports are valuable, pitchers must also be able to gain real-time information by assessing the hitter's stance and position in the batter's box, the hitter's swing type, and the game situation. The ability to process these factors in a timely fashion and make an appropriate pitch is a significant mental skill that pitchers should be taught.

Hitter's Stance and Position

For a pitcher to read the stance and position of the hitter in the box effectively, he must be able to think like a hitter. Each hitter has a reason for assuming a certain type of stance and positioning himself where he does in the box.

- **Upright versus crouch.** Hitters who assume an upright stance in the box are revealing their desire to keep the ball as low in their hitting zone as possible. Hitters with an upright stance tend to be better low-ball hitters than high-ball hitters. Conversely, hitters in a crouched stance are indicating their preference for having the pitch high in their hitting zone. Crouched hitters tend to be high-ball hitters. If a pitcher is making a decision based on this information, he'll choose to challenge upright hitters with fastballs up in the zone, and he'll try to work down in the zone to those who are crouched.
- **Vertical bat versus flat bat.** The manner in which a hitter holds his bat often indicates the types of pitches he can most easily handle. A hitter who starts with his bat in a more vertical position tends to prefer pitches down in the zone. He might struggle to handle good fastballs at the waist or higher. A hitter who starts with his bat at a flatter angle can often handle pitches up in the strike zone more effectively. A flat-bat hitter usually has more trouble covering pitches down in the zone.
- **Off the plate versus on the plate.** A batter's stance in relation to home plate can also indicate his preferences. A hitter who stands off the plate is indicating his desire to have the pitch out or away from his body in the hitting zone. Hitters who stand off the plate usually have a slightly longer swing path and want pitches that allow them to get their arms extended. In contrast, hitters who crowd the plate are indicating their preference to keep pitches as close to them as possible. Pitchers who fail to recognize these stances often misread the preference of the hitter and pitch away to those who are off the plate and in to those who are on the plate, which is precisely what these hitters want.

• **Up in the box versus deep in the box.** Where a hitter positions himself in the batter's box is another indicator of his preferences. For example, a hitter positioned deep in the batter's box usually wants more time to react to the fastball and prefers off-speed pitches. A hitter who moves up to the front of the box tends to want to hit fastballs. Pitchers who understand these signals won't hesitate to challenge the hitter deep in the box with fastballs and to use off-speed pitches against the hitter who's up in the box.

Hitter's Swing

The hitter's swing also signals the types and locations of pitches he prefers and those he finds difficult to hit. Reading swings is valuable for all defensive players, not just pitchers, because a batter's swing informs them how to position defensively.

Dead pull, or rotary, hitters prefer pitches on the inner half of the plate. They often cheat on fastballs in an attempt to start the bat early. Force dead pull hitters to hit fastballs and breaking pitches away. A good change-up is also an effective pitch against a dead pull hitter.

Lift hitters prefer pitches down in the zone. They often either stand upright in the box or have a high back elbow. When facing a lift hitter, keep the fastball above the waist and try to avoid throwing the breaking ball for strikes. Instead, throw the breaking ball down and out of the strike zone.

Slow-bat hitters are most effective hitting fastballs on the outer half of the plate and off-speed pitches in the strike zone. Keep the fastballs close to the hitter and throw the breaking ball and other off-speed pitches in the dirt. Like rotary hitters, hitters with slow bats will eventually try to cheat to catch up with the good fastball. By starting their swings early they'll have difficulty making adjustments, such as checking their swings, and will be very susceptible to chasing good off-speed pitches out of the strike zone.

Poor breaking ball hitters are found in almost every lineup. They either struggle with seeing spin or have problems with their approach and find it extremely difficult to wait long enough to read the pitch. Good pitchers take advantage of this type of a hitter by throwing breaking balls for strikes and throwing fastballs in locations just outside the strike zone.

Make-hit players are the hitters in the lineup who will rarely, if ever, hit the ball out of the park. They are typically guys who are not yet strong enough to drive a ball into the gap and are strictly at the plate to make contact. Pitchers should challenge these hitters with hard stuff, trying to force contact early in the count.

The best hitters are usually able to make pitch-to-pitch adjustments, wait longer before committing to a swing, and use the whole field—and they rarely miss a pitcher's mistake. Pitching to hitters with these types of abilities makes pitching both challenging and fun. The keys to pitching effectively to an opponent's best hitters are to continually mix pitches and learning to pitch "backward."

Fooling a good hitter on a particular pitch one time doesn't mean you should double up and repeat that pitch. Good hitters make adjustments, and doubling up on pitches increases the hitter's opportunity to adjust. Pitchers must mix both pitches and locations. It's difficult for even good hitters to cover the entire strike zone, so pitchers who can vary their location well have greater success against these hitters.

In addition to mixing pitches, pitchers should become adept at recognizing when to pitch backward, which means throwing the opposite of what the count would ordinarily indicate. Instead of throwing fastballs when behind in the count (1-0, 2-0, 2-1, 3-1), the pitcher should resort to an off-speed pitch. Instead of throwing breaking balls when ahead in the count (0-1, 0-2, 1-2), the pitcher should throw a well-located fastball, usually in on the hitter.

Game Situation

Another important factor to consider when selecting pitches is the game situation: the score, number of outs, pitch count, number of runners on base, and inning.

Experienced pitchers understand that pitching to contact is usually good strategy, but in some situations it's best to pitch around a hitter. For example, one pitch-selection rule of thumb that a pitcher should follow throughout a game is not to throw a pitch on a 2-2 count that he wouldn't be willing to throw on a 3-2 count. In other words, if he wouldn't throw a breaking ball on a 3-2 count, he shouldn't throw it on a 2-2 count, either. Instead of pushing the count to 3-2 with a breaking ball, go at the hitter on the 2-2 count with a fastball. If the situation is such that you need a strikeout or have a base open with runners in scoring position, use your best strikeout pitch on the 2-2 count and, if necessary, repeat it on 3-2.

Early in the game, the pitcher should have his best stuff. He will likely be more count-oriented in his pitch selection. As opposed to pitching backward, he should be willing to challenge the hitter in the strike zone. By doing so, he'll have a better chance to keep his pitch count down and pitch deeper into the game. He should work to establish command of his fastball to both sides of the plate and get as many outs "in" as he can. As much as possible, he should try not to show all his pitches the first time through the opposing team's order. A pitcher's effectiveness in accomplishing these goals early in the game will undoubtedly help him as the game progresses and he begins to tire.

Later in the game, pitch selection is likely to be more situation-oriented, and pitching backward becomes more important. If the starter is still in the game, he might find it necessary to get more outs "away" because the quality of his stuff probably will have diminished.

Physical ability is extremely important, but only by commanding the mental side of pitching can a pitcher become complete.

4

Catching Techniques

Jim Penders

The catcher is the foundation of the defense, the one everyday player who's an indispensable part of any good team. In many ways that most people don't notice, the catcher's stances are the groundwork on which championship teams are built. To best understand the three different catcher stances, you must first recognize that the position entails three distinct duties, each of which is very important to the outcome of a game:

1. To communicate pitch selection clearly, yet covertly, with the pitcher and middle infielders
2. To make the pitcher look good by receiving the ball softly with the body, not just the glove
3. To stop or change the direction of the baseball

Although the catching position demands much more than these three duties, everyone who has played the position successfully has understood these three basic responsibilities and learned to perform them with proficiency. Each of the three stances has its own utility. Each is a position an effective catcher must assume prior to a pitch in order for him to perform various techniques and tactics effectively.

Once a catcher is familiar with his role, he'll likely adopt the necessary stance almost automatically, as dictated by circumstance; he develops a kinesthetic sense for proper body posture and positioning. In short, he not only knows what he's supposed to do in certain situations—he can also *feel* what his duties are by the markedly different stances he uses. A catchphrase helps describe the purposes for the three stances: "The catcher must be stable, and then he will be able."

Each stance provides the catcher the best position from which to execute four distinct duties: to communicate accurately and confidently with the pitcher and involved infielders, to give the umpire a clear view of each pitch, to allow the catcher to block pitches in the dirt, and to improve the catcher's ability to throw.

Signal-Giving Stance

The catcher's first duty is to communicate pitch selection clearly, yet covertly, to the pitcher and critical fielders. The signal-giving stance is taken more often than the other stances because a catcher uses it before every pitch of the game. The other two stances are employed in specific situations, but the signal stance is generally taken 100 to 160 times per nine-inning game. It is used prior to assuming the primary or secondary stances described later. The signal stance is uncomplicated and easy to assume—thus, it's also the one most likely to be fouled up. The simplicity of the posture can lead to laziness in execution.

A catcher assumes the signal stance by placing his feet about 12 inches apart and parallel to one another. This is a stance that most people use every day, such as when standing and talking to someone. The feet are even and beneath the hips. The catcher then lowers his center of gravity so that his butt is resting on his calves (figure 4.1). The toes point straight ahead. People who naturally stand with their feet flared might have difficulty assuming this stance. On an imaginary clock, the feet are positioned correctly if the clock reads 10 minutes to 2 o'clock. A tighter angle, say, 5

Figure 4.1 Signal-giving stance.

minutes of 1 o'clock, will work, but any angle greater than 10 minutes to 2 o'clock presents an open look at the signals to base runners or opposing first- and third-base coaches.

The knees should be closed and pointed straight ahead. The right knee can be closed off a bit more significantly than the left, but both should be closed. The hips and shoulders should be perpendicular to the shortstop (not to the pitcher), which creates a natural blinder that prevents the first-base coach from seeing the catcher's fingers.

Many catchers are paranoid about the third-base coach, but they should be thinking more about the first-base coach. The glove provides an extension of the left-leg blinder for the third-base side. Moreover, the coach at third is preoccupied with the number of outs, the play situation, and the signs he needs to relay, so he's less likely to be trying to pick up signs from the catcher. Meanwhile, the first-base coach has less to do, and his view is not blocked by the catcher's mitt, so he's the one the catcher should worry about. Thus, a good signal stance should close off the right leg from the first-base area. The catcher should check with the first baseman. If the first baseman can see the catcher's signs, the catcher needs to close his right leg off better or pull his fingers deeper in.

Another common error catchers make in the signal stance is to bend their bodies forward, as if to protect their signals from those watching from the sky. Nobody can pick off the signs from *above* the catcher, but many catchers lean forward to hide their secrets from the pesky satellites and spy planes overhead. This is a problem for several reasons. First, the proper stance is compromised; the catcher becomes unbalanced and unathletic. He'll have difficulty moving from this posture to the primary or secondary stances. Second, the posture looks wimpy. When a catcher leans forward, he looks shorter, less sure of himself, and much less authoritative. A pitcher is more apt to believe in a guy who looks like he's in charge back there. Third, this hunched-in position creates unnecessary shadows between the legs in the signal-giving area that might lead to mix-ups with the pitcher or critical fielders. For all these reasons, the catcher needs to crouch with his shoulders back, chest out, and head up. This posture suggests authority and confidence and presents the best view to those who need to see the signs.

The catcher's belly button, or center of the body, should be behind the midpoint of the plate. Any favoring of one side of the plate could tip pitch location or selection to the opposition, particularly to the batter. The catcher's mitt obstructs the third-base coach and runners at third base by acting as a rigid and straight extension of the left thigh. The mitt should not drop to the ground or fall below the knee.

The catcher's throwing hand and fingers should be in contact with his right inner thigh or groin area. Depending on the length of the catcher's arms, his right elbow should be tight up against his side or right hip while the hand is in contact with the groin (figure 4.2). The fingertips when extended should be touching the catcher's protective cup. If the fingers are

Figure 4.2 The catcher's elbow is tight to his side or hip as he gives the signal.

any lower, the opposing runners, coaches, players in the dugouts, or, most commonly, players behind the backstop with clipboards and radar guns will have a view of the pitch selection and location.

It is critical to present the signs crisply and with no hesitation. An effective catcher knows the pitch and location he wants to call before he puts his hand down. While executing the signals for sign and location, he should alternately shift his eyes from the hitter's head to the pitcher's face. He needs to know if the hitter is peeking and if the pitcher agrees with the pitch and location.

If the catcher's hand is down there, the pitcher is watching. If the catcher hesitates, the pitcher might be less likely to believe in the pitch because the catcher didn't sell it with authority. The instant his hand goes down in front of the cup, a sign and location must be given.

Although each coach has his own preferences on which signals to use for pitch and location, some absolutes are accepted. The catcher must use his index finger when calling an inside fastball to a right-handed hitter or outside fastball to a left-handed hitter without a runner at second (figure 4.3*a*), and he must use his pinky finger when calling an outside fastball to a right-handed hitter or inside fastball to a left-handed hitter (figure 4.3*b*). This prevents the wrist from turning. If he were to call an outside fastball to a right-handed hitter with his index finger, his wrist would roll, and his elbow wouldn't stay in contact with his side or hip. He could tip location and ultimately pitch selection. For instance, if a left-handed pitcher is facing a left-handed hitter, and the bench player in the first-base dugout notices that the catcher's elbow flares out, he might use a verbal signal to communicate to the hitter the high probability that he's about to see a fastball. After all, how many inside breaking pitches or off-speed pitches

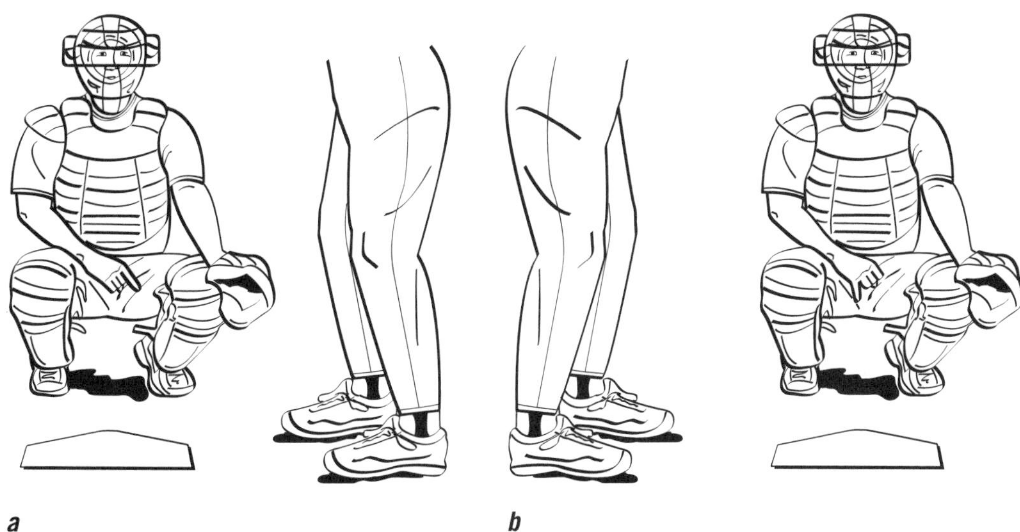

Figure 4.3 Prevent the wrist from turning when flashing signs: *(a)* the catcher uses his index finger to signal an inside fastball to a right-handed hitter or an outside fastball to a left-handed hitter; *(b)* he uses his pinky to signal an outside fastball to a right-handed hitter or an inside fastball to a left-handed hitter.

are called inside? By using his pinky, the catcher eliminates the possibility of a benchwarmer affecting the outcome of the game.

For the same reasons, a catcher should also use an "OK" sign (rather than a pitchfork-style sign) to signal a 3 (figure 4.4). The elbow must flare out slightly for the pitchfork 3, but it won't flare with the okay sign. With so much information available to the opposition from web-based stat pages,

Figure 4.4 Use an "OK" sign to signal 3.

advance scouts, video, and the like, opponents have enough data already. The catcher should never help them even more.

Some of the other absolutes of showing signs include flashing more than one location with a runner on second base. A single sign for location tips the pitch off to the hitter through the base runner at second. Also, when using a sequence of signs, the catcher must go slowly enough for his pitcher and middle infielders to read the signs and yet maintain a rhythm that expedites the game. He should also bring his fingers back into a fully closed fist between flashes to indicate a clear delineation between first, second, third, and fourth signs. Tell your catcher to speak in short sentences, not run-ons. Pitchers and middle infielders like their signs to be clear, concise, and direct.

One suggestion for maintaining the rhythm of the game is to ask pitchers to change the location of a pitch call with a stare instead of a shake of the head. If a pitcher shakes his head, the catcher must go through an entire set of pitches to find the one the pitcher wants. This can be eliminated in cases in which the pitcher likes the pitch call but not the location. If the pitcher stares at the catcher, the catcher knows to set up on the other corner and that the pitch he just called is about to be thrown. This process makes for a clear and easy way to maintain rhythm among the pitcher and the defense.

The signal stance and presentation communicates pitch selection and location to the pitcher and middle infielders while shielding the signs from everyone else. The middle infielders need to know the pitch and location so that they can "cheat" as they creep forward to areas at which the ball is more likely to be hit. They can also broadcast the signs and locations to their outfielders with hand signals behind their backs (being wary of opposing outfield bullpens) and with verbal cues to corner infielders. A proper signal stance by the catcher increases the chance of success for both the pitcher and the rest of the defense.

Overall, the signal position speaks stability, authority, and confidence. Catchers should feel little or no strain when assuming this position. Comfort is a priority. This is the one stance the catcher takes before every pitch. If he can't get comfortable in the signal stance, he probably won't be catching long.

Receiving Stance

The main function of the receiving stance is to make the pitcher look good. In this stance, the pitch is absorbed with the body, not just received by the glove. The receiving stance (also called the primary stance) is used exclusively with no men on base and fewer than two strikes on the batter. This stance is a stable position that gives the catcher some lateral mobility and force absorption. The stance is athletic but comfortable.

In this posture the feet should be shoulder-width apart or slightly wider, with the toes pointed at first and third base (figure 4.5). The weight of the body rests on the inside of the feet; the spikes on the outside of the feet really shouldn't even be in the dirt. The body should be as close to the plate as possible. A good rule of thumb is to be an arm's length from the batter's back knee, but no further than that.

Figure 4.5 Receiving stance.

Unlike in the signal stance, the knees in the receiving stance are closer together than the feet. The catcher's butt should be on or just barely above the ground. Leaning forward slightly makes for a nice, low target. The bare hand is behind the right heel or back far enough to protect it from foul tips and wayward bats. The glove arm should be outside or above the left leg, about 90 percent extended, with the index finger of the glove pointed at 1 o'clock and in front of the catcher (we'll discuss the importance of this point later). The eyes are peering just above the top of the glove; the head is erect.

Many catchers accustomed to simply setting up in a primary stance as a derivation of the signal stance will have difficulty getting their knees inside their feet and their butts low to the ground. If they can't get low enough, widening the feet often drops the butt sufficiently. If they still can't get their knees inside their feet enough to sway sideways in this stance, their hip and quadriceps flexibility will need to be improved. Swaying is a necessary part of this stance. Lateral mobility is what allows the catcher to receive the pitch not just with the glove but with his entire body.

If there were no umpire, a catcher would really be just that—a catcher. In reality, he does a lot more than simply catch the pitch. The word "receiver" actually describes the catcher's duties more accurately. The act of receiving includes framing and dressing up the pitch to offer the umpire the look that the catcher wants the umpire to have of the pitch. The catcher wants to make sure that all strikes are indeed called as strikes and that borderline pitches are called strikes as often as possible.

Because the umpire plays such a large role in the game by calling balls and strikes, the catcher must have a system of receiving to help the umpire do his job well. Of course, no umpire would ever admit to needing help, but catchers are a charitable, giving, and selfless lot. It's their nature to want to help those who can't always help themselves.

The four major facets of receiving a pitch include

1. catching the pitch;
2. framing the pitch with the body;
3. using the glove to turn, bring, and stick the pitch; and,
4. understanding, combating, and using gravity's influence on the pitch.

Catching the Pitch

Catching the pitch might seem simple enough but is in reality an art form. The catch, like the pitch or the swing, must have a trigger. That trigger is initiated with the index finger beginning at 1 o'clock.

As the pitcher releases the baseball, most big-league catchers dump the glove. The next time you watch a big-league game on TV from the center-field camera, watch the catcher drop, dump, or dunk his target. Nine times out of 10, that precious target that the catcher worked for and the pitcher aimed for goes bye-bye just as the pitch is being released. At the lower levels of baseball, this dump of the glove can really be a detriment to a pitcher's command. Imagine aiming at a dart board in your local tavern and having some drunk rip the bull's-eye out of the board just as you release the dart.

Pitching is tough enough. Catchers shouldn't make it tougher. That's why we have a trigger for the catch that keeps the glove open, relaxes the catcher's forearm to move quickly, and helps to overcome inertia. This trigger is undetectable to the pitcher about to release the ball.

The trigger is performed with a slight wave of the hand. The index finger simply moves from 1 o'clock to 12 o'clock on the dial—just enough movement that the hand is moving when the pitch is released but not so much as to be detected as a moving target by the pitcher. The Queen of England wave is a suitable analogy for the desired movement. Or think of the old clocks on elementary school walls that had minute hands that clicked backward before moving forward. This is the action you want to keep the glove open, get it moving, and maintain the target as long as possible. This motion also helps prevent the dreaded thumb bruises that come with the hard inside tailing fastball to a right-handed hitter. The glove-hand simply continues to rotate so that the index finger goes to 9 or 10 o'clock when the catch is made, taking the thumb out of harm's way.

All catches in the primary stance are one-handed catches. The old-timers who caught with the pillows and no breaks in the mitts will say it's wrong to catch this way, but they also went back there with no cups, shin guards, or even masks in some cases. Why would anyone listen to a guy with five broken knuckles on his right hand, anyway? Today's mitts are made to catch one-handed, and that's the way we do it in the primary stance (and usually in the secondary stance as well).

Body sway helps get the glove into the right position for the one-handed catch. Bringing the pitch with soft hands is also important. This means not funneling the ball to the middle of the body or vacuuming it toward the chest protector. The catcher should be firm and beat the pitch to the spot with his body sway and glove position, and then (and only then) should he bring the pitch or absorb its force with a slight flexion of the elbow. An analogy here is to envision a doctor's reflex hammer hitting the catcher on the underbelly of the wrist and the elbow serving as an airbag to absorb the force. The ball is brought, or absorbed, straight back to the catcher, maybe an inch or two at the most. It should not be moved in closer to the middle of the plate.

Framing the Pitch

Framing used to be thought of as turning the glove a certain way to make a pitch look better. But framing really refers to using the entire body to make the pitch look as good as it can to the umpire. Framing begins with the stance itself. The catcher must set his target where he wants the pitch thrown. That target is made not just with the glove but with the entire body. The nose, belly button, and glove should all be in alignment. This means that if the catcher wants a pitch on the corner, half his body, half his glove, and half his head are outside the zone. If the glove is there and the body isn't, the catcher is giving a less than authoritative and somewhat sheepish sell to his pitcher. As a pitcher, you want your target to say, "Right here, babe—fill me up. Throw that heater in *this* spot." You don't want a target that portrays, "I think I kind of want you to maybe place this pitch sort of near where my body and glove are—I mean, if that's okay with you."

If the glove, belly button, and nose are in alignment on target, why shouldn't they be in alignment on the catch itself? By swaying to a pitch that doesn't hit its target, the catcher is simply remaining consistent and showing the umpire that while the pitcher may have missed his spot, it wasn't that bad because he just centered it with his whole body. In swaying, the catcher should try to get the call only on pitches 6 inches or less outside the strike zone. If he tries to sell every pitch, the umpire is less likely to trust him on those critical borderline calls.

The sway is simply moving the body sideways or laterally by putting one knee up while the other goes down. Sometimes the sway is slight enough that it looks as if the knees slide sideways. The main point to remember is to try to catch the baseball with the ball, glove, nose, and belly button all lined up. This is centering or framing with the body.

To help your catcher understand this concept correctly, ask him what a frame hanging on a wall does. Most likely he'll say that the frame highlights the picture, makes the picture look better, or makes the art "pop." He's right. The frame doesn't change the artwork. In baseball, the artist is the pitcher. The catcher is the framer. Just as the frame on the wall highlights the picture, the frame behind the plate highlights the pitcher.

Using the Glove

The final part of the frame is the glove. In dressing up a pitch for the umpire, the glove needs to turn, bring, or stick the pitch for final presentation. None of these things can happen if the glove doesn't beat the ball to the spot. That means body sway must be complete and the glove in position to catch the pitch after stopping. It can't be on the move toward the catch and still be effective.

If the pitch is on the inside corner to a right-handed hitter and the catcher's body must sway to beat it there (meaning the pitcher didn't hit his spot), the thumb inside the glove should be pointed up, allowing for the entire glove to be in the zone. Conversely, if the catcher must sway to the other corner, the first-base side, his thumb should be pointed down. Both of these pitches require turning the glove so that the entire glove is inside the strike zone on the catch.

Understand that the umpire calling balls and strikes sees only the back of the glove. He can't see where the ball entered the glove. Thus, the catcher must eliminate any doubt from the umpire's mind by showing him that the entire glove is in the zone upon presentation of the pitch. The pitch to the first-base side is the most difficult because the thumb must rotate clockwise to the right and down to 6 o'clock. The pitch on the third-base side corner requires a more natural counterclockwise quarter-turn to 9 o'clock.

A good rule for all pitches except for the low pitch is that the thumb is the last part of the hand to touch the baseball on the catch when the pitch is just barely high, just barely inside, or just barely outside after the catcher's sway. The catcher needs to remember not to turn a pitch that hits him in the midline of the body, regardless of where he's set up on the plate. He shouldn't complicate that call for the umpire. If he catches it as if it's down the middle, it's easier for the umpire to call it a strike than a ball. So, the catcher's body position and not the plate itself will dictate whether or not a turn is necessary. In other words, if the catcher is set up on a corner and the pitcher hits that corner, the catcher should catch it as if it's down the middle of the plate. He shouldn't turn the glove.

Another absolute is that the palm should face the interior of the strike zone unless the pitch is low. This is another way of saying the catcher should catch the top half of the barely high pitch, the outside half of the barely outside pitch, and the inside half of the barely inside pitch. The bring after the turn is used on borderline high, borderline inside, and borderline outside pitches. The bring refers to the soft hands that are essential for absorbing the force and presenting the pitch to the umpire unobstructed without funneling the ball.

A final absolute about turning and bringing is to use the midline of the left knee as a line of demarcation for whether to turn or to catch and bring. If the pitch is outside the midline of the left knee, the catcher should shake hands with the pitch and point the thumb up to 12 o'clock. This keeps a riding fastball or slider to a left-handed hitter a strike. Once the pitch gets outside the midline of the knee and the sway is exhausted, strength and leverage are lost. Thus, the best way to keep the pitch a strike is to turn. Conversely, if the pitch is inside the midline of the knee after the sway is completed, just catch the ball as if it's down the middle and cushion or bring it an inch or two back for presentation.

When all's said and done, turning and bringing really aren't all that necessary if the catcher does a good job swaying when his pitcher misses the spot. By swaying, he's framing and presenting the pitch.

Think about it this way. If a catcher sets up on the corner closest to third base and the pitcher misses his spot and throws to the opposite corner to a right-handed hitter, the umpire is set up in the chute between the hitter and the catcher's left ear. If the catcher doesn't sway, he must reach all the way across his body with an extended and unathletic arm that's unable to bring or turn. The pitch will undoubtedly take the glove out of the zone with it. The umpire is also screened on the catch by the catcher's own body. Conversely, if the catcher sways, beats the ball to the spot, turns his thumb counterclockwise to 6 o'clock, and catches the pitch with a bend in his arm and a soft bring, the umpire has a clear view, and the catcher will be able to keep a strike, albeit a missed-spot strike—exactly that: a strike.

The stick is an advanced move for a catcher who has mastered the turn and bring. The technique behind the stick really spits in the face of the concept of turning and bringing for presentation. The stick is designed to keep a low strike a strike. The stick is part of the glove action, but it really belongs in the next section on using gravity's influence on the pitch.

Understanding the Influence of Gravity

Sir Isaac Newton didn't catch the apple when it fell on his head, but if he had been a catcher, he would undoubtedly have agreed with the principle that the longer a pitch travels from the hand of a pitcher standing on a 10-inch mound, the lower the pitch is. Said another way, a pitch tends to get lower, not higher, as it covers distance. Perhaps this basic principle wouldn't have held true if Neil Armstrong had thrown a baseball on the moon back in 1969, but as long as baseball diamonds exist only on our planet, gravitational pull will influence pitches. With that understood, it's the catcher's duty to know how to use gravity and also how to combat it to make his pitchers look as good as possible.

"Sticking" really means going to get a low strike before it becomes a ball and to keep it a strike. A catcher can't bring this pitch. If he brings it straight back, it's only going to look lower to the umpire. If he can beat it to the spot with a nearly extended catching arm and stick or kick it up a hair, he has a much better chance at having the pitch stay a strike and be called a strike.

The stick begins just like all other pitches being received. The catcher must identify it as a low pitch. Once doing so, he rotates the thumb of his catching hand all the way to 7 to 8 o'clock on the dial. The only way to do this is with a clockwise rotation. If he can do it any other way, he should quit baseball and join the circus. At any rate, the rotation is critical.

After rotating his thumb, his glove is in position to stick the pitch with the only soft part of the glove when the hand is moving toward the pitch and not bringing it—that is, the web. The web is used, and no fingers or thumbs are in the way. The catcher must catch the bottom half of the ball. In drill work from a short distance at less than game speed, the catcher will actually lift the ball upon fully extending his catching arm on the catch itself. At game speed, while trying to keep a 90-mile-per-hour downhill fastball a strike, that same catcher's lift will look just like a stop. However, the action of the lift is required to combat the downward force of a power breaking ball, a sinking fastball, or a diving splitter. Also, catching the ball as far out in front of the body as possible with a strong or bent arm is integral to making this pitch look good. After all, the longer the pitch travels, the lower it will be. Visualize a successful stick as a 59-foot pitch—that's how the catcher wants it to look.

On the flip side, the catcher should be taught to catch the borderline high pitch as deep and as close to his mask as possible. Many catchers go out to get this pitch, and they really just keep it high. They might turn and bring well, but they're not using gravity to help them.

Although gravity is the enemy on the low pitch, necessitating the stick, it's the catcher's friend on the high pitch. Use it. The successful reception of the high pitch is executed by catching the top half of the ball and not letting the horsehide hit the cowhide until the pitch reaches 63 or 64 feet. The bring is not even necessary if the pitch is received deep enough. Indeed, if the pitch is at the mask when caught, the catcher has nowhere to bring it. Some successful catchers even tuck their chins and bring their heads back on the catch as if to lengthen the pitch by a couple more inches.

Secondary Stance

The main function of the secondary stance is to stop or change the direction of the ball. Use this stance with a man or men on base or with no men on base and two strikes on the batter. This is the stance for which the best catchers get paid—which makes sense because it's the one that hurts the most.

Using this stance and throwing, or changing the direction of, the ball is covered masterfully by Coach Scott Stricklin in the next chapter, so I'll keep this section brief. However, a basic explanation of the secondary posture should be a useful supplement to Scott's information. All aspects of the catcher's throw are best accomplished from this more mobile and anticipatory stance.

The premise behind the secondary stance is that it's necessary to sacrifice some of the stability of the primary stance in order to gain the mobility needed to block balls and throw effectively, safely, and efficiently. Mainly, the butt is higher in this stance (figure 4.6), yet the target must be as low as it's kept in the primary stance. This is accomplished by standing with feet parallel and slightly wider than shoulder width. The feet are just about as wide as they are in the primary stance; the difference is that the heels kick out to align with the toes, which are pointed straight ahead. The feet are flat on the ground, and the body weight is on the middle of the feet, not on the inside of the feet, toes, or heels. All spikes are in the dirt. The knees are wider than they are in the primary stance, and the butt is slightly below

Figure 4.6 Secondary stance.

the knees and not resting on the ground or calves. Part of the hamstring may rest on the upper calves, but the butt needs to be up. The higher the butt, the more mobile the catcher.

The target must stay as low as it's kept in the primary stance; the glove and eyes are at the same height as in the primary stance. The butt is the only thing that's higher. This posture is managed simply by leaning forward with the upper body and flattening out the back. If the catcher is unable to lift his face in this position and keep his head erect, he probably won't be catching long. Some younger catchers assuming this position for the first time make the mistake of looking out of the top of their masks. The head must be erect and the back must stay flat for the target to look as good as possible and for the catcher to be balanced and agile.

The glove-arm is above the left knee, and the bare hand is in a loose fist behind the mitt with the thumb inserted and protected within the fist. (Make sure when teaching this position that the catcher knows not to hit anyone with his fist this way. If he enters a brawl, he'd break his thumb!) This positioning works well to protect the thumb from foul tips. The target is still in the middle of the body with the index finger pointed to 1 o'clock, just as it is in the primary stance. Eyes should be just over the top of the glove and the head erect. This position allows greater mobility and anticipation than the primary stance does.

When catching the pitch (figure 4.7), the catcher should retain his goals of the primary stance. When he doesn't need to block or throw on the pitch, he applies all the same techniques he uses in his primary stance.

Figure 4.7 Catching the pitch from the secondary stance.

Of course, with his knees wider, his sway will be more limited, but all the same absolutes of the primary stance also apply here. The catcher should be able to judge whether a block or throw will be necessary by the time the pitch is in mid-flight.

Should neither a block or a throw be necessitated by a ball heading for the dirt or a first baseman yelling "going!" the catcher should pull his bare hand back to the crease of his chest protector and right armpit to shelter it in case of a foul tip. This also allows him greater range to sway and beat pitches to spots with the glove because he doesn't have to bring both hands to the pitch. Just as a first baseman has better range when catching one-handed, the catcher is better equipped with his unnecessary bare hand out of the way.

The secondary stance is best for blocking because the knees are still slightly inside the hips. Throwing the hips allows for lateral movement when the catcher has to go to his knees to block. Once the knees get outside the feet or the catcher takes a step, his range is predetermined, and the catcher, like a hockey goalie moving his skate, has already exhausted his range. The lateral movement or slide necessary to stop errant pitches comes from the hips and knees, not the feet. Blocking takes heart and repetitions. Anyone can do it, but not everybody loves it. To do it well, a catcher needs to have a screw loose and to take pride in it. He needs to love to do it.

The catcher needs to be an athlete here and react by centering the ball with the middle of his chest protector. He shouldn't try to catch the ball. Remember—the catcher's duty is to stop the ball, not necessarily catch it. The glove and knees plug the hole between the knees. Knees are pressed to the ground and stay on the ground throughout the execution of the proper block. The chin is tucked to the chest to protect the neck and make the ball visible to the catcher. Shoulders curve forward to create a concave chest and a natural airbag effect with the chest protector bubbling out from the chest surface. The air between the chest and the protector helps absorb and control the baseball, which helps significantly to limit the carom. A helpful tip in mastering the block is to have the catcher exhale as he drops to his knees and takes the hit. By blowing the air out, his body should naturally relax and better absorb the ball.

In mastering the technique of sliding to the location to center the baseball, the effective catcher will also corral or turn his body with a slight curve to best contain the baseball. If he moves linearly, like a soccer player on a foosball table, the blocked ball might be centered on the protector but won't be contained. A crescent moon or banana path should be taken to balls thrown to the left or right in the dirt. On breaking balls on right-handed curves or sliders, the catcher's left shoulder should fire or curl in on contact with the protector. The right shoulder should curl in on left-handed breakers. Mastering this skill while the body is sliding into the blocking slide and while maintaining balance is perhaps the most difficult part of blocking.

A final point of emphasis in blocking is gaining ground while staying soft with the body. On breaking balls or off-speed pitches, the catcher should anticipate a dirt ball every time. He should also be able to propel his body forward to limit the hop between the dirt and his body. The catcher should imagine tiny rockets in his heels that fire whenever an off-speed pitch is significantly short of the plate. This is nearly impossible to do on a good fastball because there won't be time to cut the distance. In this scenario, he must simply get down and plug the holes.

Mirror Drill

The catcher faces a mirror and reviews signals to himself while perfecting the stance in a home environment.

Partner Drill

The catcher faces a partner standing about 10 feet away. The catcher is critiqued for any mistakes in giving signals, including mistakes in tempo, hand movements, and stance. The catcher goes through different situations, including pitchouts, throws to first base, various signal systems, and so on. Catchers alternate roles.

Catch With the Step To

The catcher's partner throws in front of him about 30 feet. The catcher receives balls by stepping at a 45-degree angle (with pitchout-step work) to practice centering the baseball. The partner throws outside the catcher's body frame.

Catching Tennis Balls With a Bare Hand

The catcher gets in his stance with no glove. His partner flips tennis balls firmly to different locations in and out of the strike zone. The catcher uses soft hands to catch and bring the tennis balls. Emphasize trying to make no sound on the catch.

Using a Machine for Repetitions

Crank the pitching machine up to its highest velocity. Have catchers catch one pitch after another, using the proper trigger for the catch. Once they have mastered this skill, move the machine on its highest setting up to 55 feet, then 50 feet, then 45, and so on. The catcher will teach himself the right technique.

Rapid Fire

A partner flips balls to the bare-handed catcher from about 10 feet in front of him. The partner has three balls in each hand and quickly flips to different spots in the zone by alternating hands. All six balls should be flipped within 3 to 4 seconds. Repeat.

Point Drill

The catcher's partner is 10 feet in front of him. The partner points left or right, up or down, to prompt the catcher to catch an imaginary ball. With no ball, the catcher can be perfect every time.

Shadow Box

Two catchers work together. They face each other at a distance of about 10 feet. One mirrors or shadows what the other one does, swaying, catching, setting up with different looks, and so on.

Shadow Box With Coach on Side

Catchers perform the shadow box drill with a coach watching from the side to provide feedback for high and low frames. The coach needs to make sure each catcher sticks in front enough and catches the high strike deep enough.

V Drill

This drill requires three or four players. The catcher is in his stance. One player is a feeder, standing 10 to 15 feet down the third-base line. Another is on the first-base line at the same distance. A third feeder can be directly in front of the catcher on the ground or on a stool. The feeder on the third-base line flips a ball to the first-base corner and watches the catcher sway to beat the ball to the spot and use the proper hand position. The first-base feeder does the opposite. The feeder up the middle works on high and low feeds. If the middle feeder is on the ground, he flips the ball up to accentuate the angle to ensure the catcher is receiving the top half of the ball. If the middle feeder is on a stool, he's accentuating the downward plane angle of a pitch to be stuck.

Two Machines

The activity is the same as in the V drill, but the reps are more consistent because the machines are more accurate than a partner.

Hold the Ball

The catcher's partner or coach holds a ball 2 feet in front of the catcher in different locations. The catcher sways, showing proper technique as if he were going to catch the ball. The catcher can be perfect with the reps here because he doesn't actually catch the ball but only visualizes it.

Rainbow Drill

The catcher's partner starts 10 feet down the third-base line and flips balls like an option quarterback pitching to a running back to the catcher's bare-hand side. The partner makes sure the catcher sways and catches the ball, then slowly walks a semicircle toward the first-base line. The partner stops in different locations and flips balls to different spots in and out of the zone to check the catcher's technique.

Shadow Drill

To ensure universal rhythm and language among the catching staff, have the catchers mirror or shadow each other to make it easier for the pitching staff. Each catcher faces a partner and copies the partner's signal, location, and setup.

No Block, No Going Combo Drill

The catcher's partner is 40 to 50 feet in front of the catcher with a bucket of balls. The partner throws pitches to the catcher. If the pitch is in the dirt, the catcher blocks using proper technique. If the pitch is in the air and the partner yells "going!" the catcher pounces and uses good throwing footwork to receive, transfer the ball, and get his body in position to make a throw. If the feeder says nothing and throws a strike, the catcher simply catches the ball and pulls the bare hand back with sway and presentation.

Blocking Point

The catcher's coach or partner points to different locations. The catcher slides to the spot indicated using proper technique.

Glove Leads Down

The catcher is in a secondary stance, but the glove is already on the ground in proper blocking position. As a dirtball is thrown, the catcher drops to his knees, plugging up the hole between his legs.

Softer Balls

Using a softer ball, the catcher's partner throws five dirtballs to the middle, five to the left, and five to the right. The partner then moves back to 60 feet and lets it rip for five in different locations. Occasionally, the partner should throw a strike so that the catcher doesn't cheat and get to his knees too early. Then the partner throws five breaking balls in the dirt to check for technique.

Circle Containment Drill

Draw a circle 5 feet in diameter in the dirt in front of the plate. The catcher's partner throws real balls in the dirt. The blocking catcher tries to keep as many blocked pitches in the circle as he can. He must recover them before they roll out of the circle. He competes with others for best score.

Hard-Guy Drill

To emphasize gaining ground on breaking balls and off-speed pitches and to cut the distance between the dirtball and the catcher's body, a feeder stands about 50 feet in front of the catcher and throws tennis balls to the five hole. The catcher blocks the ball and gets to his feet in the secondary stance. Another ball is thrown. This pattern is repeated more and more quickly until the catcher reaches the feeder by propelling himself forward. The thrower scores a point if he gets the ball through the five hole. The catcher scores a point if he tags the thrower without taking a step but just by blocking and gaining a little bit of ground each time. Close to 20 dirtballs should be thrown. This is an exhausting drill.

The construction of any good ball club begins with the construction of the catcher. Championships begin with the catcher's stances. Without those critical groundings, the catcher can't perform the duties critical to the success of a good team. The signal-giving, primary, and secondary stances are positions from which the catcher can best perform his responsibilities. A construction foreman wouldn't build his dream house on stilts above the San Andreas Fault; a baseball coach shouldn't try to build a dream team without first making sure the foundation is sound. That foundation is the stable and able catcher.

5

Stopping Steals From the Catcher Position

Scott Stricklin

The stolen base is an offensive tool that can create havoc for a defense. Not only does the offense gain a base via the steal, but the defensive alignment is compromised when the middle of the infield is on the move, opening more holes for the hitter. Potential steal situations also force the pitcher to rush his delivery to home plate, which often translates to the hitter seeing more pitches elevated in the strike zone. For these reasons, every successful defense devotes a significant amount of time to tactics that prevent opponents from stealing bases.

To be truly effective in defending a team from stealing bases, the pitcher must do a great job of holding the runner (see chapter 6). This can be accomplished by pickoff attempts, changing the timing on pickoffs or pitches to home plate, and using the slide step to home plate. Everything starts with the pitcher. If a pitcher ignores the base runner or gets into a consistent rhythm with either his pickoff attempts or his move to home plate, good base runners will steal bases.

Catchers know the importance of the pitcher when it comes to throwing out base runners. In fact, most baseball experts place most of the responsibility for catching stealers on the pitcher. However, the catcher plays a major role as the anchor of a team's defense.

In this chapter we'll focus on the catcher's duties in preventing steal attempts. The key technical points to cover are the secondary stance, the transfer of the ball from the glove to the throwing hand, footwork fundamentals, and the throwing motion. In addition to these techniques, we'll also address the catcher's tactical decisions in defending specific steal situations, such as runners at first and third attempting to execute a double or delayed steal.

Secondary Stance

When runners are on base or the hitter has two strikes against him, the catcher must be positioned in his secondary stance (or his ready stance), as described in chapter 4. When no one is on base and the hitter has fewer than two strikes, the catcher can be in his primary stance, which is more relaxed. The main goal in the primary stance is to stay low and relaxed. The shoulders and knees square up to the pitcher, and the throwing hand is protected behind the right calf, with the thumb tucked inside a loose fist.

The secondary stance is a more athletic stance, similar to a basketball defensive posture (figure 5.1). From his secondary stance, the catcher must be ready to go right, left, up, or down. This position puts a lot of stress and pressure on the legs, but a catcher must be prepared both to block and to throw.

The feet straighten out a little in the secondary stance. Body weight is on the balls of the feet. The right foot can be slightly behind the left foot, but the catcher must not drop the right foot too far back (called "cheating with the feet"). A catcher drops the right foot back so that he can get a head start on the footwork when throwing the ball to second base. Yes, the feet may be in a better position to throw, but what about being able to block

Figure 5.1 Catcher in secondary stance.

the ball in the dirt to the right or left? If the catcher cheats with the feet, he'll struggle to block the ball in the dirt properly. The toes of the right foot should be even with the instep of the left foot.

The target the catcher gives the pitcher must remain low, but notice in the figure how the throwing hand is now behind the glove. The thumb is still protected by the other fingers. This method is preferred because the hands must work together during blocks and throws. The catcher runs the risk of getting hit with a foul tip, but if the fingers shield the thumb, making a loose fist, the hand should be somewhat protected. Some catchers prefer to put the throwing hand on the right thigh, and others keep it behind the calf. Again, this is a personal preference, but it's tough for the hands to work together when they're apart.

The knees are parallel with the rear end, which keeps the catcher low enough to prevent blocking the umpire's view. Although the secondary stance is similar to a basketball defender's stance, the catcher must be a little lower than the average basketball defender. He must stay low in an athletic stance.

The catcher needs to keep his shoulders as square to the pitcher as possible, which is more easily accomplished when the feet are close to even. This is a very strenuous position to assume, so it's important for the catcher to stay relaxed. One way to accomplish this is to slouch the shoulders, which allows the upper body to stay as loose as possible.

The saying goes that if a catcher has good feet and good hands, he can throw effectively. Having a cannon for an arm certainly helps, but that's not the most important criteria for a catcher. If his feet are quick and he can get his body into the throwing position, and if the transfer of the ball is clean from the glove to the hand, a catcher will have success throwing out runners. Few base runners can outrun a thrown baseball. The trick is to get the ball into the air and to be accurate. It does a catcher no good to wind up and throw a 90-mile-an-hour fastball to second base. While the catcher is winding up, the runner is taking another step toward second. A quick release is the key. A quick release comes from proper footwork and a smooth transfer from glove to hand.

The word *efficient* is sometimes used in reference to the catcher's throw from behind the plate. Nothing in the throwing motion can be wasted if a catcher wants success in throwing out runners. The hands and feet must work together. Getting the ball from the mitt to the throwing hand as quickly as possible improves a catcher's throwing as much as any other factor and should be practiced daily. If a catcher is successful throwing out base runners, he most likely has a quick transfer. Transferring the ball smoothly from the glove to the throwing hand requires good, soft hands. If a catcher has a good transfer, he can get rid of the ball more quickly.

The transfer should occur out in front of the body. The arms remain bent, but the transfer needs to be out front. The idea is to get the ball into the throwing hand as quickly as possible. Sometimes catchers are taught to take the ball to the right ear and then to transfer the ball. This method is not preferred because a catcher can't throw the ball to any base if the ball is still in the glove. He needs to get the ball into his throwing hand. Getting the ball into the hand early also allows a better grip on the ball.

Because the catcher will be in a secondary stance any time he's throwing to the bases, the throwing hand should be close to the glove when the ball is caught. This allows his hands to work together. If the ball is received in the middle of the catcher's body or to his right, the hands should be together (figure 5.2). Notice how the thumb of the throwing hand and the thumb of the catcher's mitt are together in figure 5.2*a*. This creates a smoother transfer because the glove doesn't turn. The hand can go directly to the throwing position after the transfer.

If the catcher catches the ball to his glove side (to the left for a right-handed catcher), the throwing hand stays in the middle of the body, waiting for the glove to bring the ball back to the middle (figure 5.3). The thumbs are still pointing up. The catcher's throwing hand does not go with the glove to catch the ball to the catcher's left because that makes the shoulders turn too far, and it takes too long to move the shoulders back into position. The hands are much quicker than the shoulders. The catcher gathers the ball back into the middle with the glove instead of reaching with the throwing hand.

Figure 5.2 The ball is received in the middle of the catcher's body: *(a)* thumb of throwing hand and thumb of mitt are together; *(b)* the catcher smoothly transfers the ball to the throwing hand.

Figure 5.3 Catcher catches the ball on his glove side.

Once the ball is in his throwing hand, the catcher must go directly to the throwing position. Remember the word *efficient*? To be efficient, the catcher must not loop with his throwing arm. He moves the ball up in a straight line. It might not seem like much, but even a small loop in the throwing arm adds an unwanted delay when making a throw.

The catcher must concentrate on using his hands and not his shoulders. If he takes the ball to throwing position with his hands, his shoulders will follow. Again, the hands are much quicker than the shoulders. The catcher shouldn't worry about pointing his front shoulder at the target. If the hands do their job, the shoulders will get to a good throwing position. When a catcher thinks about pointing his front shoulder at his target, he can overcompensate, and his shoulders go too far. Use the hands!

Footwork

The importance of footwork in a successful throw from behind the plate is often underestimated. If a catcher can't get his feet into proper position quickly, he'll struggle to throw out base runners. Even a catcher with a tremendous throwing arm will have problems. The feet must take the body into throwing position.

A key to the catcher's footwork is that the feet can't move until the ball is caught. The feet must remain stationary until the ball hits the glove.

If the feet move too quickly, they'll set before the hands are ready. If the lower half of the body is ahead of the upper half, a lot of energy is wasted. Think of a hitter being out in front of an off-speed pitch. All the strength from his lower half is gone, and his body is out of sync. His hands and feet must work together.

Don't think that because the feet are stationary when the ball is caught that the body is stationary as well. The momentum of the body is very important. Body motion must start as the pitch is in flight. When the ball is caught, the body is moving, but the feet are stationary. The body should be leaning forward toward the ball, creating momentum.

Once the ball is caught, the feet explode toward the target. The right foot moves forward in a short, powerful step. This foot should be in line with the tip of home plate. If the right foot goes too far to the left, the catcher's rear end goes with it and takes the body off line. The left foot should move in front of the right so that the catcher is in an athletic position (figure 5.4). If the catcher is stepping on home plate, his steps are probably too long. When throwing to the bases, his footwork should be short, quick, and explosive.

It can be difficult to keep the body moving in a straight line toward a target. If the body is moving to the left of home plate, the right foot might be going too far to the left when the catcher takes the initial jab step. The

Figure 5.4 Athletic throwing position: catcher's feet aligned with the tip of home plate.

ball may be on the glove side, and as the glove reaches for the ball, the body might go with it. Just remember that the more the body is going toward third base, the more the throwing arm will drop. When the arm drops, the ball will sink as it flies to second base. Middle infielders don't like trying to catch the ball where the base stealer is sliding. To keep the ball straight, the catcher's momentum must stay on line to the target. Draw a straight line in the dirt right behind the tip of the plate to help keep the catcher on line.

The footwork described so far is for a ball caught on the glove side or down the middle of the plate. When the ball is on the throwing-arm side of the catcher, he uses a different technique.

If his feet move forward on the ball to his throwing-arm side (the right side for a right-handed catcher), his body will move in the opposite direction of the ball. It's as if the ball is passing by the body. That's why the catcher must pivot on his right foot and swing his left foot around. His body will then be slightly to the right and behind the plate (figure 5.5). The energy stored in his right leg is enough to create the momentum he needs to throw to second.

Some catchers try to pivot on their right feet for all their throws. This technique takes an extremely strong arm and is also very hard on the arm. Use the feet to create momentum except when the pitch is caught on the right.

Figure 5.5 The catcher makes the catch on his throwing-arm side. To get in throwing position, he pivots on his right foot and swings his left foot around.

Throwing Motion

Now that we've covered proper transfer and footwork, let's turn to proper throwing mechanics. Creating backspin on the baseball is very important when throwing to the bases. When the ball has backspin, it goes straight and tends to carry. If the ball has any sort of sidespin, it will sink. A catcher needs the ball to carry if he wants it to travel the 127 feet to second base. Catchers need to think in terms of throwing downhill. When throwing a ball downhill, the catcher has his fingers on top of the ball and he keeps his arm up high.

The arm can't drop down during the throwing motion. If the arm were an hour hand on a clock, it should go from 11 o'clock to 5 o'clock (figure 5.6). This helps create backspin.

The glove-hand (left hand for a right-handed catcher) pulls into the body during the release. This helps pull the body through and takes some strain off the throwing arm.

The lower half of the body must also be used. The legs are very strong and must be in a position to push the body toward the target. This means the catcher must get into an athletic position when throwing. His knees remain bent so they can push, but the upper half of his body must stay tall. Keeping his upper body tall allows him to stay on top of the ball and throw it downhill.

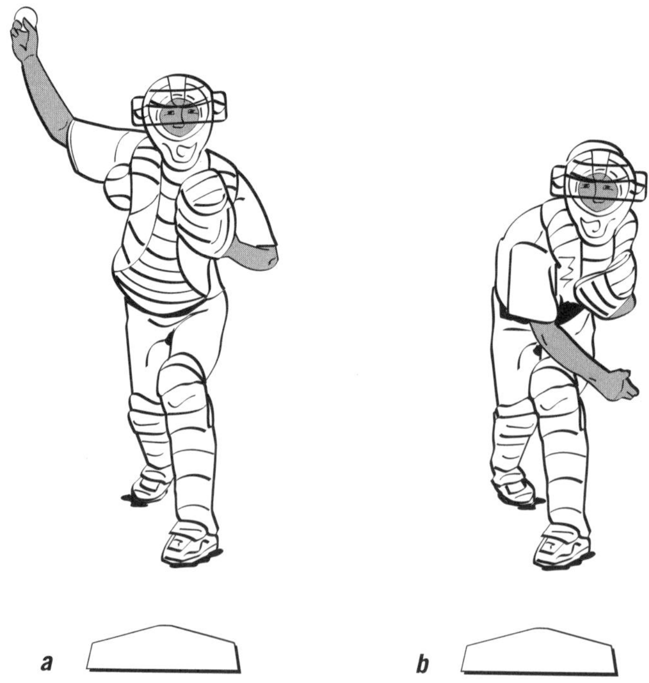

Figure 5.6 When throwing, the catcher's arm moves from *(a)* 11 o'clock to *(b)* 5 o'clock, creating backspin on the ball.

The catcher's head remains straight and on target once the ball is in his glove. If his head tilts, his body will follow. Many catchers tilt their heads to the left when they throw, which causes their right arms to drop.

Catchers should always remember to follow through after the throw. The short and quick arm action required to throw the ball to second base is tough enough on the arm. The body follows the arm to the target while decelerating.

Throws to Bases

Throwing to all three bases requires variations in footwork and arm action and a variety of mind-sets based on game situations. With continual practice, catchers can improve their arm strength, accuracy, and quickness.

Throwing to Second Base

A catcher can build quite a reputation based on his throwing arm. There's no better way to show off this ability than by throwing runners out at second base. Quickness of both hands and feet, arm strength, and accuracy are needed to throw the ball effectively to second base.

Many coaches don't have catchers throw to the bases very much in practice because the repetition strains the catcher's arm. However, a catcher needs to throw to the bases as much as possible to build up his arm strength and to perfect his accuracy. Catchers should be timed in between innings when they throw to second base. Keep a stopwatch handy to record their times. Knowing their times makes them more competitive and hungry to improve. In many games, no one attempts a steal. By throwing in between innings, the catcher is getting repetitions on game day. With increased practice, his arm will get stronger.

A good time for a high school catcher's throw from home to second base is 2.0 to 2.1 seconds. A good college catcher will throw 1.9 to 2.0. Be honest when working the watch. Being just a fraction early on the button can change a 2.0 to a 1.85, giving the catcher a false sense of security. It's rare for a catcher outside the big leagues to throw a 1.85.

Throwing to Third Base

Throwing the ball to third base is obviously easier than throwing to second because third base is only 90 feet from home plate. However, because catchers don't throw to third base between innings, they need to work on their throws from home to third during practice.

When a left-handed hitter is in the box (figure 5.7), a throw to third base is easy because nothing obstructs the catcher's view. The runner is in the catcher's field of vision, so the catcher can see the runner heading

Figure 5.7 The throw to third with a left-handed hitter at bat: *(a)* the pitch is caught in the middle of the catcher's body; *(b)* the catcher takes two explosive steps toward third and throws downhill.

for third. Once the ball leaves the pitcher's hand, the catcher can start his momentum toward third base *if* the ball is in the middle of his body or to his left. If the ball is to his right, he must wait a little longer to start his momentum. He still won't move his feet until he catches the ball. Once he has caught the ball, he takes two short, explosive steps toward third base. The throw to third base is much shorter than the throw to second base so throwing downhill is easier.

When a right-handed hitter is in the box (figure 5.8), the catcher has a much tougher throw. The hitter has a right to retain his stance and doesn't

Figure 5.8 The throw to third with a right-handed batter at the plate: *(a)* catcher makes the catch in the middle of his body; *(b)* he drops his right foot behind his left foot to clear the hitter and make the throw.

have to move out of the way. To clear the hitter, the catcher must drop the right foot behind the left foot. The left foot then moves toward third base. The catcher should never try to throw over the hitter. It's too easy to throw the ball into left field, and he risks hitting his fingers on the batter's helmet or bat.

The only time the catcher moves in front of a right-handed hitter when throwing to third is when the pitch is way outside. In this case, he must recognize the wide location of the pitch and meet the ball with his right foot. This step should take him slightly in front of the hitter. His left foot then goes directly toward third base, making this throw very difficult.

Throwing to First Base

Throwing the ball to first base to pick off a runner is another difficult throw for the catcher. It's much tougher for a catcher to get momentum toward first than it is toward second or third. Most important, the catcher needs a good pitch to throw from. A pitch located on the outside part of the plate to a right-handed hitter (or an inside pitch to a left-handed hitter) is the best pitch to throw to first from. This location allows the catcher's shoulders to open toward first base as he catches the ball. Once he has caught the ball, the catcher's right foot must open. He takes a short jab-step toward first base, which turns his shoulders completely. His left foot then moves toward first. Calling for the right pitch and getting the shoulders around to face the target are the most important things to remember in the throw to first.

Catchers with strong arms sometimes try this throw from their knees. Again, the catcher will want to look for a good pitch to throw from. After the ball is caught, the right knee opens and the left knee drives the body toward first base. The shoulders must turn for the catcher to make this throw effectively.

Double Steal Defense

A double steal puts pressure on a defense, especially the catcher. Almost all double steals are attempted with runners on first and third or runners on first and second. Either of these situations makes it tough on the catcher.

Runners on First and Third

The toughest situation for a catcher is when the offense has runners on first and third in a close game. If the game is close, the runner on third must be the priority, but the runner on first shouldn't be allowed to take second freely. The situation is further complicated when a right-handed hitter is in the batter's box because now the catcher can't easily see the runner on third. This situation can call for several different plays, including the look and throw, the throw to third, the pump fake, or the no-look and throw.

• **Look and throw.** The catcher looks at the runner at third before throwing to second. He hopes to freeze the runner at third before making the throw to second. The extra time he takes to look at the runner at third of course makes it difficult to throw the runner out at second. The main objective of this play is to have at least a chance to throw out the base stealer while not allowing the runner from third to score. The third baseman can help in this play by raising his hands in the air if he thinks the runner on third is too far down the line. The look and throw is often used early in a game. In the later innings, the score dictates if the play can be used. In a close game when a runner on third can't be allowed to score but allowing the runner to freely take second also causes problems, the look and throw is a play to consider.

• **Throw to third.** The catcher comes up out of his stance and throws directly to third base. It's crucial that the catcher keeps his throw to the inside of third base in fair territory because the runner will be in the baseline. If the ball hits the runner, it might be deflected away from the third baseman, allowing the run to score. Use this play when the runner on third is an important run and throwing the ball to second is too great of a risk. This play can also be used when the base runner at third is very aggressive.

• **Pump fake.** The catcher fakes a throw to second and looks for the runner at third to come off the base. The fake must be realistic to fool the base runner. A catcher with small hands might choose to keep the ball in his glove when using the pump fake. This keeps the ball from flying out of his hand on an aggressive fake. Employ this play when the runner at third represents an important run or when he's too aggressive coming down the third-base line.

• **No-look and throw.** The catcher tries to throw the runner out at second without worrying about the runner at third. This play is used when the team on defense has a lead and is willing to trade a run for an out. Don't ever give the run away. Make sure you have a good chance of throwing the runner out at second before trying the no-look throw.

Runners at the corners put pressure on a defense, and most of all the catcher. When the runners have good speed and the hitter is right-handed, the catcher has his work cut out for him. This situation must be practiced repeatedly so that when it occurs in a game, the defense knows how to respond.

Runners on First and Second

When runners on first and second attempt a double steal, the catcher must quickly decide where to throw the ball. As a rule, if a left-handed hitter is in the batter's box, the catcher should throw the ball to third base. In this case, the catcher has an open lane to throw into, and the throw to second is generally tougher with a left-hander at bat.

With a right-handed hitter in the box, the catcher can make a backdoor throw. He throws the ball to second base to catch the runner stealing from first. Because the right-handed hitter makes the throw to third tougher, the throw to second is often a better option. Generally, the runner at first base won't get as good a jump as the runner at second. Of course, the speed of the runners always influences the catcher's choice of where to throw the ball.

When runners are on first and second, the catcher should signal the infielders where he intends to throw the baseball if a double steal occurs. With two runners stealing, you don't want both bases being covered because this leaves too many holes in the defense. Something to watch for when considering the backdoor play is that the runner at first doesn't attempt to steal when the runner at second does. In this case, the third baseman must react and get to the bag, while the catcher adjusts to make the throw to third.

Delayed Steal Defense

The delayed steal is a tactic some coaches use against teams that tend to let their guard down. The base runner on first takes his secondary lead and then steals the base. The delay in his departure toward second base sometimes goes unnoticed until it's too late to throw him out. If the catcher neglects to check the runner or the middle infielders put their heads down after a pitch, a runner might try a delayed steal.

To defend against the delayed steal, the catcher should always check the runner before dropping to his knees. Many catchers automatically go down to their knees after they receive a pitch. If an opposing coach sees this, he might put on the delay. This play is usually attempted when a left-handed hitter is in the batter's box because it's tougher for the catcher to see the runner at first. Remember to always check the runner!

The middle infielders also play an important role in defending the delayed steal. After the pitch, the second baseman and shortstop should pick up the runner and step toward second base. If the middle infielders put their heads down and don't pick up the runner at first after the pitch, a delayed steal attempt will likely succeed.

Pitchouts

When a catcher or coach suspects that a base runner is going to try to steal a base, he might call for a pitchout, which can be effective in slowing down an opponent's running game. Typically, catchers are taught two ways to receive a pitchout. One involves fewer steps and allows the catcher to wait a bit longer before popping out; the other requires a few more steps but gets the catcher in a better position to receive the pitchout.

The catcher always sets up on the outside corner after he calls the pitchout. This gives him a little more separation from the hitter and makes it easier to pop out.

The quick pitchout involves fewer steps. When a right-handed hitter is up and the ball is released from the pitcher's hand, the catcher takes an angled step toward first base with his right foot to get away from the hitter and gain some momentum toward second base. After catching the ball, his left foot moves toward second, and he throws the ball. Only two steps are needed with this technique.

When a left-handed hitter is at the plate, the catcher takes an angled step toward third base with his left foot as the ball is released. After catching the ball, he takes two steps toward second base, his right foot preceding his left, and then releases his throw. Three steps are used here.

This method allows the catcher to retain his stance a bit longer, and he won't tip off the base runner. However, this technique also requires the pitcher to throw a perfect pitchout. The catcher is not in a position to adjust to a pitchout that's off line.

The longer pitchout requires the catcher to begin his footwork a little earlier because more steps are involved. Against a right-handed hitter, as the pitcher releases the ball, the catcher takes a step straight out to the right with his right foot (figure 5.9*a*). This keeps his body squared up to the pitcher. The catcher meets the pitch with his left foot (figure 5.9*b*) and then takes two steps (right foot first, then left) to get into position to throw (figure 5.9*c*). This technique requires four steps.

When a left-handed hitter is at the plate, the catcher has to step straight out to the left with his left foot and then step straight to the left with his right foot when the pitcher releases the ball (figure 5.10*a*). Again, his body should now be squared up to the pitcher. Once the pitcher releases the ball, the catcher meets it with his left foot (figure 5.10*b*) and then takes two steps with the right and then the left feet to get in position to throw (figure 5.10*c*). This method requires five steps.

The five-step method allows the catcher to get his body in position and create a lot of momentum toward second base. It also gives the pitcher a better target. A catcher with good feet can use this style with no problem. A slow-footed catcher might also use this method because it allows him a little extra time. The only drawback to the long pitchout is that the catcher's early movement might tip off an alert base runner. Honestly, few base runners have strong enough instincts to correctly read a pitchout. If a catcher crosses paths with a runner who has those kinds of instincts, the catcher can adjust and try the quick method instead.

Defending the stolen base successfully can be the difference between winning and losing a close baseball game. Teach pitchers to hold runners

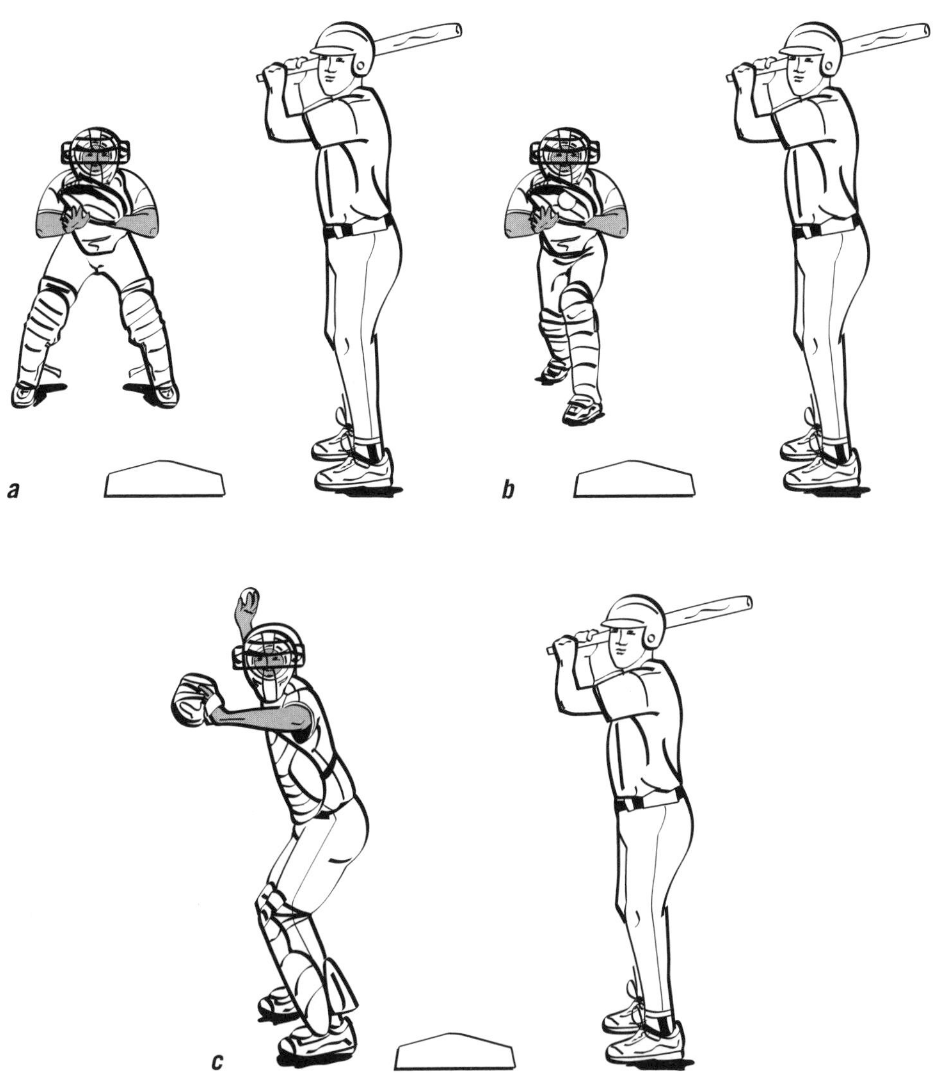

Figure 5.9 Long pitchout, right-handed hitter: *(a)* when the pitcher releases the ball, the catcher steps to the right; *(b)* the catcher makes the catch with his left foot forward; *(c)* the catcher takes two more steps to get into position to make the throw.

effectively by changing their timing and looks. Teach catchers to use the proper fundamentals when throwing to the bases. Prepare your team to handle first-and-third situations, double steals, and delayed steals.

The techniques and philosophies presented in this chapter must be worked on and discussed daily in practice. Preparing a team with gamelike situations during practice will improve the team's performance in games. Attention to detail and repetition of drills are the keys to successfully defending the stolen base.

Figure 5.10 Long pitchout, left-handed hitter: *(a)* catcher steps to the left; *(b)* catcher catches the pitch with his left foot forward; *(c)* he takes two more steps to get into position to throw.

Catcher Drills for Preventing Steals

Drills lead to the improvement of skills required to curtail an opponent's running game. Drills must be performed frequently with gamelike intensity and with several repetitions. The quality of drills should yield near perfection, but take care not to overdo them because too many repetitions can be counterproductive. Watch your players carefully and monitor their focus.

For a catcher to improve, he must work on certain fundamentals. The skills he needs to become a good thrower include quick feet, soft hands, a strong throwing arm, and accuracy. The following drills should improve these skills and increase his ability to throw out would-be base stealers.

One Knee

The catcher kneels on his right knee, facing his target. The target is about 30 to 40 feet away. The coach is in front of and off to the right of the catcher at a 45-degree angle (figure 5.11). The coach throws a baseball underhand to the catcher. The catcher catches the ball and transfers it into the throwing position. Move the ball around to work on different pitches. Make sure that the ball is going in a straight line to the throwing position. This drill checks for efficiency. Notice how the catcher's hand has turned the ball to face in the opposite direction of the target and how the glove stays in position so that the front shoulder is pointing to the target. Concentrate on a quick, smooth transfer and on hands working together.

Figure 5.11 One-knee drill.

Transfer Drill

Two catchers stand about 30 feet apart in athletic stances (figure 5.12). Feet stay in place during this drill. The catchers throw the ball back and forth quickly. The object is not to throw the ball hard but to get rid of it quickly. The drill is similar to the children's game Hot Potato. If the ball stays in the glove or hand too long, the catcher gets burned. Don't do this drill at a distance further than 30 feet because the arm needs the rest of the body to help on longer throws. This drill is meant to give the catcher a high number of repetitions in a competitive atmosphere.

Figure 5.12 Transfer drill.

Dry Runs

The catcher is in his secondary stance; a coach stands about 20 feet in front of the catcher on one knee. The coach throws the ball to different locations while the catcher works on getting to the throwing position as quickly as he can. This drill is meant to quicken the feet as the catcher works to develop proper footwork. The catcher won't throw during this drill, but he should be short, quick, and explosive with his feet.

Coach in the Middle

Use two catchers in this drill. Have them stand about 90 feet apart, with a coach midway between them. One catcher is in a secondary stance, and the other is standing up. The coach throws the ball to the catcher in the secondary stance; the catcher makes the catch and throws the ball to the standing catcher. The ball is then thrown back to the coach, and the catchers switch roles. This drill gives the catchers many repetitions at a shorter distance.

Triangle or Square Drill

You need three catchers for the triangle drill and four for the square drill. All the catchers stand in an athletic position approximately 60 feet apart. The ball is thrown around clockwise as catchers work on getting rid of the ball and setting their feet. Switch the direction of the ball to counterclockwise. Catchers must meet the ball with their left feet and then take the two steps to get their momentum going in the direction of the target. This simulates the footwork of a home-to-first double play.

A variation of the square drill is to allow catchers to throw in any direction, including diagonally. Everyone must be ready to react to the ball. If a catcher doesn't have the ball, he may squat down. If a catcher is squatting, he's off limits. The ball must go to someone else. The catcher must reset his feet and throw to another catcher.

6

Executing Pickoffs and Rundowns

Mike Maack

The consistent success of top-notch sports teams has long been credited to the high value these teams place on defense. The ability to consistently stop the other team from scoring, or to limit their scoring opportunities, allows a team's ever-fluctuating offense to play a lesser role in determining the outcome of a contest. Defense has a reliability factor that offense doesn't enjoy. An offense might score up to 20 runs, or even more, on a given night, but you'll rarely see a defense make more than four or five errors in a game, and even that many is quite unusual. Even with wind, wet surfaces, and bad hops on a rough infield, defense is more predictable than offense and can be more easily practiced to something resembling perfection. Offense, meanwhile, with its high degree of variability, is impossible to perfect. Your team is in a groove, on an eight-game winning streak, and then you're two-hit by a soft-throwing junk ball pitcher, your big hitters start to slump, and your winning streak turns into a five-game skid. That's offense for you. Fortunately, you can combat the unpredictable nature of your offense with a solid defense known for its grit and reliability.

The more defensive weapons a baseball team has in its arsenal, the greater its chances of success over a long season. Pickoff plays and rundowns are two such weapons. Proper execution of the pickoff move and the ensuing rundown is vital to any defense. Every team should address these two phases of the game in their daily practice plan.

Left-Handed Pitcher's Pickoff Zones at First Base

The best move to first base can be achieved by breaking the process down into three zones, each one vital to the development of a good pickoff move. The key is the left-handed pitcher's ability to blend the movements of all three zones into a smooth and controlled delivery identical to his delivery to the plate. By coordinating all three, a pitcher can consistently make runners believe that he's delivering the ball to the plate when in fact he's coming to first base.

Breaking the whole into three parts makes it easier for the coach and pitcher to analyze the pickoff move and make proper adjustments. Once the pitcher understands how to control his body, he'll have success in developing a good move.

Zone 1

This is the most important zone, in which the pitcher is selling the runner that he's throwing to the plate. Zone 1 involves the pitcher's head, glove, and shoulders. All three should remain pointing directly at the catcher even while the ball is being thrown to first base. The head looks to the base once the ball has been released, but not before.

Many coaches teach their pitchers to vary their head looks to a base, but too many times, the pitcher unconsciously develops a pattern that tips off runners when he's going to throw over. I suggest that a three-look sequence be taught instead:

1. The first look is at the catcher to pick up the pitch signal.
2. The second look is to the base as the pitcher comes to the set position.
3. The third look is back to the catcher as the pitcher reaches the top of his leg lift, but not before.

Effectiveness lies in the consistency of the delivery, eliminating any possible patterns the pitcher might otherwise develop. As the body begins to drive down the 45-degree line, the head, glove, and shoulders should be pointed at the catcher. At this point, 99 percent of runners are already picked off. A common mistake pitchers make is to reach with the glove somewhere between the 45-degree line and the base, which forces the shoulders to turn, thus tipping off the runner.

Zone 2

Zone 2 involves footwork, leg lift, balance position, and body drive down the 45-degree line.

The pitcher's feet should always be in a staggered position with the heel of the stride foot lined up with the toes of the pivot foot. The pivot heel should be about 2 inches in front of the rubber. This allows the pitcher to turn his body slightly toward the runner, increasing the pitcher's angle within the imaginary 45-degree line and decreasing the chance of a balk. Still, this isn't enough of a turn for the runners or coaches to notice or to affect the pitcher's delivery to the plate.

Staggering his feet helps the pitcher control his leg lift. Maintaining control of the body is crucial during this stage of the delivery. All the pitcher has to do is lift his foot straight up. It's also important that he keep his stride foot relaxed. Tension in the foot often causes the pitcher to reach out with it rather than allowing it to move naturally with the body. Very often, this little reaching motion is enough to tip off the runner at first. A pitcher who begins with his feet side by side instead of staggered tends to kick his foot out on the leg lift, causing his back to arch. This creates balance problems and makes it easier for the runner to detect when the pitcher is throwing to the base and not the plate.

A controlled leg lift makes it virtually impossible for the runner to steal on the pitcher's first move. Remaining balanced during this phase allows the pitcher to step down and throw to the base when the runner takes off. The balanced position at the top of the leg lift is the most important position in the delivery. Up to this point, the pitcher has not given any indication that he's going to throw over to the base. His next move will determine whether the runner will be picked off. At this point, the pitcher is going to look home and begin the move.

As the pitcher's body begins to drive down the 45-degree line, the pickoff move to first base mirrors the delivery to the plate. Everything must be similar. The pivot leg pushes the body down the line, and the stride foot is closed and relaxed and ready to catch the body as it lands.

Zone 3

Zone 3 involves the throwing arm and the follow-through. The pitcher is responsible for getting the ball to the base accurately without using the glove side of his body to generate power and to follow the throw to the base in the event the runner is picked off. Enough power will be generated from the momentum of his body moving down the 45-degree line.

Complete Pickoff Move

1. The pitcher looks in for the signal from the catcher.
2. The pitcher comes to the set position with his feet staggered and looks to the base (figure 6.1*a*).
3. The pitcher begins a controlled leg lift (figure 6.1*b*).
4. Once in a balanced position, the pitcher's body drives down the 45-degree line and his head, glove, and shoulders point to the plate (figure 6.1*c*).
5. As his weight is transferred to the stride foot, the pitcher throws the ball. His head keeps looking home until the ball is delivered. At this point, his body pushes off the stride foot and follows the ball to the base in the event of a pickoff (figures 6.1*d*-*f*).

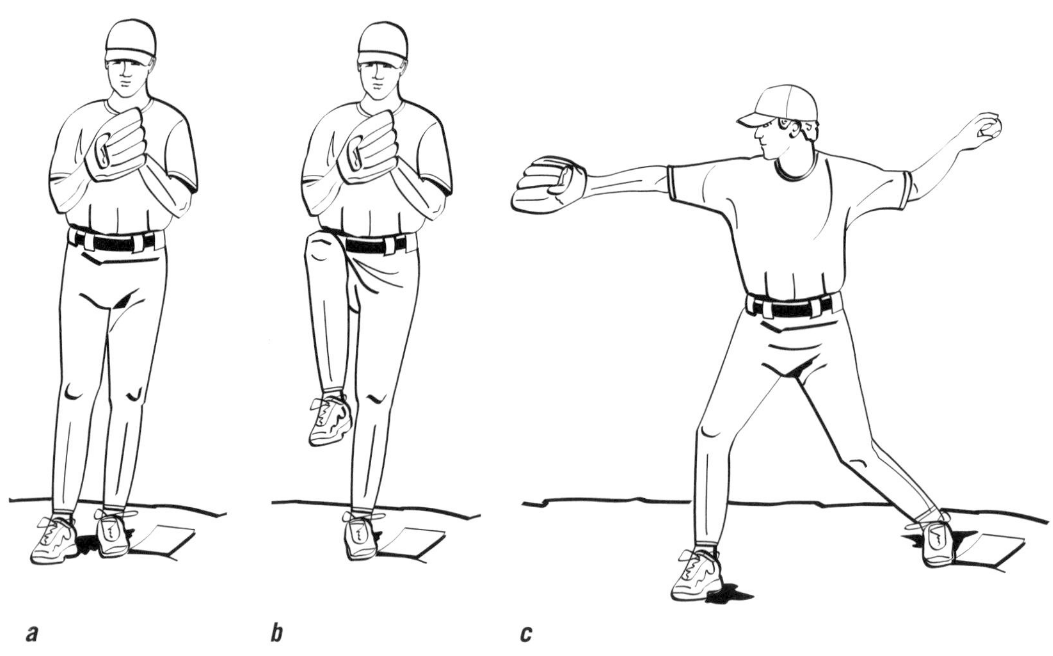

Figure 6.1a-c Pickoff move: *(a)* pitcher looks to base; *(b)* controlled leg lift; *(c)* body drive down 45-degree line with head, glove, and shoulders turned toward home plate.

Figure 6.1d-f Pickoff move (continued): *(d)* weight shifts to stride foot in anticipation of the throw; *(e)* pitcher throws to the base; *(f)* pitcher follows his throw to the base.

Because the runner is picked off before the throw is made, the throw must be accurate but not hard. The harder the pitcher tries to throw the ball, the more his body turns to gain velocity. Emphasize to pitchers to get on top of the ball as much as possible without turning the shoulders. The throwing elbow should be slightly lower than the shoulder at the release point. The throw is actually more of a wrist-snap with a good follow-through. It's common for pitchers first learning the move to throw the ball in the direction their body is moving. This is easily corrected through progressive teaching drills.

The follow-through is important for two reasons. First, the pitcher doesn't want the umpire to get a good look at where he landed. Second, in the event the runner is picked off, the pitcher must assist in the rundown.

A good habit for a pitcher to establish is to push off the stride foot and move toward the base as the throw is made. In the event the pitcher violates the 45-degree line, this push-off will give the appearance that his body was going to the base in a legal direction.

Left-Handed Pitcher's Pickoff to First Base

The threat of a pickoff is the only way to keep runners from getting too large of a lead off the base. To execute the pickoff efficiently and effectively, a left-handed pitcher must master three facets of the move.

The first and most important is balance. When talking about balance in pitching, the focus is on a pitcher's ability to maintain consistent body control throughout his delivery, resulting in consistent ball control. Without balance, a left-handed pitcher has no defense against a runner who takes off on the pitcher's first move. A poorly balanced delivery to the plate gives the base stealer a huge advantage because the pitcher is unable to throw over to first base. However, a balanced delivery freezes the runner and won't allow him to get a good jump.

The second factor is direction. Direction is the ability of the pitcher to control the movement of his body when throwing to first base while appearing to be delivering a pitch to the plate. Direction is the most difficult factor for pitchers to learn because it requires them to move their body in one direction (45 degrees) while throwing the ball in another without tipping the motion off with the shoulders or legs.

The third element is the follow-through, which involves pushing off the inside of the stride leg and following the throw to the base in case the runner is picked off. An effective follow-through is vital because in the event the runner is successfully picked off, the pitcher is the only backup to the first baseman in a rundown.

The delivery when throwing to first base should be a mirror image of the delivery when throwing to the plate. The obvious objective is to make the runner think the pitch is being delivered to the plate. When throwing to first, the throw doesn't have to be hard, but it must be accurate. The tempo of both throws, to the plate and to first base, must be identical.

The runner will be picked off before the throw is actually made to the base. One of the biggest problems pitchers have is trying to throw the ball too hard, which forces them to turn their shoulders toward the base, which tips off the runner.

Setting Up the Runner

The decision to attempt a pickoff is made before the pitcher steps on the rubber. Once the plan of attack is in place, the pickoff is simply a matter of setting up the runner and keeping the delivery consistent. A left-handed pitcher will set up the runner by looking to the catcher at the beginning of the leg lift.

A certain amount of strategy is involved when a left-handed pitcher picks a runner off first base. A series of setup moves are required before the pitcher uses his best move. The number of setup moves is usually determined by the pitcher. He'll use his bad moves until he feels good about his read on the runner. He might use these moves consecutively or alternate them with pitches to the plate. In any case, he should try to get a feel for the runner during his delivery to the plate. If he sees the runner leaning away from the base or beginning his secondary lead, this tells him to go immediately to his best move. But in most cases the pitcher has greater success if he sets up the runner with one or more bad moves and then goes to his best.

The series of setup moves is something each pitcher develops for himself. Setup moves should range from an obviously bad move to a move that could be mistaken for his best move. There are two important things for a pitcher to do in his setup move:

1. He must turn his head toward home plate the instant he begins to lift his stride foot.
2. He must always reach with his glove hand and point his glove shoulder directly at first base when making the throw.

The runner will start to identify the head turn on the first movement and the glove hand and shoulder turn as initiating the throw to first. Once the runner thinks he has the pitcher figured out, it's easier for the pitcher to pick him off.

Left-Handed Pitcher Drills

These drills help a lefty develop a good pickoff move to first base. Practiced daily, the drills make for quicker progress. They're designed to break a delivery down into segments so that the pitcher gets a good feel for the necessary body movements.

For best results, do the drills in the order in which they're presented here. Doing so will produce the greatest results in achieving the feel of the delivery to first base. It's also good practice for the pitchers not to look at all to the base while throwing. This helps develop a better feel of the arm slot during the move.

Chair Drill

The pitcher sits in a chair facing his partner, who's standing about 30 feet away. Sitting in the chair minimizes the use of the lower half of the body, allowing greater use of the shoulders and head. The emphasis is on the shoulders remaining in line with the plate, the head and glove-hand pointing toward the plate, and the throwing arm making the toss to the partner (figure 6.2). This drill is excellent in developing the proper feel of the throwing action.

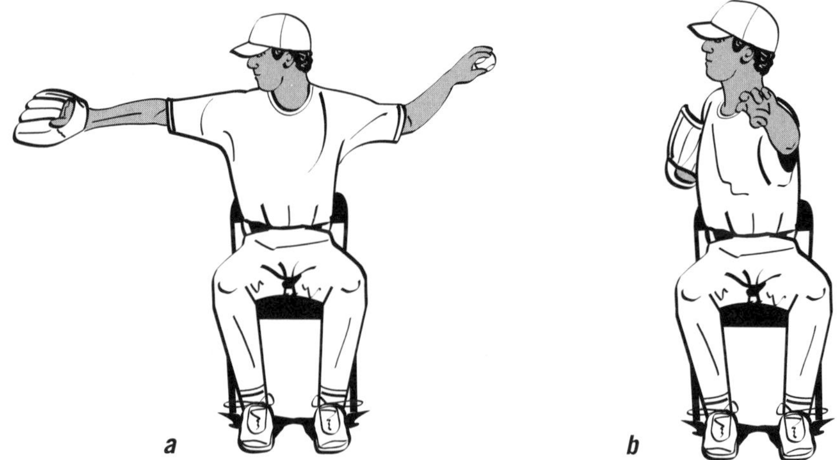

Figure 6.2 Chair drill: *(a)* pitcher sits in a chair; *(b)* as he throws to his partner, his shoulders, head, and glove-hand stay in line with home plate.

Stand-Up Drill

The pitcher stands with his feet shoulder-width apart, facing a partner 30 feet away. The pitcher's feet remain stationary throughout the drill except for the rotation on the balls of his feet as the pitcher transfers his weight. Emphasize keeping the shoulders in line with the plate; the glove-hand and head point toward the plate as the arm makes the throw to the base (figure 6.3). The lower half of the body has more movement and hip rotation than it does in the chair drill.

Figure 6.3 Stand-up drill: *(a)* pitcher stands with feet shoulder-width apart; *(b)* he throws to his partner, keeping his shoulders, glove-hand, and head in line with home plate.

Stand-Up 45-Degrees Drill

The setup is the same as for the stand-up drill except the feet are at a 45-degree angle (figure 6.4). The pitcher starts with his weight on his back leg so that he can feel the weight transfer from his back leg to his stride leg during the delivery to the base.

Figure 6.4 Stand-up 45-degrees drill: *(a)* pitcher stands with feet staggered, front foot at a 45-degree angle; *(b)* he throws to his partner at the base.

Step 45-Degrees Drill

The pitcher stands on the mound with his feet in proper position for the leg lift (figure 6.5*a*). He steps directly down the 45-degree line without the leg lift. The purpose of this drill is for the pitcher to feel his weight being transferred by his legs down the 45-degree line. At the same time, the pitcher should reach his glove-hand toward home plate (figure 6.5*b*), turn his head toward the plate, and make the throw to the base (figure 6.5*c*). Once he has made the throw, the pitcher pushes off his stride leg and begins running toward the base. This procedure makes it look as if the body were going to the base throughout the delivery and gets the pitcher in position to be the next man in line in case of a rundown.

Figure 6.5 Step 45-degrees drill: *(a)* pitcher stands on mound with feet together for leg lift; *(b)* without doing the leg lift, he steps down the 45-degree line, reaching toward home plate with his glove-hand; *(c)* he throws the ball to the base.

Balance Drill

The pitcher stands on the mound with his stride leg lifted to the balance position and looks toward first base (figure 6.6*a*). He holds this position for 3 to 5 seconds, feeling totally in control of his body. The pitcher starts the delivery by looking at the plate. At the exact same time, he reaches with his glove-hand toward the plate and begins his drive down the 45-degree line (figure 6.6*b*). He must make sure his shoulders remain parallel to first base. After making the throw to the base (figure 6.6*c*), he pushes off his stride leg and runs to the bag.

This drill should start in the set position. Work on a balanced leg lift and hold it at the top for 3 to 5 seconds before continuing.

Figure 6.6 Balance drill: *(a)* pitcher holds the balance position for a few seconds; *(b)* he reaches toward home plate with his glove-hand and drives down the 45-degree line; *(c)* he throws the ball to the base.

Right-Handed Pitcher's Pickoff to First Base

Why do most right-handed pitchers have a difficult time holding runners at first base? The problem is twofold. First, they don't work on their deliveries to the plate with runners on first base, and second, they don't work properly on setting up runners before trying to pick them off. Not every pitcher is going to be great at picking off runners, but every pitcher can be effective in holding runners close.

All base runners fall into one of three categories. The base-stealing threat will usually attempt to steal within the first two pitches. The average to above-average runner is a situational base stealer. He'll usually attempt to steal on breaking-ball counts only. Finally, nonrunners don't attempt steals very often. Obviously, pitchers will pay most attention to runners in one of the first two categories.

Pitchers must learn to categorize runners. Not every runner is going to be a threat to steal. In fact, any given team probably has only a couple of runners that pitchers need to be concerned about. But runners who are a threat to steal instantly attract attention and put pressure on the pitcher.

Perfecting the art of holding runners takes the pressure off the pitcher and replaces it with confidence because the pitcher knows that he's in control of the situation and the runner isn't dictating his thoughts. When the pitcher knows who these runners are, he's less likely to lose focus on the hitter.

To effectively hold runners close, a right-handed pitcher must first vary the timing of his delivery to the plate with runners on first or second base. Second, he needs to practice the proper technique for setting up runners before attempting to pick them off at first base. When attempting to pick a runner off at second base, the pitcher should use only his best move.

Varying the Delivery Time

Timing a pitcher's delivery to the plate is a key fundamental for runners attempting to steal. Many pitchers tend to do the same thing when a runner is on base. His delivery seldom changes, and it becomes easy for the runner to time his break to the next base. The pitcher needs to vary his delivery to disrupt the runner's timing and make it more difficult for him to get a good jump. A pitcher has eight primary options when executing this tactic.

1. Hold the ball until the batter calls for time out. An aggressive base runner is waiting for the pitcher to do something so that he can get a jump and attempt to steal a base. The pitcher, by coming set and holding the ball, forces the runner to make a choice. In most cases, this makes the runner nervous. He'll get anxious and begin to move his feet rapidly in an attempt to go, take off early, or retreat to first base. In any case, the pitcher is not to break from the set position until the umpire calls time out or the runner breaks early.

2. Set and hold 5 seconds, then attempt a pickoff with his best move. This is a great follow-up to the set and hold with no throw. Many times, this catches the runner off guard and off balance, resulting in a pickoff.

3. Set and hold 5 seconds, then step off the back of the rubber quickly while separating the hands and checking the runner, but making no throw. Many times, a runner will tip off his attempt to steal by flinching toward second base. The hitter might also tip off a bunt attempt on the pitcher's first movement.

4. Set and hold the ball 5 seconds, then pitch. This catches the runner off guard and makes it hard for the runner to time the delivery and get a good jump.

5. Attempt a pickoff before getting to the set position. This might catch the runner off balance while he's taking his primary lead.

6. Come to the set position with no look to first, and pitch. Because looking over to first or second base is a natural thing for the pitcher to do, the no-look and pitch makes it difficult for the runner to time the delivery, thus making it hard to get a good jump.

7. Come to the set position, look one, two, or three times, and then pitch. The pitcher must vary this maneuver. He needs to avoid developing a pattern of looking the same number of times when going to the plate.

8. Come to the set position, look one, two, or three times, and then attempt a pickoff. Setup moves to first base can be executed here, as well as the pitcher's best move. Remember that any attempt to pick at second base should be done with the intention of picking off the runner. Keep in mind that the pitcher must throw to first base when attempting a pickoff but doesn't have to throw the ball to second or third base if he doesn't want to.

Note that options 6 and 7 should be practiced and executed the same way with runners on first or second base.

Setting Up and Picking Off the Runner

As is true for left-handed pitchers, balance is the key for every right-handed pitcher in developing a good pickoff move. Because it's much more difficult for a right-handed pitcher to pick off a runner at first base, he must develop a quick delivery from the set position to the plate and to first base. It's imperative for the right-handed pitcher to have quick feet and develop a quick snap throw to be successful in his pickoff attempt.

The right-handed pitcher must also do a good job of not tipping his move by keeping his body language in the set position consistent. Pitchers often give away their move by doing something different when they're getting ready to pick to first base.

Unlike a left-handed pitcher, who's trying to force a runner to shorten his lead before the pitcher uses his best move, the right-handed pitcher must try to make the runner feel comfortable enough to extend his lead before the pitcher uses his best move. This is best done through a series of moves that allow the runner ample time to get back safely to first base as the pitcher sets him up for his best move.

Note that in every setup move the action of the throwing arm is long, simulating a normal throwing motion, to allow more time to release the ball, thus allowing the runner to get back safely. This is all part of the plan to set up the runner. In addition, each setup move should be gradually quicker, and one of them should be the move that the runner mistakenly thinks is the pitcher's best. Once the runner thinks he has figured out the pitcher, he'll gain enough confidence to extend his lead another step or two.

For a right-handed pitcher, the main objective for setting up a runner at first base is to get the runner to feel secure that he can get back to the base on an attempted pickoff. The goal is to allow time for the runner to comfortably and confidently extend his lead. To do this, the pitcher must practice patience when throwing over to first. Too many times, the pitcher shows his best move too soon and alarms the runner, making it almost impossible to set him up or pick him off. The pitcher can't be in a rush to show his best move because the runner needs a few throws before he gets into his comfort zone.

It takes less than 1 second for a runner taking a normal lead to dive directly back to first base. With this in mind, the pitcher must develop a series of setup moves to entice the runner to extend his lead. In addition, the pitcher's best move must be executed in less than 1 second from first movement to tag. This can be mastered by following these two rules:

1. On all setup moves, the throwing arm must go down to make the throw. No matter what the feet do, this makes the delivery longer and permits the runner to get back safely.
2. On his best move to first or second base, the pitcher must execute his turn with quick feet, and the throwing arm must come up to the ear to make the throw. The momentum of the body turning allows plenty of energy to make an effective throw.

Remember that the key is not the speed of the ball thrown to the base but how quickly the ball is released.

The three setup moves that follow gradually get better and give the runner a chance to gain confidence in his lead:

1. Step off the back of the mound and throw to first with a long throwing motion. This should be executed slowly, but not too obviously slow.
2. Do the same as in move 1, but speed up the feet and the throw.
3. With quick feet, hop-turn and throw to first with a long throwing motion. The pitcher must execute this move a few times to allow the runner to get comfortable and mistakenly think that this move is the pitcher's best.

Once the pitcher has set up the runner, it's time for him to use his best move, which must be executed quickly. The feet turn swiftly on the hop turn, and the ball is released as quickly as possible. Obviously, the sooner the ball is on its way, the better chance of picking off the runner.

Right-handed pitchers need to practice pickoff moves to first base to make sure they can effectively hold the runner and entice the runner to make a move. Drills for right-handed pitchers are included later, under Drills for Pickoffs to First and Second Base (page 106).

Pickoff Plays to Second Base

Regardless of which hand the pitcher throws with, pickoffs to second base are executed the same way. With the exception of the inside move, which the pitcher executes by turning toward his throwing side, all other moves are executed by turning toward the glove side.

Coaches use many different variations of pickoff plays in their defensive schemes. Here are a few basic pickoff plays practiced and executed most often by both left- and right-handed pitchers.

Pitcher Reacting to Middle Infielders

This is one of the most common pickoffs in baseball. Execution depends solely on the pitcher's ability to react quickly to the middle infielder breaking to the bag.

Once the pitcher comes to a set position in his delivery, he begins his look to check the runner at second base. During this time, one of the middle infielders, most commonly the shortstop, prepares to break to the bag as the pitcher takes one of his looks at the runner.

The universal indicator used by the shortstop to signal the pitcher to throw is showing the glove-hand as he breaks to the bag. The indicator used by the second baseman is the open throwing hand as he breaks to the bag. Immediately upon seeing this signal, the pitcher quickly turns, following his glove-hand, and attempts to pick off the runner. The throw should be made accurately over the bag and slightly to the third-base side.

Timing Play

Another commonly practiced pickoff move is the timing play. This play requires a lot of practice for the pitchers and middle infielders to coordinate the timing between the pitcher looking home, the infielder breaking to the bag, and the pitcher wheeling to pick at second base.

The basic execution of this move is simple. The pitcher usually has a predetermined number of looks he'll make to second base before the play is executed. Once the pitcher looks to the runner the set number of times, the pitcher turns his head toward the batter and begins to count 1001, 1002. At the right time, the designated infielder breaks quickly to the bag. As the pitcher says 1002 to himself, he quickly turns toward his glove-hand and attempts to pick off the runner. Again, the throw should be over the bag and slightly to the third-base side.

Inside Move

The inside move is probably the most difficult for the pitcher to make look natural. It is usually attempted on counts when the runners will run, such as a 3-2 count with two outs and runners on first and second base. The pitcher must emulate his normal leg lift from the stretch position, making it look exactly like his delivery to the plate. At the top of his leg lift, he turns inside to his throwing side and steps toward second base to make his throw.

The middle infielder breaks to the bag as the pitcher reaches the top of his leg lift. He must be careful not to tip off the move by breaking to the bag too early. The pitcher must be aware of the runner as he turns to make the throw. If the runner is in his secondary lead, the pitcher continues with his throw to the bag. If the runner is running hard toward third base, the pitcher comes off the mound and runs directly at the runner, running him back toward second base before throwing the ball to the middle infielder covering the base.

No-Look Pickoff

This move can be executed from the stretch or the wind-up and must be done as the pitcher is getting his signs without his ever looking at the runner at second base. The move must be carefully coordinated among the pitcher, catcher, and middle infielders. It requires a lot of practice to perfect the timing between the middle infielders breaking to the base, the catcher giving the signal to the pitcher to pick, and the pitcher attempting the pickoff.

As the pitcher is in position to receive the signal, the middle infielder breaks to the base. At the exact time the middle infielder breaks, the catcher alerts the pitcher by giving him the predetermined signal to pick. The most common signal is the catcher flipping his glove-hand toward his right leg. Immediately upon seeing the signal, the pitcher turns to pick at second base.

This is a great move to use when the base runner at second has lost focus and seems to be drifting too far off the bag as the pitcher is getting his signals from the catcher. It can be used with runners on second, first and second, second and third, or with the bases loaded.

The coach should create a signal to put the play on without tipping off the opposing team or runner. He can do this between pitches using a verbal signal from the dugout or from the shortstop without the pitcher ever having to make eye contact with the runner. The less attention the pitcher gives the runner, the better his chance of catching him wandering off the base.

Drills for Pickoffs to First and Second Base

This drill series is effective in developing the mechanics necessary for a right-handed pitcher's pickoff move to first base as well as developing both the left- and right-handed pickoff moves to second base. The only difference is that the right-handed pitcher works on making a quick quarter-turn for his pickoffs to first base. On pickoffs to second base, both left- and right-handed pitchers work on making a quick half-turn.

Repetition is vital in mastering the pickoff move. Run these drills in the order in which they're listed and make them part of your pitchers' daily workout routine.

Line Drill

Most right-handed pitchers who don't have good moves to first base struggle with their footwork and tend to magnify the problem with a long throwing delivery. This drill is effective in helping the pitcher develop quick feet. Pitchers can practice it individually or in a group. There's no throwing motion in this drill, so the pitcher focuses completely on footwork.

The pitcher straddles the foul line in the outfield. A right-handed pitcher working on his pickoff move to first base turns a quarter-turn as quickly as he can to his glove side and lands with both feet on the foul line. When working on his pickoff move to second base, he turns a half-turn as quickly as he can to his glove side and again lands with both feet straddling the line. He must do this quickly while maintaining his balance. Many pitchers find this drill easy, but others have difficulty at first. All pitchers, regardless of skill level, should perform this drill until they show consistency in turning quickly and maintaining balance.

Line Drill With Loading Up

This drill is executed the same way as the line drill except the pitcher simulates the proper throwing motion. Regardless of whether the pitcher is working on his pickoff move to first or second base, he executes the drill the same way. This time, however, his throwing hand comes up out of his glove, and he gets into the proper loading phase of the delivery (figure 6.7). Because the throwing action during the pickoff is different from his normal arm action, the pitcher needs to practice this drill with a lot of repetition to develop the throwing action he needs for a quick delivery.

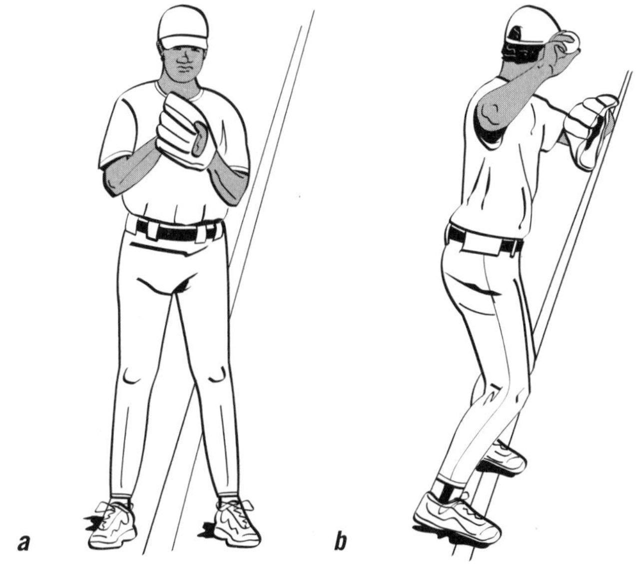

Figure 6.7 Line drills with loading up: *(a)* pitcher straddles foul line; *(b)* he makes a quarter-turn and loads, ready to throw.

Line Drill With Quick Toss

This drill is done the same as the line drill with loading up except the pitcher begins with his throwing hand in the loaded position next to his chin (figure 6.8*a*). As he makes his quick turn to first or second base, he works on throwing the ball from this position (figure 6.8*b*). This might feel awkward at first, but through repetition he'll begin to feel more comfortable and natural throwing the ball from this position. Again, because this throwing action differs from the normal arm action, repetition is vital to develop consistency in the delivery.

Figure 6.8 Line drill with quick toss: *(a)* pitcher straddles the foul line with the ball in a loaded position next to his chin; *(b)* he makes a half-turn and throws from the preloaded position.

Line Drill Loading Up With Quick Toss

Pitchers can do this drill with a partner or by throwing the ball into a net. Emphasize quick feet, balance, and proper throwing action. Because the pitcher is now putting it all together, it's common for him to revert back to a more normal throwing motion. Make sure he brings the ball up out of the glove before making his throw (figure 6.9). This movement takes a lot of repetition to develop but becomes natural over time.

Figure 6.9 Line drill loading up with quick toss: *(a)* pitcher straddles the foul line; *(b)* he quickly makes a half-turn, bringing the ball up out of his glove; *(a)* he throws the ball to a partner or into a net.

Right-Handed Pitcher's Pickoff Move to Third Base

This move is also a great weapon for the right-handed pitcher picking a runner off third base. The best time to try it is when the runner at third base gets too comfortable and begins to take his secondary lead as the pitcher begins his leg lift. When executed with success, this move can demoralize an offense.

Unlike the left-handed pitcher, the right-handed pitcher must use his best move without attempting to set up the runner. Setup moves to third base only alarm the runner. The runner then knows the pitcher is thinking about him, which eliminates the chance of a pickoff. The pitcher's delivery to third base must be a mirror image of his delivery to the plate. The movements should be identical in both sequence and timing.

The only significant difference from a left-handed pitcher's move to first base is that the left-handed pitcher is throwing to a stationary target, and the right-handed pitcher going to third base must have a pre-throw signal because the third baseman will be away from the base and moving on the throw. This signal is usually given by the third baseman in an inconspicuous way, but the coach, catcher, or another designated player can also give the signal.

The person giving the signal must take care not to alert the runner or the third-base coach. The signal must have been practiced and rehearsed several times so that it looks natural during the game.

The right-handed pitcher's pickoff move to third base is identical to the left-handed pitcher's best pickoff move to first base. Once the designated player gives the predetermined signal, the pitcher goes through his natural delivery. Everything, from the number of times he normally looks at the runner to his delivery, must be the same as in his natural delivery. Any deviation might alert the runner that a pickoff attempt is coming.

In addition, the third baseman must conceal any difference in where he plays defensively so that the runner or third-base coach won't catch on to the pickoff. Once the pitcher gets to the top of his leg lift in his delivery, the third baseman casually walks to the bag, preparing to receive the throw. The third baseman's movement can't be sudden or rushed because it might alert the third-base coach and possibly the runner.

The most important thing to note about the pickoff attempt by a right-handed pitcher to third base is that it must be practiced regularly so that the sequence of events that take place from the signal being given to the actual move are well orchestrated. When executed with perfection, this move can be a game saver.

Rundowns

When a runner is picked off base, he often gets caught in a rundown between the base he occupied and the base he wants to advance to. Defensive execution of the rundown play is critical in taking advantage of the opportunity to record an out. Failure to practice this play regularly results in embarrassing miscues and runners safe on base. With proper practice, the execution of the rundown is quick and effective, with few throws required.

The goal of the defensive team is to limit the number of throws to one or two. In the event the runner ends up safe, you always want that runner safe at the base he originally occupied.

To learn how to execute a successful rundown, first note these details. You want to split the base path into two lanes—the lane between the bases for the runner and an inside lane for the defenders. Always give the runner the lane between the bases. The defender with the ball and the receiving defender should occupy the lane on the infield side of the base. This ensures that there will be no throwing over, or around, the runner and gives the defenders a clear path to make the throw, whether they throw with the left or right hand.

Once the throw is made, the defender should always break in toward the pitching-mound side of the infield and advance to the base he was heading to in case he needs to take another throw. Again, doing this prevents collisions with the runner and a possible interference call.

Fielders must never dance with the runner. That is, the defender with the ball should never speed up or slow down with the runner. Running hard at the runner forces the runner to commit to one direction and prevents him from dictating the rundown. If he slows down, the defender with the ball can either catch him and make the tag or feed the ball to the receiving defender as he begins running hard toward the runner to receive the throw.

The guidelines that follow increase the chance of successfully executing the rundown with a limited number of throws.

- **Always run hard at the runner with the ball in the air, forcing the runner to commit.** Getting the runner to run hard makes it more difficult for him to stop and change direction quickly and gives the receiving defender a better chance to catch the ball and tag the runner. Even the fastest runners have difficulty changing directions when forced to go hard one way.
- **Always look at the defender receiving the ball, not at the runner, to see when he moves his feet, signaling that he wants the throw.** If you're running hard at the runner and force him to commit to run hard, it's easier for the receiving defender to judge when he needs to take off to receive the throw. By looking at the receiver, the defender with the ball will see the receiver's feet move, which is the signal to deliver the ball.
- **To feed the ball, simply execute a soft snap-throw aiming at the receiver's chest.** This throw must be accurate and easy for the receiver to catch because it will allow him to continue moving toward the runner without slowing down to receive the throw.
- **The receiver should never slow down to receive the throw.** Once he moves his feet to begin running to receive the throw, he must continue gaining ground and momentum toward the runner. If the runner is able to change direction, the receiving defender will have enough momentum to catch even the quickest runner and apply the tag.

Every team should work on the rundown during practice. For such a seemingly easy play, several parts must be perfected to execute it properly. Everything from the feeds to proper execution and timing to receiving the throw and making the tag must be rehearsed repeatedly so that they come automatically in game situations. Figures 6.10, 6.11, 6.12, and 6.13 illustrate the most common rundown plays.

Once a runner is picked off, the pitcher must follow his throw to first base (figure 6.10). If the runner is not tagged out by the first baseman during the rundown or by the middle infielder who receives the throw from the first baseman, the pitcher must be in position at first base to receive the throw from the middle infielder as he forces the runner back toward first base. This is the only pickoff play in which the pitcher will run to the base he attempted the pickoff to. On pickoffs at second base, the pitcher will run to third base; on pickoffs at third base, he runs to home plate. The

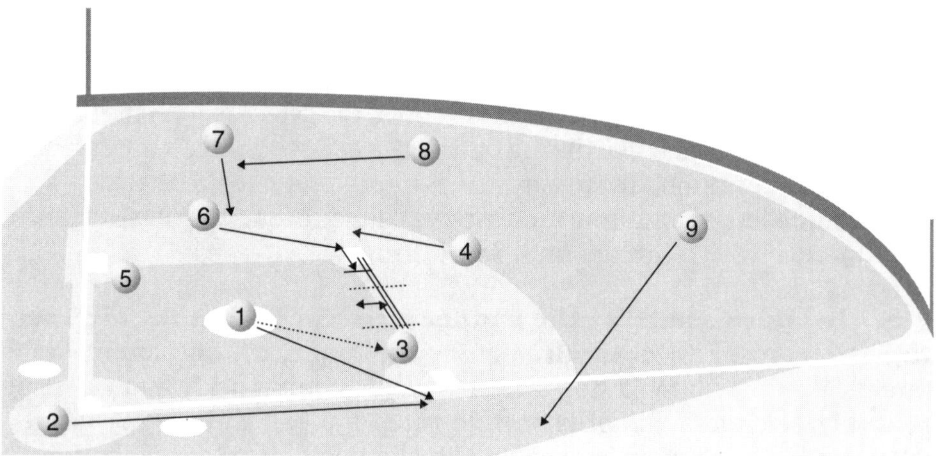

Figure 6.10 Rundown play after pickoff at first base, normal execution.

outfielders play an important role in backing up bases as well. On pickoffs to first base, the left fielder and center fielder back up second base in case of an errant throw, and the right fielder must hustle to back up first base in case a ball gets away and ends up coming down the first-base line or hitting the fence in foul territory.

In the play shown in figure 6.11, the runner at first has been picked off while taking his secondary lead, or he deliberately drew the pickoff throw to create a situation in which the runner at third base could potentially score during the rundown. When the runner at first base delays running after being picked off, the second baseman should run directly to the baseline

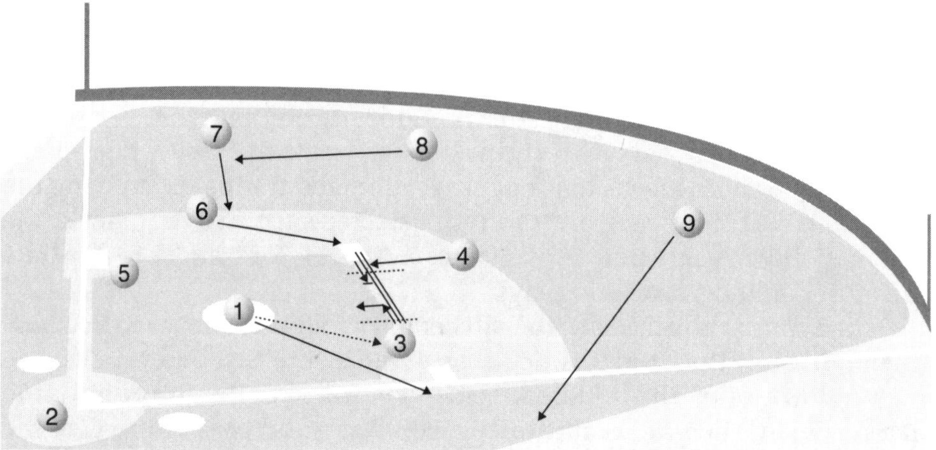

Figure 6.11 Rundown play after pickoff at first base with runners on first or first and third. Runner at first delays.

to shorten the distance between himself and the first baseman, creating a shorter running lane and a shorter throw. This will speed up the rundown process, making it more difficult for the runner at third base to get a good jump in his attempt to score. The outfielders need to back up the bases: left fielder backs up third base, center fielder backs up second base, and right fielder backs up first base.

Another possible first-and-third rundown play occurs when the runner at first base breaks early while the pitcher is in his set position. When this happens, the second baseman must again run directly to the baseline to receive the throw from the pitcher and shorten the distance of the running lane. The pitcher should step off the rubber, check the runner at third base with a fake throw, then turn and throw the ball to the second baseman who is now in the baseline about 20 to 25 feet from second base. The fake throw toward third base forces the runner back to the base and makes it more difficult for him to get a good jump in his attempt to score on the rundown between first and second base.

In the rundown play after a pickoff to second base (figure 6.12), once the pitcher delivers the ball to second base, successfully picking off the runner, he must run to third base to back up the third baseman. Since there are already two defenders at second base—the shortstop and second baseman—the pitcher doesn't need to follow his throw to that base. The right fielder and center fielder must back up second base in case of an errant throw. The left fielder backs up third base in case a ball gets away and ends up down the third-base line or against the fence in foul territory.

On the pickoff play to third base (figure 6.13), after delivering the ball to third base and successfully picking off the runner, the pitcher runs to home plate to back up the catcher. The shortstop breaks toward third base

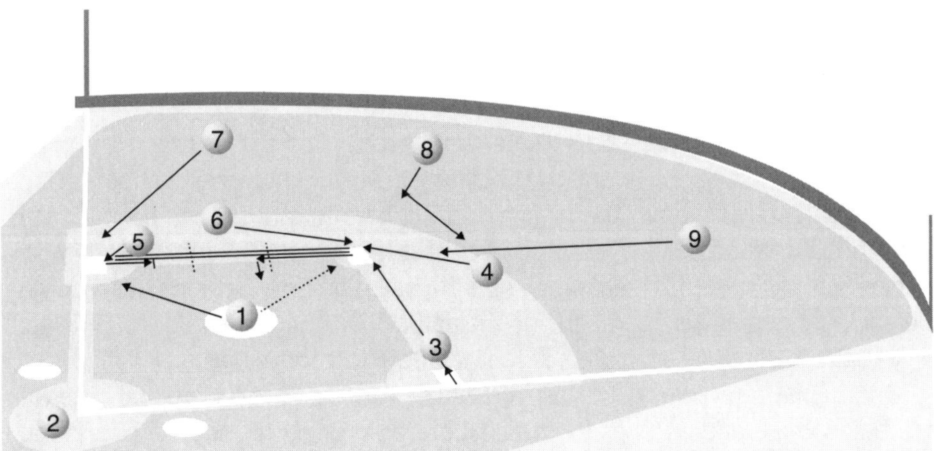

Figure 6.12 Rundown play after pickoff at second base.

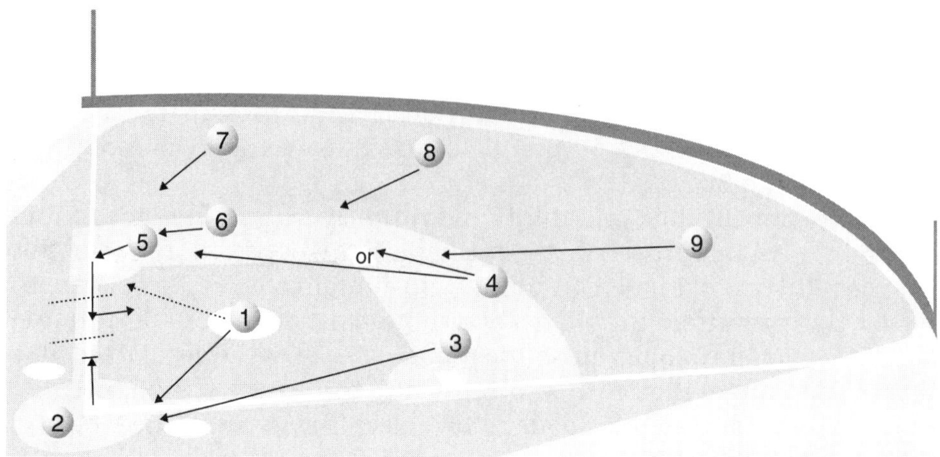

Figure 6.13 Rundown play after pickoff at third base.

and becomes the back up for the third baseman. The catcher must shorten the running lane by moving up the third-base line so a potential tag play at the plate doesn't happen too near the plate. The third baseman must get the ball to the catcher soon enough so that the runner is forced back to third base. If the rundown doesn't result in an out, at least it should make the runner retreat to third base rather than allow him to score a run. The left fielder backs up the third baseman in case an errant throw gets by both infielders at third base.

Rundown Drill

This drill is effective in developing every facet of the rundown. You can run it between any two bases, but in this example we'll use first and second base. It's best to run the drill a few times through without a runner, and then include runners to make it more gamelike. Run this drill at game speed.

Split infielders, catchers, and pitchers into two groups and put each group at a base. The coach begins the drill by simulating a pickoff attempt at first base. Once the player receives the ball, he begins running hard toward second base with the ball up high. When the player at second base wants the ball thrown to him, he begins running toward the defender with the ball. The time between the receiving defender beginning his approach and the actual feed should be minimal. The goal is to make the feed as soon as the receiving defender moves his feet.

Once a player receives a throw, he continues running hard toward first base with the ball up high and watches for the next player to begin his approach, and then feeds him the ball. Players continually rotate, returning to the back of the line they were feeding to.

After a few run-throughs, add runners to the drill (usually the outfielders). The coach again simulates picking off the runner, but now the goal is for the defenders to get the runner out in one throw. Again, this drill should be practiced at game speed to be effective. With the runners in place, the defense must now work on beginning their approach with correct timing, receiving the throw while running at full speed, and applying the tag.

This drill might start out looking sloppy, but over time you'll see improvements. Within a few weeks, you should observe that your defense's confidence in performing the rundown effectively has been significantly strengthened.

7

Defending Bunts

Jerry Weinstein

Baseball is a game of precious outs. When an offensive team attempts to move runners into scoring position with a sacrifice bunt, the defensive team would like to get the lead runner whenever possible. But what they really *don't* want to happen is to get neither runner. When this happens, a precious out—one that the offense has been willing to give them—has been squandered.

Most teams today use overcomplicated bunt defenses. Teams practice these defenses in nongame situations, usually at a low intensity, but because sacrifice bunts are used infrequently in game situations (fewer than three per game, on average) they seldom use them under real-game pressure. This lackadaisical approach to bunt defense can lead to botched sacrifice bunt defenses or a base on balls to the sacrifice bunter.

The primary goal of any bunt defense is to get an out. The consequence of not doing so is illustrated in table 7.1. As the stats clearly show, an offense usually gains no real advantage when giving up an out to advance a runner, so the defense needs to get the sure out. Obviously, the more base runners and the farther they are along the base paths, the greater chance the offense has of scoring.

Getting outs on bunts and sacrifices even if runners advance allows a team to avoid the big inning. In many games, the winning team scores more runs in one inning than the losing team scores in the entire game. Too often those big innings involve a poorly executed bunt defense. Thus, as I've said, the primary goal of any bunt defense is to get an out.

In this chapter I'll explain how bunt defense *should* be practiced. I'll also talk about how bunt defense should be simplified to increase the probability of successful execution in game situations. Keep bunt defenses simple and practice them at game speed. Use a stopwatch to time defensive execution.

Table 7.1 Runs Scored Based on Outs and Base Runners

	NUMBER OF OUTS		
Runners on base	**0**	**1**	**2**
None	.537	.294	.114
Runner on first	.907	.544	.239
Runner on second	1.138	.720	.347
Runner on third	1.349	.920	.391
Runners on first and second	1.515	.968	.486
Runners on first and third	1.762	1.140	.522
Runners on second and third	1.957	1.353	.630
Bases loaded	2.399	1.617	.830

Based on Major League baseball stats 1945 through 2004.

The defenses that follow stress the simplest way to get an out. More complex bunt defenses might make you look like a genius on a play or two during the season, but will cost you the game in other instances. The approach here is that simpler is better; simpler defenses are much easier to execute consistently and take less time to learn.

Putting on a Bunt Defense

First, understand the offense's tendencies regarding sacrifice bunts when preparing for the game. Most teams that use sacrifice bunts do so only in specific situations, such as no outs, a close game, a good bunter at the plate, or quick runners on the base paths.

It's also important to identify game situations in which a sacrifice bunt attempt is likely. Knowledge of personnel and tendencies can be picked up through scouting and statistical analysis. Be aware of physical indicators, too, such as the hitter's positioning in the batter's box or an early show prompted by a move to first base or an inside move to second.

Typically, the coach signals the bunt defense from the dugout to the catcher. The catcher signals the rest of the defense either verbally or with hand signals. Another option is to signal directly from the dugout to the field with no middleman.

Offenses are getting smarter about baiting the defense into defending the bunt. They force the defense into a disadvantageous defensive alignment by showing bunt and then instead hit away.

A bunt defense can't be so aggressive and so committed to the lead runner that it puts the defense in jeopardy of being out of position to defend a batted ball. If the defense is surprised by an offense showing bunt when no bunt defense is on, the pitcher steps off. If the bunt is shown late, the defense automatically goes to the most basic bunt defense.

The defense must get an out in every bunt situation, which often means the lead runner will get the base he wants. The pitcher must pitch to contact in bunt situations, throwing his highest percentage strike pitch to his highest percent strike location. Review bunt defenses at least once a week during the season and more if necessary.

Sometimes a defense will want to deke a bunt defense to encourage the offensive team to hit. Some offenses take off the bunt after a bunt defense is put on, hoping the defensive team will be out of position to defend a batted ball. Any time a bunt defense is put on with a runner on first only, the first baseman confers on the mound with the pitcher. Some defenses involve the first baseman telling the pitcher how many picks he wants. To avoid giving a defense away, have the first baseman go to the mound on every bunt defense with a runner on first.

Pitch Selection

The key in any bunt situation is to throw strike one, and as mentioned, the way to do that is to throw the highest percentage strike pitch to the highest percentage strike location. Low mid strikes are best because you can never be 100 percent sure the offense is bunting and you want to avoid giving the hitter an elevated pitch to hit. Also, elevated pitches are often called balls, and walks add to the possibility of a multiple-run inning. Most bunters have trouble going down to get the ball and handle balls up in the zone better, just as most hitters are able to handle high pitches better.

Throw high velocity pitches to bunters, including power breaking balls that have depth. Few batters practice bunting breaking balls. Depending on personnel, after strike one is thrown, an elevated fastball can be effective. Be sure that the opponent is still bunting. Many teams will switch from bunt to hit after strike one, especially when a bunter looked bad in his first attempt. When in doubt, pitch down in the zone.

A batter who's switching from bunt to fake bunt and hit will sometimes make an earlier turn than usual and will not fully rotate. He often holds his bat at a flatter angle or stands deeper in the box. The pitcher and infielders should pick up on these cues that the hitter is going to swing rather than attempt another bunt.

Fielder Decisions

The defensive player fielding the ball is usually in the best position to make the decision where to throw the ball. Some coaches prefer that their catchers direct the play, but catchers are often indecisive, and the fielder has already decided where to throw the ball, anyway. The catcher's late call only creates problems. There's more commitment and decisiveness when the fielder makes decisions based on his prepitch preparation and his awareness of the game situation.

The fielder should know the inning, number of outs, count, score, hitter's position in the batting order, hitter's running speed, base runner's running speed, run scoring potential for the opposition, run scoring potential for his team, and field conditions. Once all this data is factored into the defensive player's personal computer, he's in a better position to throw to the correct base, depending, of course, on how hard the ball is bunted and its direction.

If the fielder's initial body alignment and mind-set is to get the lead runner, he generally has plenty of time to retire the bunter if there's no play on the lead runner. This is especially true with only a runner on first. The key is for the fielder to align his body toward second before fielding the ball. He'll still be in position to throw to first base if he has no play at second.

Also, even if the defender quickly throws to second or third, there's probably still time to get the bunter out. To find out, time bunt throws in practice at game speed with live pitching and with all plays ending up at first base. If the play (throws to second to first or to third to first) can be completed in 4.1 seconds or less, go after the lead runner. This approach is obviously more risky, so the scoreboard really comes into play.

Bunted pop-ups can be intentionally dropped, depending on the game situation and the height of the pop-up. Remember that the infield fly rule doesn't apply on a bunted ball. If a bunted ball is popped up, the bunter doesn't run (as often happens), and the runner (or runners) is close to his base, the catcher should holler, "Drop! Drop!" The fielder can also see the situation on his own by taking a quick look at the batter and runner(s).

The fielder should call for the ball with big arm action to sell the catch and then let the ball drop to the ground without touching it with his glove or body. If he touches the ball in the air, the drop will be ruled intentional, the batter will be ruled out, and all base runners will return to the bases they occupied at the time of the pitch. But if the fielder lets the ball drop without touching it, he provides the defense multiple options for double plays because the batter is *not* automatically out and the base runners have been forced to hesitate at their bases. The intentional drop is especially effective with runners on first and second because even if you don't turn a double play you're likely to get the lead runner. The intentional drop can also be used when it's advantageous to trade a fast runner at first for a slower runner at bat.

Defending the Bunt With a Runner on First Base

With a runner on first base, the sacrifice bunt is used to move the runner into scoring position at second. The odds greatly favor getting the bunter out over the lead base runner. As in all bunt defense situations, be sure to get an out. Only go for the lead runner if you know you can get him.

Pitcher Covers First-Base Line

This is the most basic bunt defense with a right-handed pitcher on the mound and virtually guarantees the defense its best chance of getting one out. This is not the case with a left-handed pitcher because a left-handed pitcher tends to rotate toward the third-base line as the pitch is completed.

This defense (figure 7.1) provides better coverage in cases when the offensive team doesn't bunt but instead hits away, puts on the hit and run, slashes, or puts on the fake-bunt hit and run. The second baseman doesn't have to cheat as much to get to first base because the first baseman is not crashing.

This defense has other benefits as well. It provides opportunities to pick off an overly aggressive runner on first base on a missed bunt. It doesn't give the runner at first a chance to get aggressive primary or secondary leads (because the first baseman isn't vacating early to close the gap on a potential bunt). It's also safer to have the first baseman cover first in this defense because he's not on the move. That isn't the case for the second baseman, who will have to take the throw on the move. The second baseman usually presents a smaller target than the first baseman and lacks the first baseman's expertise around the base.

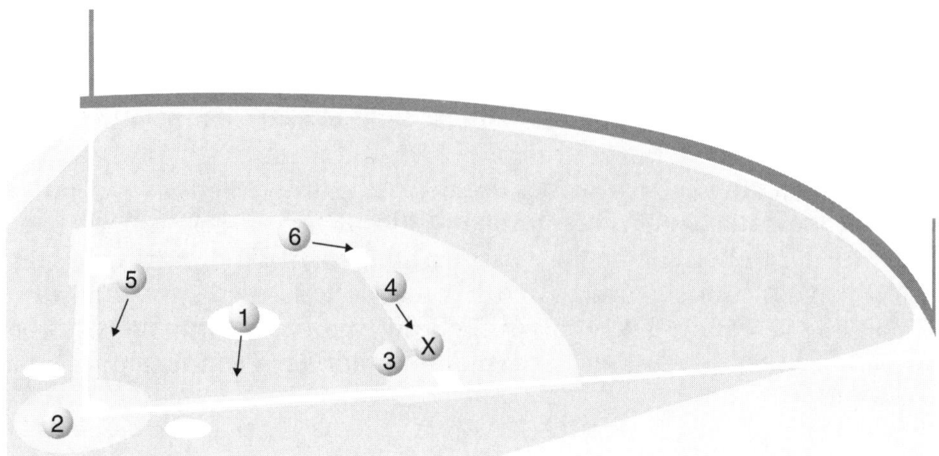

Figure 7.1 With runner on first base, pitcher covers the first-base line.

Third baseman. The third baseman starts in front of third base and positions off the line so he's in a position to cover the 5.5 hole in case the hitter swings or slashes. He walks aggressively toward the plate if the hitter is in a bunt stance, continuing as the pitch is in flight as long as the hitter stays in a bunt stance. If the hitter pulls back, he stops, lowers his center of gravity, and readies to field a batted ball. He makes all his throws with his feet under his body and not on the run. If the ball is bunted and he doesn't field the ball, he retreats to cover third base. If the ball is bunted toward the third-base line, he will most likely have to throw to first base. If the ball is bunted firmly at him or to his left, he'll likely have a play at second. After fielding the ball and making the play, he changes positions with the catcher who covers third while he covers home.

Shortstop. The shortstop starts in his normal double-play position and breaks to cover second base only after the ball passes the hitter or the ball is hit or bunted. Although it's not imperative, in most cases the shortstop covers the steal in this bunt defense. (The second baseman may cover the steal against a team that frequently slashes or fakes the bunt and executes hit and runs in traditional bunting situations.) When the ball is bunted and the throw goes to first base, he gets into position on the infield side of second base and readies himself for a throw from first in case the runner takes too big a turn at second. Should the catcher pick the runner at first, the shortstop must be the first baseman's eyes in case the runner breaks to second. His verbal cue is "two, two" because the right-handed first baseman has his back to the runner as he receives the catcher's throw.

Second baseman. The second baseman cheats slightly toward first base. If the hitter shows bunt, he side-shuffles toward first. When the pitch is in flight and the hitter is still in a bunting stance, he moves toward the hitter in case the hitter pushes the ball hard past the pitcher. When a bunted ball is not going to pass the pitcher, he breaks to back up or, if necessary, he covers first. Against a slash, fake bunt hit-and-run, or hit-and-run, he holds his double-play, steal-coverage positioning and has no responsibility to cover first base. He may or may not cover second base if the runner starts early, depending on the pitch and the spray chart tendencies of the hitter in like situations. He retains push-bunt responsibility and will break toward first when the ball is bunted in case of an errant throw at first or because he has to cover first when the first baseman vacates to field a ball close to the line. He should receive the throw with his left foot on the base and his body squared up to the thrower. After receiving the throw, he looks for back-door possibilities at second if the runner from first takes too aggressive a turn at second.

First baseman. The first baseman shuffles off toward second on the pitch and readies himself for a pick from the catcher. If the ball is bunted close to the line, he goes to get it and tags the runner out or throws to the second baseman, who's covering first. If the ball is really close to the line and he's unable to tag the runner, he'll need to pull the ball away from the line to throw to first to avoid throwing through or over the runner. In most cases, he will be able to tag the runner, or else the pitcher will be able to cover the line, making it unnecessary for the first baseman to come get the ball. If the runner stops in the baseline and starts to backpedal to avoid being tagged, he's not out until he backpedals past the plate. In this case, it's best to throw to first as soon as the runner starts to backpedal.

Pitcher. The pitcher delivers the pitch and breaks toward the first-base side. If he's going to field the ball, he should put his glove up and call for the ball as early as possible so that the first baseman can hold his position at first base.

Catcher. The catcher can field the bunt, cover third if the third baseman fields the bunt, or be ready to pick to first in case the bunt is missed or the bunter takes the pitch.

First Baseman Charges Late

Use this defense when you have a left-handed pitcher who has trouble getting to the first-base line. The late-charge defense (figure 7.2) also gives both right- and left-handed pitchers a better chance to get the force at second and for the first baseman to field a popped-up ball on the first-base side.

This is not an overly aggressive defense. Most of the defensive movement comes when the pitcher starts his glide to the plate. The game situation (especially the score) and the direction and speed of the bunt will tell the fielders (pitcher, catcher, first baseman, and third baseman) where to throw the ball. When in doubt, be conservative and get an out.

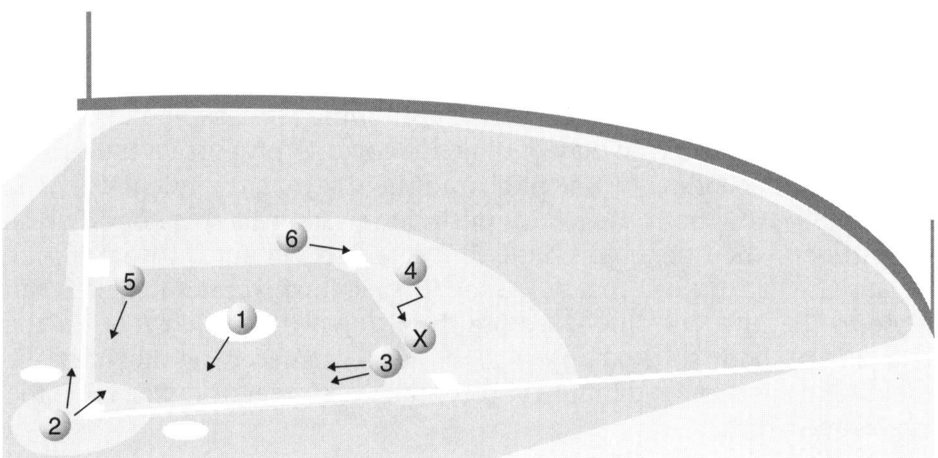

Figure 7.2 With runner on first base, first baseman charges late.

It's preferable for all pitchers to use a "knee-to-knee six cleat" move out of the stretch. This move helps both right- and left-handed pitchers keep runners closer to first base because it produces a 1.2-second or better break time from the pitcher's first move to the ball arriving at the plate. This technique allows the pitcher to be quick to the plate without sacrificing stuff. It's useful with runners on any base and will shorten the runners' leads because the ball reaches the plate sooner.

The move involves a scissors-like action by the stride leg and back leg. As soon as the front knee moves toward the back knee, the back knee moves toward home plate. The six cleats on the stride foot are visible to the hitter. The pitcher must refine this move because most of his big pitches come out of the stretch. Whether pitching out of a windup or stretch, velocity and strike percentage must be the same.

Third baseman. The third baseman starts in front of third base and positions off the line so he can cover the 5.5 hole in case the hitter swings or slashes. He walks aggressively toward the plate if the hitter is in a bunt stance, and then comes forward more quickly as the pitched ball is in flight. If the hitter pulls back, the third baseman stops, lowers his center of gravity, and readies to field a batted ball. He must call off the pitcher and throw to first unless the pitcher is camped in front of the ball.

Shortstop. The shortstop starts in his normal double-play position and breaks to cover second base only after the ball passes the hitter or is hit or bunted. The shortstop covers the steal in this bunt defense.

Second baseman. The second baseman cheats his initial positioning toward first base and shuffles toward first when the hitter shows bunt. He breaks to cover first when the ball is bunted. If the hitter doesn't show sacrifice bunt but push bunts, the second baseman comes straight up to field the ball.

First baseman. The first baseman breaks straight to home as the pitcher's foot moves toward home. If a left-handed pitcher is on the mound, the first baseman will take more of a loop to be able to cover the push bunt. He must not vacate early because this would give the runner a chance to get an extended primary lead or even to steal second. He'll delay a little longer if a left-handed pitcher is on the mound to make sure the pitcher is throwing home. The first baseman can call for a set number of picks when he goes to the mound, but it's preferred to allow the pitcher to pick or not pick based on the base runner's lead and how the pitcher feels at the time. The first baseman retreats to cover first base if the hitter shows base-hit bunt to third base. In the case of a push bunt, the first baseman might have a play at second or have to feed the pitcher covering first base. He must be under control so that he gets an out for sure.

Pitcher. The pitcher breaks straight to home, slightly favoring the first-base line to cut off a potential push bunt or to cover first on a push bunt that he doesn't field.

Catcher. The catcher fields the bunt or covers third if the third baseman fields the bunt.

First Baseman Charges Early

This defense (figure 7.3) is similar to the late-charge defense but is more aggressive. When the first baseman goes to the mound, he alerts the pitcher to a designated number of pickoffs at first. After the pitcher makes his last pickoff move, the pitcher quick-sets (making sure to stop completely) while the first baseman breaks hard to the plate.

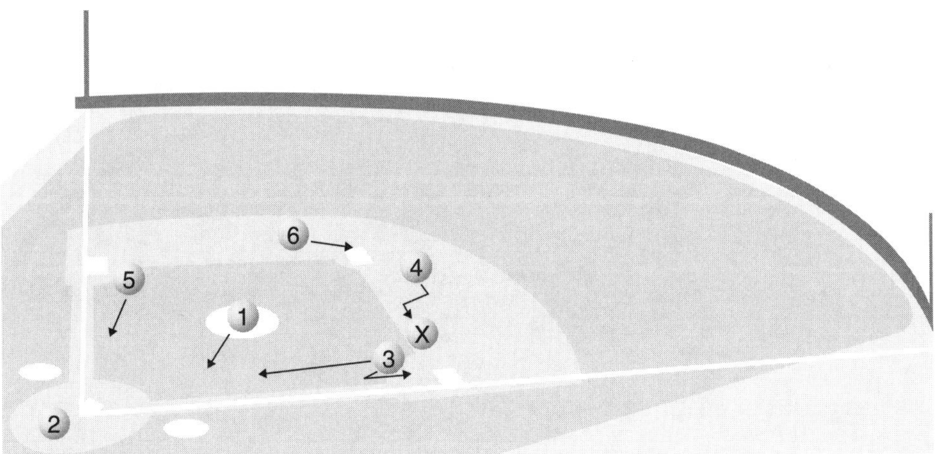

Figure 7.3 With runner on first, first baseman charges early.

Using an "off and back" pick at first keeps the base runner from breaking when the first baseman vacates. On the off and back pick, the pitcher picks to first after the first baseman takes his second step toward home. An early break by the runner at first won't be a problem if the pitcher and first baseman time things correctly.

Runner on Second Base or Runners on First and Second Bases

Once a runner reaches second base, the situation becomes more critical. A runner on second can score on a base hit or advance to third easily on a deep flyout. Because a runner on third is close to scoring, preventing the runner from getting to third base is crucial.

Pitcher Goes to Third-Base Cut

The third-base cut is where the grass starts in fair territory down the third-base line. This defense (figure 7.4) is conservative, meant to get an out. The worst thing that can happen with runners at first and second is to fail to get any outs. Most outs made using this defense are at first base. With just a runner on second, the probability of getting the tag-out at third is low unless the ball is popped up or bunted extremely low and hard directly back at the pitcher.

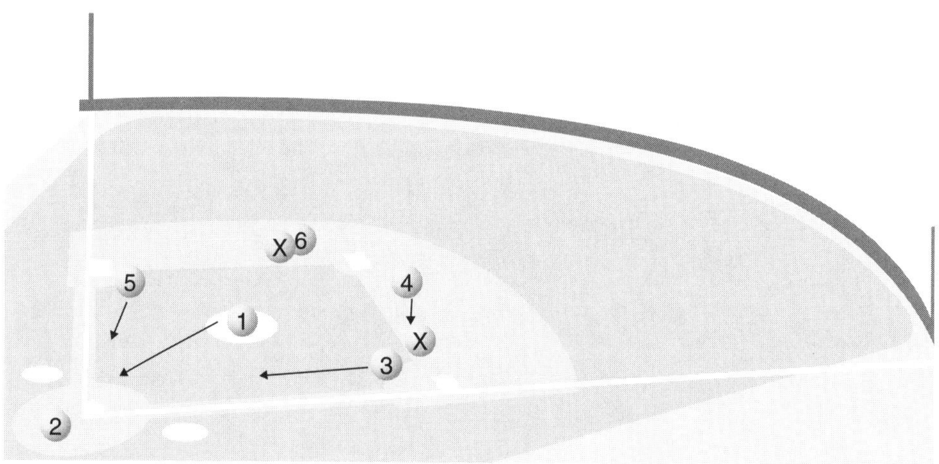

Figure 7.4 With runners on first and second, pitcher goes to the third-base cut.

Third baseman. The third baseman starts three to four steps off the line and two steps in front of the base. As the hitter shows bunt, he creeps up under control, taking care not to stray so far from third that he can't get back to cover the steal in case the ball isn't bunted. As soon as the ball is bunted, the third baseman goes to get it. The only time he would retreat to third base is on a pop-up or on a ball bunted hard and low back to the pitcher. He must call the pitcher off the ball and throw to first unless the pitcher is camped in front of the ball. If the pitcher is camped in front of the ball, the third baseman should let him know to throw to first. There's an outside possibility that the third baseman will have a play at second if runners are on first and second and the ball is bunted sharply to his left.

Shortstop. The shortstop starts on the left shoulder of the base runner at second. If the base runner extends his lead so that there's daylight between the runner and the shortstop, the shortstop breaks to second with an open glove to initiate a pitcher's pick. Common sense rules the day here. If there's daylight and the runner has a still and short lead, don't use the open-glove pick. This becomes a feel play between the pitcher and shortstop. The defense must not be so consumed by the runner at second that the pitcher fails to throw a quality strike to the hitter. No one expects to throw the runner out at third, so don't get too invested in the runner at second. If the ball is taken, popped up, or bunted through, the shortstop must be ready to receive the catcher's throw at second. If the ball is bunted hard to the third baseman's left, the shortstop must be ready to receive the throw at second.

Second baseman. The second baseman cheats toward first and shuffles toward first as the hitter shows bunt. He breaks to cover first as the ball is bunted. He has no push-bunt responsibilities once the hitter is in a bunting stance with the ball in flight.

First baseman. The first baseman starts in front of the base and off the line. He slowly closes in on the hitter, accelerating as the hitter continues to show bunt. If the hitter doesn't show bunt or comes out of his bunt stance to hit, the first baseman stops and lowers his center of gravity to prepare for a batted ball. If the ball is bunted hard, pushed to his right, or is bunted low on a line, he may have a play at second. If the ball is bunted softly at him, he should most likely throw to first because the third baseman is closing on bunt contact.

Pitcher. The pitcher comes set, looks at home, and makes a half head turn toward second. The half head turn is enough for the pitcher to see the shortstop and runner but allows a quicker transition back to the plate to pitch than a full head turn allows. This prevents the runner at second from getting a long secondary lead or reestablishing momentum toward third base before the pitch. If the runner at second has a short lead or is going back toward second, and the shortstop is not open-glove picking, the pitcher looks home and delivers the pitch. If the base runner at second is moving toward third and there's no open glove, the pitcher holds the ball until the base runner walks into a daylight pick or overextends and can be frozen and picked by an inside move. After the pitch is delivered, the pitcher immediately breaks to the cut at home plate (the spot where the dirt stops and the grass starts at the base path running from third to home). This area is somewhat of a defensive Bermuda triangle in that it's too far away from the third baseman and catcher for either of them to field the ball and throw out most bunters. The pitcher must field the ball and throw without a shuffle step. To do this, he must be under control (low center of gravity), and his pivot foot should be at a right angle to first base. The pitcher needs to get the ball airborne as soon as possible.

Catcher. The catcher will aggressively field any ball that he can get to and throw to the appropriate base. If the catcher doesn't field the ball, he stays home for a potential play in the event of an errant throw by the third baseman, first baseman, or pitcher.

Pitcher Breaks at a 90-Degree Angle to the Third-Base Line

This defense is similar to the pitcher-to-the-cut defense but gives the defense a greater opportunity to get the force at third base. The difference lies in the routes and responsibilities of the third baseman and pitcher (figure 7.5).

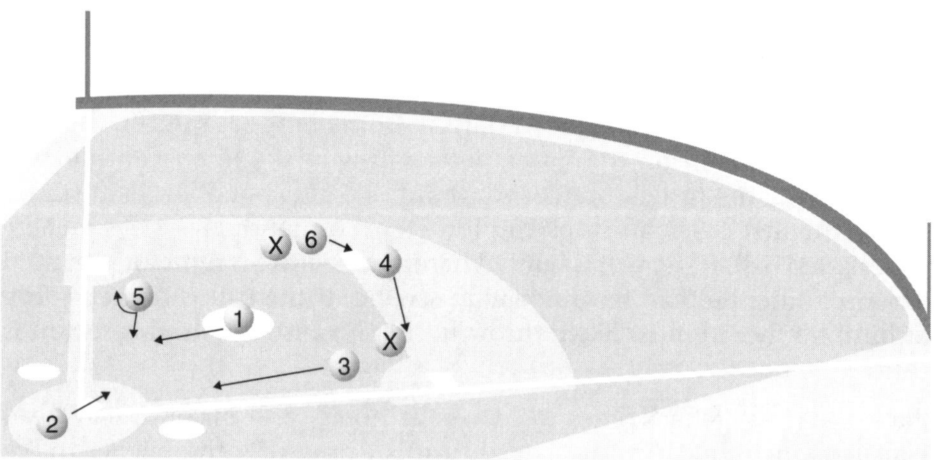

Figure 7.5 With runners on first and second, pitcher breaks at a 90-degree angle to the third-base line.

Third baseman. The third baseman starts three or four steps off the line and two steps in front of the base. As the pitch is in flight, he moves toward the plate with a right step and then a left step. He draws an imaginary line from his left knee to the outside corner of home plate; he goes after any ball bunted firmly into the cylinder formed by this imaginary line. The third baseman must be keenly aware of the game situation and factor in the pitcher's defensive abilities. He'll give a left-handed pitcher who has quickness and agility more latitude to field balls bunted into the cylinder than he will a less agile right-handed pitcher. When in doubt, the third baseman should go get the ball. He also has the option to throw to second on a ball bunted hard to his left when runners are on first and second. When he decides to get the ball, he should call off the pitcher or yell, "one, one" so that the pitcher knows that there's no play at third. If the ball is not bunted, the third baseman retreats to cover the steal of third. If he's retreating to cover third base, he steps right, left, right. When runners are on first and second and the play is to third base, the third baseman looks to complete the double play at first base. If there's no play at first, he arm fakes and looks to backdoor the runner at second if the runner takes an overly aggressive turn. If the hitter draws back to slash, the third baseman stops moving and lowers his center of gravity to field the ball.

Shortstop. The shortstop starts on the left shoulder of the base runner at second. If the base runner extends his lead so that daylight appears between the runner and the shortstop, the shortstop breaks to second with an open glove to initiate a pitcher's pick at second. If there's daylight and the runner is still and has a short lead, the shortstop doesn't use the open-glove pick. This becomes a feel play between the pitcher and shortstop.

Second baseman. The second baseman cheats toward first and shuffles toward first as the hitter shows bunt. He breaks to cover first as the ball is bunted. He has no push-bunt responsibilities once the hitter is in a bunting stance and the ball is in flight.

First baseman. The first baseman starts in front of the base and off the line. He slowly closes on the hitter, accelerating as the hitter shows bunt. If the hitter doesn't show bunt, the first baseman stops and lowers his center of gravity to prepare for a batted ball. If the ball is bunted hard, is pushed to his right, or is bunted low on a line, he might have a play at second or third with runners on first and second. If the ball is bunted softly at him, he'll most likely throw to first.

Pitcher. The base runner at second and the shortstop dictate what the pitcher does. If there's no open glove from the shortstop and the runner at second has a short lead or is going back, the pitcher will pitch. After he delivers the pitch, he breaks on a 90-degree angle to the third-base line. If the ball is bunted hard at him or takes him toward third base, he'll most likely throw to third base. When throwing to third base, he should compress, keeping his center of gravity low to ensure good body control and prevent overrotation. The foot on the throwing-arm side should be nearly perpendicular to the third-base line, and he should follow his glove to throw. The ball is normally thrown from a three-quarter arm slot. If he has to move toward home plate to field the ball, he'll most likely throw to first.

Catcher. The catcher aggressively fields any ball he can get to and throws to the appropriate base. If he doesn't field the ball, he stays home in the event of an errant throw by the third baseman, first baseman, or pitcher.

Squeeze Plays

Most teams don't like to squeeze because of the inherent risks involved. The teams that do squeeze do it mainly to catch the other team off guard.

Presented with any type of defense or an occasional pitchout with a runner on third base, most teams won't squeeze. Those that do usually have someone with a large ego making decisions or have decided the risk is worthwhile because the offensive team is otherwise overmatched. Most squeeze plays are attempts to add to a lead. Few teams squeeze when tied or behind.

Anti-Squeeze

It's difficult to defend a squeeze unless the offense somehow tips it off. Watch for the signs. Here are some common tip-offs the offense might let slip out:

- The dugout suddenly becomes very quiet.
- The hitter goes outside his normal routine to answer the squeeze signal; for example, he taps his spikes, reaches for the top of his bat, or pushes his helmet down.
- The base runner at third shows different body language.
- The hitter shows bunt too soon or the base runner at third breaks prematurely. If this happens, the pitcher should pitch out or throw hard, low, and inside to a right-handed hitter.
- The hitter shows bunt early or the runner at third breaks early in response to a double-pump wind-up from the pitcher. A slow leg-lift move to third or a third-to-first move with runners on first and third might force the offense to tip their intentions.

The best way to defend the squeeze against a team proficient in executing it is to force the runner at third into a shorter and less aggressive lead and force the batter to bunt firmly into coverage (figure 7.6).

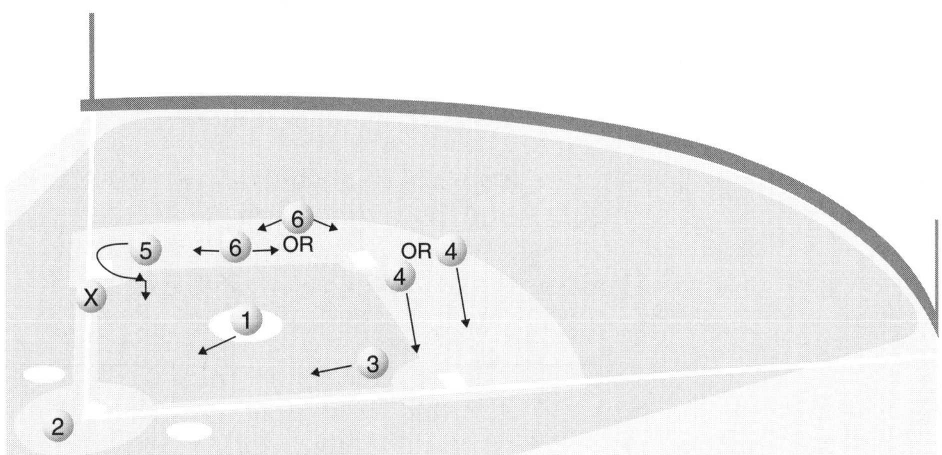

Figure 7.6 Anti-squeeze defense.

Third baseman. After the defense is put on, the third baseman goes to the mound and tells the pitcher if he wants him to pick to third. He starts on the third-base line three to four steps behind the base and breaks to the base after the pitcher comes set. If no pick is on, he touches the base and pushes off to his left, ready to field any bunted ball. Ideally, he wants to beat the runner to the ball to have a play at the plate. If there's a play at the plate, the feed to the catcher will usually be an underhand toss with the bare hand. If a pick is on with a right-handed pitcher, the ball will be delivered after he touches third base. With a left-hander pitching, the pick will occur after the pitcher's hands bottom out in the stretch. If the ball isn't bunted or hit and the defense is still on, he'll once again tell the pitcher if he wants a pick.

Shortstop. The shortstop generally plays in the up position in this defense but could certainly be back with runners on first and third or the bases loaded. If the ball is bunted or a squeeze bunt is attempted and missed, he'll break to cover third base. If there's no squeeze attempt, he needs to be ready to cover second base in case it's a fake squeeze and the runner from first is trying to steal second.

Second baseman. The second baseman may be up or back and positioned to cover first base.

First baseman. The first baseman is in front of first base unless runners are on first and third, in which case he holds the runner. He'll aggressively close on the hitter if the hitter shows bunt or if the runner breaks from third base, whichever happens first.

Pitcher. Based on prepitch communication, the right-handed pitcher will pick or pitch when the third baseman touches third. The left-handed pitcher will pitch after the third baseman touches third and pick as soon as his hands bottom out at his waist. The pitcher delivers a low mid strike and breaks straight off the mound if the hitter shows bunt. If the ball is bunted firmly to him, he'll likely have a play at the plate. He should drop his glove as he charges the ball so he can underhand flip with either hand. If he chooses to keep his glove on, he must make sure to flip the ball with his bare hand, not his glove. You risk a bad toss when flipping out of the glove.

Catcher. The catcher reacts to the bunted ball and stays home unless he can field the ball and get back for the tag. On potential tag plays at home, he stays low and receives any feed as close to the tag zone as he can. He must avoid reaching, if possible. He makes a quick tag and immediately shows the ball to the umpire. If the ball is bunted at and missed, he looks for the runner at third. Depending on the timing of the runner's break and his speed, this could be a simple tag or a rundown play. With runners on first and third, the catcher needs to be ready for a fake squeeze and a steal of second.

Anti-Safety Squeeze, First-Base Side

This is becoming a more common play in amateur baseball, particularly with runners on first and third and fewer than two outs. Most often the play is executed as a late-show sacrifice bunt or a push bunt to the first-base side. The runner on third shuffles on the pitch and runs on contact.

The key to defending this play is controlling the lead of the runner at third base and closing down the first-base side by shortening up the first baseman on the pitch (figure 7.7).

Third baseman. After the defense is put on, the third baseman goes to the mound and tells the pitcher if he wants him to pick to third. He starts on the third-base line three to four steps behind the base and breaks to the base after the pitcher comes set. If no pick is on, he hits the base and pushes off to his left, ready to field any bunted ball. If a pick is on, he'll hit third base, bounce off toward the six hole, and then retreat to receive the pickoff throw at third.

Shortstop. The shortstop covers second but is ready to break to third in case of a rundown between third and home.

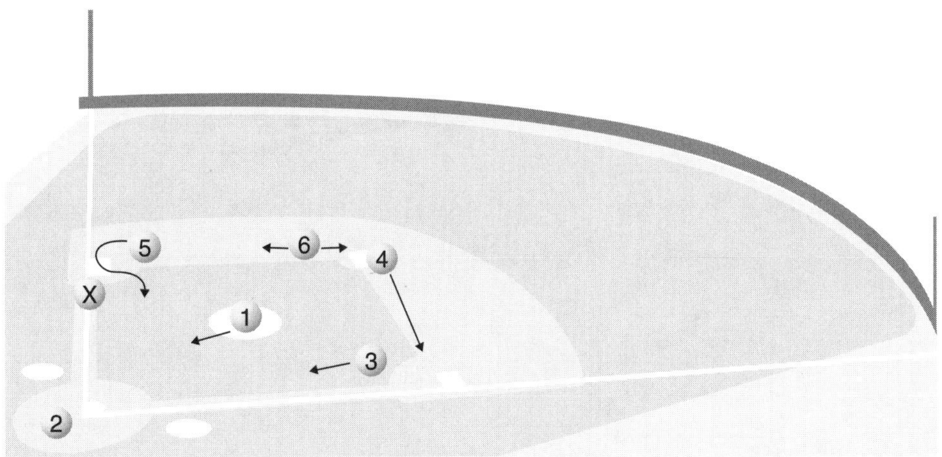

Figure 7.7 Runner at third, anti-squeeze defense, bunt to the first-base side.

Second baseman. The second baseman reacts to the bunt and covers first base.

First baseman. The first baseman charges the hitter on the pitch. He's ready to break down and stop if the hitter doesn't show bunt. He underhand flips the ball to the catcher if the ball stays down, making sure to get an out.

Pitcher. Right-handed pitchers pick to third when the third baseman touches third, as decided during prepitch communication. Left-handed pitchers pitch when the third baseman touches third base and pick when his hands bottom out at his waist. If no pick is on, the pitcher delivers a low mid strike and breaks straight off the mound, favoring the third-base side if the hitter shows bunt. If the ball is bunted to him, he'll likely have a play at the plate.

Anti-Safety Squeeze, Third-Base Side

This play is generally run with runners on first and third, usually with an early- or late-turn sacrifice bunt to third with the runner at first fake-breaking to hold the shortstop at second. The runner at third trails the third baseman and breaks toward home on the third baseman's throw to first. The runner must run 45 feet while the ball must travel 180 feet with two transfers. Some teams execute this play with a runner on third base only, usually with a base-hit bunt toward third.

At times the defense may expect the ball to be bunted to the first-base side and will then have to adjust to the ball bunted to the third-base side (figure 7.8). Pay close attention to the hitter's bat angle.

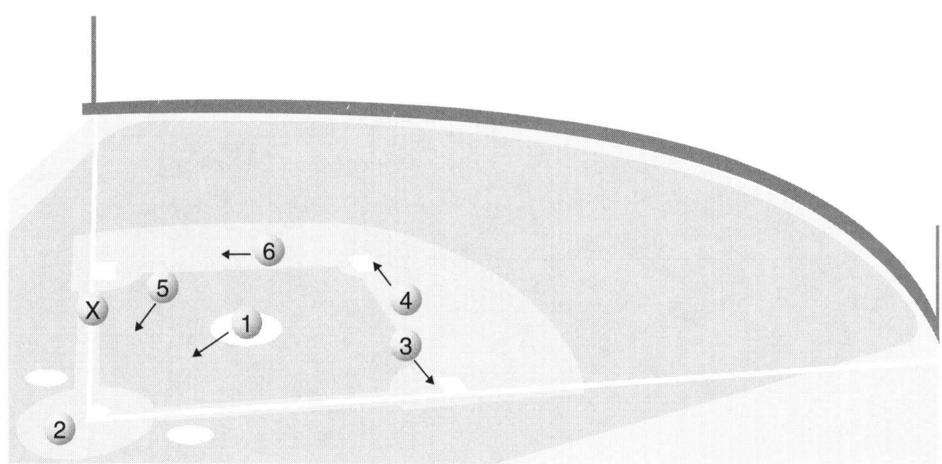

Figure 7.8 Runner at third, anti-squeeze defense, bunt to the third-base side.

Third baseman. The third baseman plays even with the base. He may be driving the runner back to third base. He anticipates the bunt and aggressively goes to get any balls bunted his way. He listens for a call from the shortstop, who rotates over to cover third base, to indicate that there is a play on an overextended runner at third. If there's a play at third, he turns toward his arm side to throw to third base.

Shortstop. If the ball is bunted to the third-base side or back to the pitcher, the shortstop breaks to third base. He lets the third baseman know to throw to third if the runner is so far off third that he'll be able to score if the throw is to first.

Second baseman. The second baseman covers second if the ball is bunted to the third-base side or back to the pitcher.

First baseman. The first baseman covers first base if the ball is bunted to the third-base side or back to the pitcher.

Pitcher. The pitcher breaks straight off the mound, favoring the first-base side. He reacts to the runner at third and to communication from the shortstop.

Catcher. The catcher reacts to the bunted ball and stays home unless he can field the ball and get back for the tag. He's ready for a rundown play if the third baseman throws the ball to the shortstop at third.

Base-Hit Bunt

The base-hit bunt is the most poorly defended play at both the amateur and pro levels, especially on balls bunted to the first-base side. The base-hit bunt is used extensively on the amateur level in lieu of the sacrifice bunt and as an offensive tool for weaker hitters in the line-up.

Ideally, the defense should be back for maximum range when the hitter is swinging and up when he's bunting. Often a cat and mouse guessing game is played between the offense and the defense. The worst place to be positioned is in no-man's land—too deep to cover the bunt and too shallow to have maximum range.

In general, the highest base-hit bunt frequency occurs with no outs and no strikes. Hitters might tip the bunt by peeking to see where the defense is positioned before or after they get into the batter's box, or else they change their position in the box relative to the plate to afford themselves a better bunting angle. Often the hitter's overall body language changes.

Base-Hit Bunt to Third Base

The base-hit bunt to the third-base side (figure 7.9) allows a speedy, aggressive hitter to get to first without getting the ball out of the infield. The defense must know each hitter and be prepared for speedy runners to try the base-hit bunt to third.

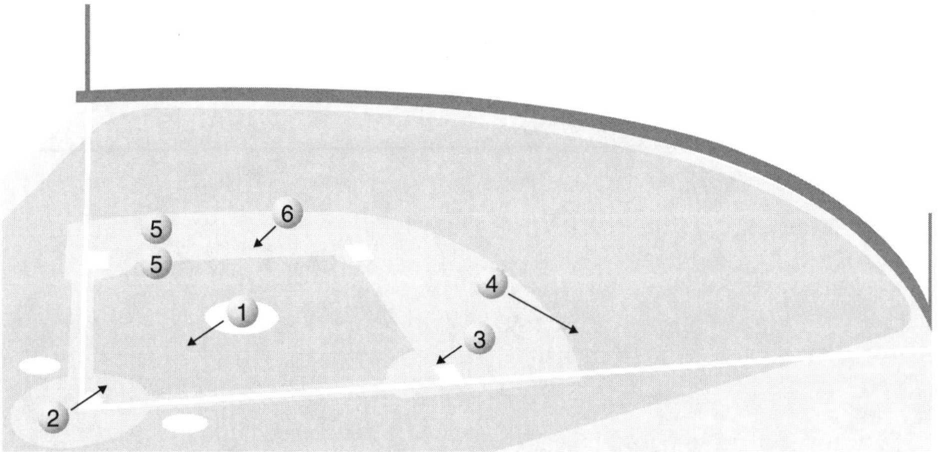

Figure 7.9 Defense against a base-hit bunt attempt to the third-base side.

Third baseman. The third baseman is the key player in defending this bunt, although the pitcher's athleticism also comes into play. The third baseman should continually change his positioning to confuse the potential bunter. He starts up and moves back; he starts up and stays up; he starts back and moves up; he starts back and stays back.

Shortstop. When the hitter, especially a left-handed hitter, shows base-hit bunt toward third base, the shortstop moves aggressively toward the hitter to field a firmly bunted ball that passes the pitcher and can't be fielded by the third baseman, preventing it from becoming a hit.

Second baseman. The second baseman backs up first base. He's ready to cover second on a ball bunted firmly at the shortstop.

First baseman. The first baseman covers first base.

Pitcher. The pitcher fields any ball he can get to unless he's called off by the third baseman.

Catcher. The catcher fields any ball in front of the plate unless called off by the third baseman or pitcher.

Base-Hit Bunt to the First-Base Side

The base-hit bunt to the right side with a left-handed pitcher on the mound or with a runner on first base is very difficult to defend at any level if executed well. The key is to anticipate, and perhaps discourage, the base-hit bunt attempt with good preparation and proper positioning (figure 7.10). Scout out bunters, even during the pregame, and pay attention to the scoreboard. Force the defense to bunt into coverage, especially to third base, by concealing that coverage.

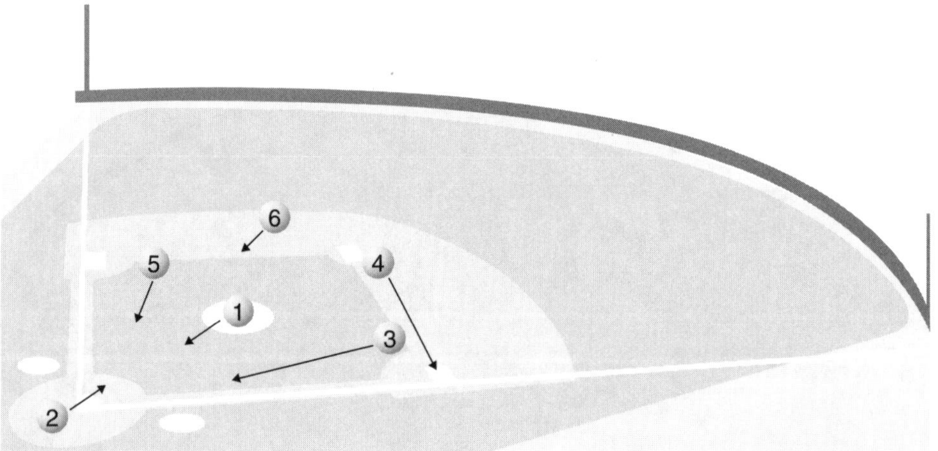

Figure 7.10 Defense against a base-hit bunt attempt to the first-base side with no one on base.

First baseman. The first baseman starts even with the base and four to five steps off the line or slightly closer to home plate, depending on the bunter's abilities. As soon as the hitter shows bunt to the second-base side, he closes on the hitter. If the hitter shows bunt to third, he covers first. When in doubt, he'll go get the ball.

Second baseman. The second baseman cheats his positioning closer to first base. As soon as the hitter shows bunt to the right side, he breaks to cover first base.

Shortstop. The shortstop breaks hard at the hitter in case the ball is bunted past the pitcher on the left side. He covers second base if he doesn't field the ball or if there's a runner on first.

Third baseman. The third baseman continually changes his positioning at third according to the situation and reacts to the ball off the bat.

Catcher. The catcher fields any bunt on the clay unless called off by the pitcher or first baseman.

Pitcher. The pitcher fields any ball bunted to the right side unless called off by the first baseman. He throws any ball that he fields to the second baseman covering first base. He has no responsibility to cover first on balls bunted to the right side.

Remember to keep defenses simple and practice them at or above game speed. Review bunt defenses at least once a week during the season and more if necessary. Get an out in every bunt situation, even if you don't get the lead runner.

8

Turning Double Plays

Rich Maloney

In our national pastime, no play has more beauty than the double play. The play has been called the "pitcher's best friend," a "twin killing," "poetry in motion," and the "double dipper." Whatever you call it, the double play is truly one of the most exciting plays in baseball. It's a tremendous momentum builder that often lifts a team to victory and is a key part of playing championship baseball.

In this chapter, we'll cover shortstop and second baseman preparation for the double play. Middle-infield play is at the heart of the defense, and turning the double play is bread and butter for the keystone combo—the shortstop and second baseman. Good middle-infield play is essential to winning a championship.

Middle infielders must have resolve and a bulldog mentality. They're going to be challenged by runners coming hard into second base and plays that need to be made in critical situations. Their teammates look to them to make defensive contributions that often determine the outcome of the game. These vital positions are not for the faint of heart but for the player who wants to be in the thick of the action.

The best infielders aren't always the most talented but are often players who have an understanding of the game and who can stay alert on every pitch. These players might not look flashy, but they have a knack for being in the correct position and making tough plays look routine. Consistency is the key. Infielders need to *always* make the routine play and, on occasion, make a great one. This is how titles are won. Infielders who make great plays but fail to consistently handle routine plays can cost their team big in critical games.

Qualities of a Successful Middle Infielder

- He's vocal; he takes charge and communicates well.
- He's a leader; he can influence others toward team goals through his words and actions.
- He's fearless; he stays in to turn the double play even when a runner is upon him.
- He's a tough player who thrives on getting dirty and playing hard.
- He's aggressive, always attacking the ball.
- He has a strong arm and a quick, accurate release.
- He has soft hands and is able to catch the baseball even when his feet are in poor position.
- He has quick feet and gets to the ball quickly.
- He has range and covers a lot of ground.
- He anticipates the play; he's a student of the game.
- He's confident; he wants the ball hit to him.
- He's agile, able to move quickly in all directions.

Proper Positions

To consistently turn a double play, each infielder must be in the proper position. Several factors come into play in determining the proper position for each player.

Infielders must be aware of both the speed of the runners on base and the speed of the hitter. This will help them gauge how much time they'll have to make a play at any base, depending on where the ball is hit. Obviously, if the hitter is slow, the infielder can play deeper. If the hitter is fast, the infielder will need to move in a few steps.

Fielders must always evaluate what type of hitter is at the plate. Is he a slap hitter who tends to hit the ball on the ground to the opposite field? Is he a power hitter who likes to pull the ball? The hitter's spot in the batting order is usually some indication of what kind of hitter the batter is. For instance, a two-hole hitter is often an up-the-middle or go-the-other-way guy who handles the bat well and bunts well. Conversely, the clean-up batter is more likely to pull and lift the ball and is typically more prone to striking out.

Knowing where each hitter usually hits the ball is also valuable. The toughest hitters to defend are those who use the entire field. In that case, infielders can't really hedge their bets and must play more or less straight up. This approach changes significantly when the batter hits a lot of ground balls to one side of the infield.

Infielders must also know their own teammates' strengths, weaknesses, and tendencies. What is the pitcher's best pitch? Does the pitcher have his best stuff that day? Is the pitcher hitting his spots? What is his strategy for that ball game and for specific hitters? Many times, knowing the type of pitch and its location improves the infielder's chances of anticipating where the ball will be hit. Off-speed pitches are generally pulled, and the hard stuff is often hit the other way. Good infielders use all the information they can gather to put themselves in the best position to make a play.

Another factor in infield positioning is the hitter's count. When the hitter has the advantage, such as 1-0, 2-0, or 3-0, he's more likely to pull the ball. If he's at a disadvantage, such as 0-1, 0-2, or 1-2, he's less likely to pull. Good infielders consider all the information available to put themselves in the best position to have a ball hit to them and increase the chance of turning a double play.

Field conditions must also be considered. Is the grass cut short and the ground hard? If so, the infielder might consider moving back and playing deeper. Is the ground wet? If so, he might move in because it will be difficult to get much on the throw.

The score and game situation significantly influence infielder positioning, as well as the amount of risk an infielder may take in turning the double play.

The depth that the infielder plays is a calculated risk. By moving closer to the hitter, he loses range but can get to the ball more quickly, which makes turning the double play easier. The general rule of thumb is one step in and two steps over. Shortstops and second basemen pinch the middle as well as shorten their depth. This is done because the easiest and most frequently turned double play in baseball is the ball hit close to the second-base bag, taken by either the shortstop or second baseman, and then completed with a throw to first.

Before every pitch and in preparation for turning a double play, a good infielder visualizes as many scenarios as he can so that when the ball is hit, he can react quickly, knowing exactly what he needs to do. For example, say a runner is on first with no outs in the first inning. The shortstop communicates coverage to the pitcher and second baseman. Before the pitcher steps on the rubber, the shortstop preprograms the possible scenarios. He visualizes the ball being hit back to the pitcher. He visualizes raising his arms to create a good target for the pitcher's throw to second base (figure 8.1).

In this case, the shortstop sees himself touching the inside corner of the bag and making an accurate throw to complete the double play. If the ball is hit to his right, he sees himself backhanding the ball using proper technique and making an accurate throw to the second baseman. If the ball is hit deep, behind second base, he sees himself fielding the ball cleanly with his glove-hand, transferring the ball to his throwing hand, and then using a quarterback flip to deliver the ball to the second baseman. This results in at least a force play but perhaps in a beautiful twin killing. The shortstop visualizes the play slightly to his left; he delivers a perfect underhand flip to the second baseman for the start of the double play. The shortstop recognizes the line-shot one-hopper and performs in his mind the proper technique of delivering the ball to the second baseman.

Prepitch preparation, concentration, and anticipation are vital in the development of good infielders and critical to teams that want to turn many double plays. And what team doesn't? Double plays have a huge role in playing winning baseball.

Figure 8.1 When the ball is hit back to the pitcher, the shortstop raises his arms to create a good target for the throw.

Techniques

When possible, infielders should catch the ball with two hands and use a short arm circle, which will help them get rid of the ball quickly. Infielders must learn to throw from all angles, but an overhand throw is preferred because the ball stays straight longer than on throws from other arm angles.

All infielders should practice throwing the ball from the different places they catch it. There are no guarantees the feed will be where they want it, so they need to be prepared for anything. Practicing from different arm slots is important in turning the double play. A term often used in delivering feeds is *throwing uphill*. To do this, the infielder must be low, which is important to fielding the ball cleanly and to executing a good feed.

At our practices we stress that the feed is everything. Middle infielders must execute good feeds to play winning baseball.

After fielding the ball cleanly, the next important component of the double play is a good, accurate delivery of the ball—that is, the feed. If the feed is poor, the double play likely goes unturned.

In general, middle infielders like the feed below the chin, in the middle of the body, chest high. All infielders should understand this. We ask our infielders to constantly communicate with each other on where they like the feed. We want to reinforce the importance the feed plays in the execution of the double play.

When doing several repetitions in a short time, many teams practice feeds while playing the first baseman well between first and second base to emphasize the importance of good throws. This allows the focus of the drill to be squarely on good feeds. Stress that your infielders stay under control. Rushing a throw often leads to a poor feed. Maintaining control when fielding the ball and then delivering the feed is critical to turning double plays. Most errors occur when the play is rushed and proper balance is lost, creating misdirected throws. Address the importance of good feeds over and over again.

Shortstop Feeds

A ball hit right at the shortstop should be attacked and fielded in the center of the body closer to the left foot (figure 8.2*a*). The right foot steps toward second base, replacing the left. During this step, the shortstop transfers the ball from glove to hand (figure 8.2*b*). The shortstop keeps his palm up, showing the ball to the second baseman. During an underhand feed, the shortstop's wrist remains stiff.

As the ball is hit, the shortstop recognizes the flip play and communicates this to the second baseman, which prepares him for the feed. After the ball is flipped, the shortstop continues his momentum in the direction

Figure 8.2 Shortstop fields a ball hit right at him: *(a)* he fields the ball closer to his left foot; *(b)* he steps toward second with his right foot and transfers the ball to his throwing hand for the flip to the second baseman.

of second base. Many younger players try to flip and stop, which leads to poor feeds. The glove and ball must be separated so they don't interfere with the second baseman's vision as he receives the throw.

The shortstop uses the quarterback flip for a ball hit behind second base. He extends his glove hand to catch the ball (figure 8.3*a*). As his momentum carries him deeper from second base, he separates the ball and his glove (figure 8.3*b*) and then flips the ball to the second baseman (figure 8.3*c*). When completing the flip, his right thumb is pointed down (figure 8.3*d*). Remember that getting the first out is most important. Completing the double play is a bonus.

When the ball is hit a step or two to the shortstop's right, we like the shortstop to field the ball cleanly in the center of his body, drop his right knee to the ground (more advanced players won't go all the way to the ground), and bring the baseball into an overhand throwing position (figure 8.4). The shortstop's glove is out of the way on the left side of his chest where it won't block the vision of the second baseman. He uses a short arm circle to deliver the feed.

More advanced players open up slightly while fielding the ball, which permits them to get rid of the ball more quickly. We always start with fundamentals before moving into advanced play. The key is that the ball must be fielded in the center of the body and funneled slightly in toward the belt with the knees bent. Then the ball is quickly moved from the glove to the throwing position with the elbow no higher than parallel to the shoulder. In more advanced play, the elbow is lower than the shoulder, and the player

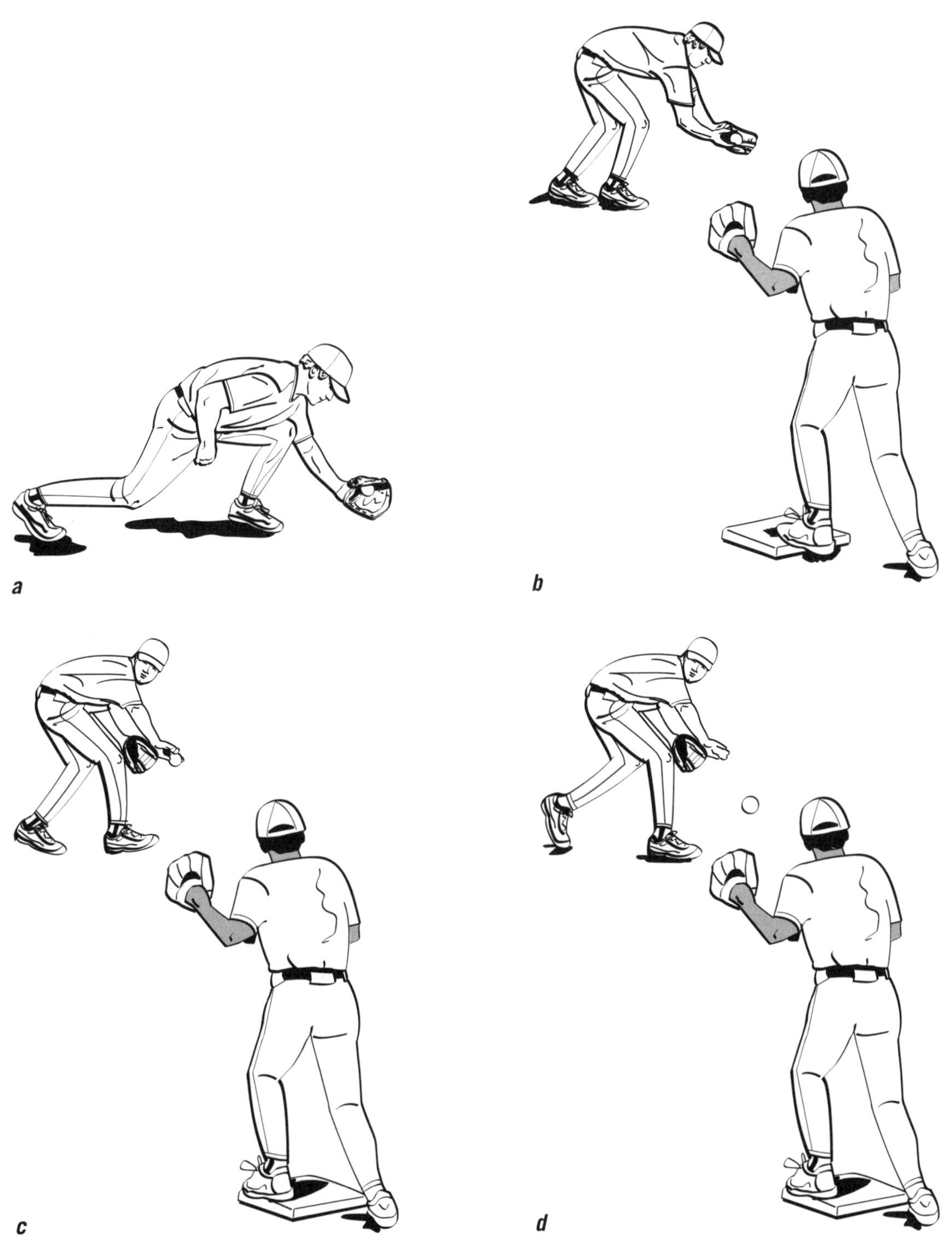

Figure 8.3 The shortstop uses a quarterback flip when the ball is hit behind second base: *(a)* he extends his glove to catch the ball; *(b)* as he moves away from second base, he separates the ball and his glove; *(c)* he flips the ball to the second baseman; *(d)* his thumb points down as the shortstop finishes the flip.

Figure 8.4 After fielding the ball, the shortstop drops to one knee and brings the ball to an overhand throwing position.

fields the ball slightly toward the right of the body. When teaching young players, we emphasize the more basic conservative route. The feed is delivered with a short arm action to get the ball to second base quickly. The feed should be delivered chest high to the front of second base, which allows the second baseman to gather momentum for completing the play.

Second Baseman Feeds

The ball hit directly at the second baseman or to his right is also an underhand flip play (figure 8.5). The only difference on this play is the second baseman steps toward second base with his left foot instead of his right. Once again, he needs to call out the flip as soon as he recognizes it. After making the flip, he continues his momentum toward second base, following through on the play.

When a ball is hit in front of the baseline, a quarterback flip is used (figure 8.6). A quarterback flip is a backhand toss with a stiff wrist. As with the underhand flip, a proper follow-through is necessary. With the quarterback flip, the thumb is pointing down at the completion of the play.

If a ball is hit slightly to the second baseman's left, he fields it in the center of his body (figure 8.7*a*). He drops his left knee as he brings the ball toward his belly, then moves into a short-arm throwing position, with his elbow no higher than parallel to his shoulder (figure 8.7*b*). He keeps his glove to his left, where it won't block the shortstop's vision of the ball. In this case, his throw needs to be to the backside of second base. The shortstop is looking for the throw to be chest high.

Figure 8.5 Underhand flip play for the second baseman: *(a)* the second baseman fields the ball; *(b)* he steps toward second base with his left foot and flips the ball to the shortstop; *(c)* he follows through, allowing his momentum to take him closer to second.

Figure 8.6 Second baseman using a quarterback flip.

Middle infielders must always be prepared for an inaccurate feed. They should not commit themselves until the ball has been released and they know where it's going.

The second baseman can also use a jump step when feeding the shortstop. The jump step is commonly used on plays to the left. Taller players and those who are stiffer in the hips seem to like this pivot better. The

Figure 8.7 The second baseman fields a ball hit slightly to his left: *(a)* he fields the ball in the center of his body and brings it toward his belly; *(b)* dropping to one knee, he raises the ball to short-arm throwing position, keeping his elbow no higher than parallel with his shoulder.

infielder fields the ball cleanly in the center of his body, slightly toward his left foot (figure 8.8*a*). He then jumps and turns (figure 8.8*b*), pointing his lead shoulder (left) toward the shortstop, who's ready at second base to receive the throw.

Figure 8.8 The second baseman uses a jump step: *(a)* he fields the ball toward his left foot; *(b)* he jumps and turns, pointing his left shoulder at the shortstop and making sure his knees stay flexed.

During the jump step, the feet basically replace each other. Younger players are encouraged to point their left shoulders directly at the shortstop. Advanced players will not close off as much. Whenever possible, a good infielder points his lead shoulder directly to where he intends to deliver the ball. While making the jump pivot, the second baseman must have quick feet, stay low, and keep his knees bent and eyes focused on the shortstop.

A second baseman might encounter situations other than those described so far, such as a play that takes him closer to first base. In this case, he extends his glove out to field the ball cleanly (figure 8.9*a*), reverse-pivots with his back toward the infield (figure 8.9*b*), squares up as best as he can with the shortstop, and makes a strong, accurate throw. This is a difficult play. The infielder should consider the speed of the base runner and the score of the game before trying it. In this situation, taking the sure out at first is often the smarter play. However, when well executed, this is one of the prettiest plays in baseball and certainly a momentum builder for the team that pulls it off.

Most infielders are quite familiar with the tag play, which is one of the easier ways to turn a double play. Here, the ball is hit to the second baseman near the baseline and the runner is running toward second base. The infielder tags the base runner with his glove and hand together, and then he throws to first to complete the double play. Of course, the second baseman knows that the base runner has been taught not to run into his tag, and this sometimes introduces a wrinkle into an otherwise almost-sure twin killing. If to avoid the tag the runner stops at enough distance from the second

Figure 8.9 Second baseman fields a hit that takes him toward first base: *(a)* he extends his glove to catch the ball *(b)* and quickly reverse-pivots to throw to second.

baseman, the second baseman can fire to first, and then the first baseman throws to the shortstop covering second to complete the double play.

Double-Play Footwork

Middle infielders need to get to the bag early because trouble occurs when they arrive late. Good infielders bend their knees, stay low to the ground, and keep their hands close together (just outside each shoulder) at chest height, with their glove open, ready to receive the throw. When receiving a throw from the second baseman, a shortstop gracefully moves toward the backside of second base (figure 8.10*a*). He squares his shoulders to the second basemen, who's fielding the ball (figure 8.10*b*). He touches the center-field side of the bag with his right foot, while stepping toward the throw with his left foot. His shoulders are squared to the player feeding him the ball.

As the shortstop receives the ball, he stays low and gathers momentum to get velocity on the throw, which will carry him toward first base. This accelerates the double play by cutting the distance of the throw. When possible, the shortstop's lead shoulder should point to first base. Sometimes this can't happen because the runner is too close to second base by the time the shortstop receives the feed, which means the throw won't have much

Figure 8.10 The shortstop quickly gets to the bag: *(a)* he moves to the backside of second base, touching it with his right foot; *(b)* he squares his shoulders to the player throwing the ball and steps toward the throw.

momentum. After receiving the throw, the shortstop (in this case) should be prepared to jump to avoid contact with the runner. All infielders should work on this kind of jump during practice.

When a ball is hit to the first baseman, the shortstop needs to yell "inside!" or "outside!" This indicates where he would like the ball to be thrown. "Inside" means he wants the feed closer to the infield; "outside" means he wants it closer to the outfield. However, the shortstop shouldn't assume the throw will come to the side of the bag he requests. He should not commit 100 percent until he sees the flight of the ball. Typically, when the first baseman is holding the runner, the throw comes on the inside of the bag. In this situation, the first baseman fields the ball cleanly, then moves his feet to create a throwing lane between himself and the shortstop.

Errors often occur when an infielder throws over the head of a runner. When the shortstop gives the inside call, he keeps his feet alive with small movements, anticipating the throw. Once the throw is in air and on target, the shortstop steps on second with his left foot and then takes a small step with his left foot that allows him to square his shoulder before making the throw to finish the double play. The other option on this play is for the shortstop to put his left foot on second base and to take a step with his right foot and another with his left as he makes the throw. This is good technique for younger players—they gain ground and the throwing distance is shorter.

Another play that the first baseman has to handle is the hot grounder that carries him to first base. He steps on the bag for the first out and yells "tag!" to the shortstop, who receives his throw and finishes the double play by tagging the runner.

The second baseman eases his way toward second base (figure 8.11*a*) to receive the first half of the double play from the third basemen, shortstop, pitcher, or catcher. He keeps his feet moving slightly to avoid becoming flat-footed (figure 8.11*b*). He heads for the outside of second base with the idea of rounding off the play as he receives a good feed that takes his momentum closer to first base as he completes the throw. He can't commit until he sees the throw.

Many second basemen precommit to coming across before they get the throw. If the feed is off line, the ball will sail into the outfield for an error that could have been avoided. Waiting and reacting to the throw is an important part of turning the double play. As the ball travels through the air and the second baseman estimates where it will land, he places his left foot on the bag and squares his shoulders to the infielder delivering the feed (figure 8.12*a*). If the feed is perfect, the second baseman can come across the bag by stepping with his right foot slightly closer to first base (figure 8.12*b*), allowing his momentum to carry him, reducing the distance he'll have to throw, and clearing himself from the runner (figure 8.12*c*).

The second baseman usually can come across the bag to receive throws from the third baseman. The throw from the third baseman must travel

Figure 8.11 The second baseman catches the ball for the first part of the double play: *(a)* he steps on second base, ready to receive the throw; *(b)* as the throw comes in, he keeps his feet moving.

Figure 8.12 The second baseman reacts to the throw: *(a)* he steps on second base and squares to the player throwing the ball; *(b)* as he makes the catch, he steps across the bag to create momentum toward first base; *(c)* he throws to first to complete the double play.

longer in the air, giving the second baseman more time to get his feet in order. When a second baseman and shortstop are in tune, the feed from the shortstop's right will often allow the second baseman to come across the bag. The shortstop and second baseman should always play catch together to develop a feel for one another.

If the feed is to the outer half of second base, the second baseman uses the bag as protection. He starts with his left foot on the bag (figure 8.13*a*), then pushes off the bag with his left foot, transferring his weight to the right and flexing his right knee (figure 8.13*b*). This allows him to load so that he can get momentum on his throw to complete the double play.

In another play, the second baseman places his left foot on the bag, drop-steps with his left foot, and completes the throw. This play often occurs when the runner is bearing down on the second baseman and he must get rid of the ball to avoid contact.

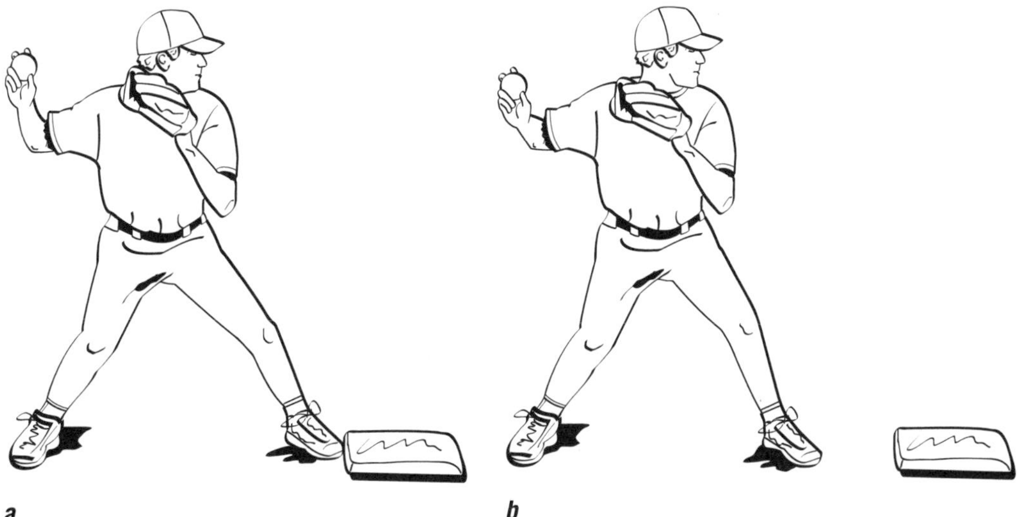

Figure 8.13 The second baseman takes the feed to the outer half of second base: *(a)* he steps on second base with his left foot; *(b)* he pushes off the bag and flexes his right knee to load for the throw to first.

Less Common Double Plays

Some double plays occur with less frequency but are just as meaningful to the defense. The 5-4-3 twin killing is exciting to watch. The third baseman shortens his depth a couple of steps, depending on the batter and pitcher. After fielding the ball, he throws to the second baseman, ideally chest high on the first-base side of second to allow the second baseman to come across the bag and avoid contact with the sliding runner. If the throw is received on the left-field side of second, the second baseman uses the base for protection but now must make a longer throw to first, which might spoil the double play. If the throw is more to the center of the base, the second baseman places his left foot on the base and holds his ground. He tries to get rid of the ball before the sliding runner makes contact. The feed means everything.

When the third baseman fields a ball over the base or when he's moving toward the base and touches the base (5-3) another kind of twin killing occurs. He should make sure he looks the ball into his glove before touching the base. Many times, he'll lift his head while in a hurry to make the play and miss a golden opportunity.

A play that should be practiced is a ball hit to any infielder or pitcher with the bases loaded and fewer than two outs. The infielders would be positioned at a shortened depth. The pitcher and the infielders must field the ball cleanly and make a chest-high throw to the plate. The catcher places his right foot on the front of the plate and steps with his left foot to meet the throw. He aligns his feet with first base and makes a strong throw to complete the double play.

Drills and Practice

Teams need to spend a great deal of time practicing feeds, footwork, and communication; learning to get rid of the ball quickly; positioning; understanding game situations; and throwing from different angles if they want the double play to be an asset for their ball club. During practice the coach should emphasize these points:

- Infielders must shorten their depth.
- Hands need to be chest high.
- Infielders must arrive at the base early.
- The defense must know the speed of the hitter and base runner.
- Players must anticipate a bad throw.
- Players need to be vocal.
- The infielder must keep his body under control.
- The player commits his feet only when he has seen the flight of the ball.
- The player cleanly fields the ball before adjusting his body to make the feed.
- The first throw is important. The feed means everything.
- Players must throw uphill.
- Practice makes perfect.
- Practice, practice, practice.

Four-Corner Flip (Four Man)

Four middle infielders position about 12 feet apart in a four-cornered box (figure 8.14). The distance may vary, depending on the age and size of the players. Player 1 has a baseball. He begins the drill by executing a flip to player 2. Player 2 has his hands up, ready to receive the feed. After he receives the throw, he repeats the flip to player 3. Each player executes quick feet and smooth hand–glove separation when making his flip. This drill moves fast, allowing for many repetitions in a short time.

Emphasize these points during the drill:

- The receiver has his hands up.
- Players use proper footwork.
- The wrist remains stiff so the ball is delivered firmly.
- Players gain ground as they flip.
- Make sure the infielder follows the flip.
- Players must be vocal and call out "flip!"

Variations

- Use two balls. Player 1 and player 3 begin with one ball each.
- Time the drill for quickness. How many flips can be executed properly in 1 minute?
- Compete with another group.

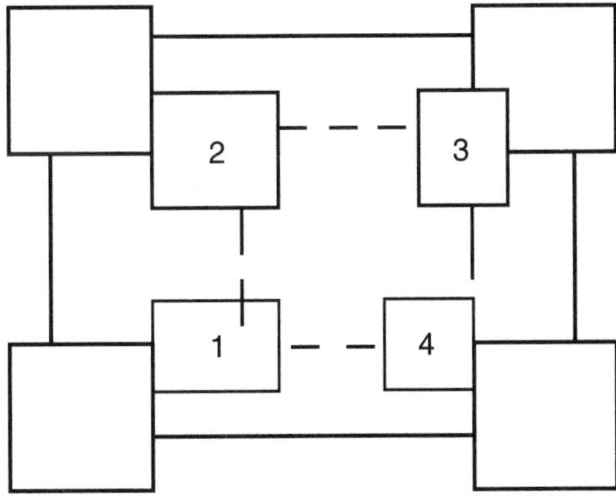

Figure 8.14 Four-corner flip drill (four man).

Four-Corner Flip (Eight Man)

Two infielders begin on each base. Start with the ball in one corner. The first infielder flips the ball to infielder 2 and then switches positions with infielder 8 (figure 8.15). Continue around all four corners repeatedly. For variation, reverse the direction and add more baseballs. Start with balls in opposite corners, and then start with balls in all corners. This is a great drill for developing quickness, eye–hand coordination, and concentration.

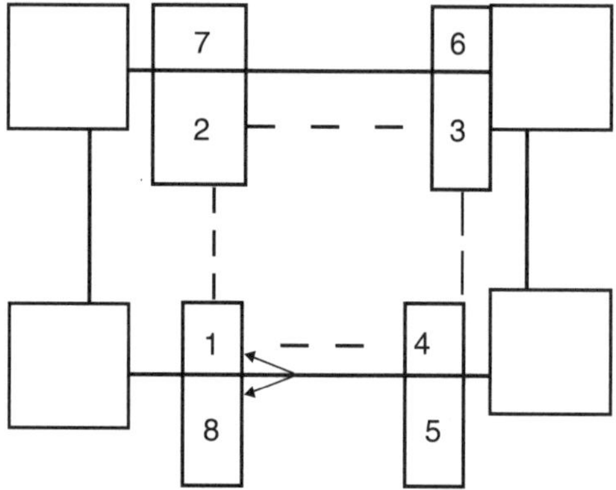

Figure 8.15 Four-corner flip drill (eight man).

Short Fungo Drill

The coach stands at the left or right of the pitching circle. He hits fungos to the shortstop, who feeds the second baseman, who turns the double play. The coach hits a different ball to the shortstop each time: to the shortstop's right and left, right at him, and behind second base. The first baseman stands with an empty bucket 45 feet from second base. This allows the coach to isolate feeds and watch footwork and double-play turns without putting too much stress on the second baseman's arm.

Emphasize these points during the drill:

- Proper footwork
- Good feeds
- Hands up
- Knees bent
- Good throws, regardless of distance
- Quickness
- Quick release
- Ground ball technique

Phantom Drill

Put a full bucket of baseballs next to each infield position. The first baseman also has an empty bucket next to him. The third baseman starts the drill when a player places a ball in his glove. The infielder then maneuvers to create whatever play he likes. He finishes the play by delivering a good feed to the second baseman, who turns the double play. After all third basemen are finished, shortstops begin creating their own plays. Continue until all infielders have made plays and their buckets are empty.

Players love this drill because they have autonomy in creating the different plays they have to make. They love diving in this drill.

The coach is at home plate, observing all plays and making comments when necessary. Emphasize these points during the drill:

- Allow players freedom to create different plays that they'll see at their positions.
- Do many repetitions in a short time.
- Incorporate gamelike throws.
- This drill provides great practice for feeds—take advantage!
- Players should use good form in turning the double play.

Note: This drill works well even with no one on base.

Quick Hands, Quick Feet

Infielders stand 45 feet from each other. Infielder 1 starts with his hands up, ready to receive the throw. Infielder 2 has the ball in his hand and throws. Once the throw has been delivered, infielder two must get his hands up, ready to receive the next throw. This drill moves quickly. Within 45 seconds of high intensity, players will begin to drag. We like to give them about 45 seconds to catch their breath before beginning again.

Emphasize these points during the drill:

- Whenever possible, catch the baseball with two hands.
- Move your feet and catch the ball on your throwing side.
- Gain ground.
- Get hands up and be ready to receive the throw.
- Throw baseball with four-seam grip.
- Always make gamelike throws (chest high).
- Catch the ball where it stings.
- The ball doesn't stay in your glove very long.
- Your glove never closes.

9

Catching Pop-Ups and Fly Balls

Charlie Greene

Championship baseball teams are built around strong pitching staffs and solid, consistent defense. More games are lost by physical or mental defensive mistakes than are won by overpowering offensive displays. Offense doesn't show up every day, whereas defense is the common thread of every successful team. Fielding averages range in the high .900 percentages, whereas batting averages hover in the .300s or below. The team that can consistently catch the ball will win a lot of games. The ability to catch pop-ups and fly balls, though apparently simpler than some defensive tasks, is not a skill to be taken for granted. Yes, some outfielders in the Major Leagues have gone a whole season without making an error, but this is quite rare at lower levels of play.

Baseball great Yogi Berra once said that half the balls hit during a baseball game are hit on the ground and half are hit in the air, while the rest are line drives. Although I question Yogi's mastery of mathematics, I know a lot of balls are indeed hit in the air. Teaching players to catch these balls requires a definite plan, combining knowledge and athletic ability. So often we witness balls being hit in the air and dropping untouched to the ground, not because players can't catch them but because of a lack of communication or confidence. Such a situation should not happen on a team well prepared in fundamentals and strategy.

Whenever you refer to a ball hit in the air, the term "pop-up" denotes that an infielder or catcher will probably have the best chance of catching the ball, whereas a "fly ball" is a ball best played by an outfielder. In either case, a ball hit in the air is caused by the batter hitting underneath the ball, creating a backspin that takes the ball into the air to a certain height before gravity causes its downward flight. If a ball is hit more solidly, it might reach the fielder in a lower trajectory and look something like a knuckleball. Or it might show some topspin that causes it to sink rapidly. The ability to catch all types of balls hit in the air is a fundamental that players at all levels should practice frequently.

As mentioned, balls hit in the air can have different kinds of movement, including backspin, topspin, or an erratic movement similar to a knuckleball's. Air balls might also slice or fade toward the foul lines, which adds another challenge to catching them. The ability to catch the many kinds of air balls players encounter in a game or over a season is a skill that needs to be included in a team's daily or pregame practice plan.

When a batted ball loses speed after leaving the bat, it will start to descend from its highest point at a more vertical angle. Contrary to what you've heard about some balls "rising" as they left a park, a baseball can travel only so far before it begins its descent. Gravity, along with any prevailing wind, is the major force influencing the flight of the ball after it has been hit. Tropicana Field, home of the Tampa Bay Devil Rays, is an indoor stadium (no wind) where the highest part of the roof is over the home plate area. The roof above the outfield fence is noticeably lower. The stadium was built this way because most pop-ups and fly balls reach their highest point relatively close to their point of origin (home plate).

Preparing to Catch the Ball

Outfielders are normally judged by their offensive prowess, but their defensive abilities are equally important. Athletic ability and a fearless confidence in going after the ball are qualities found in all good outfielders.

When selecting outfielders and determining which one will play where, you'll probably want the fastest runner in center field, the best throwing arm in right field, and the third player in left field. When possible, it's preferable to have a left-handed thrower in right field and a right-handed thrower in left field. This allows the wing fielders to be in a better throwing position after cutting down extra-base hits in the corners.

The three outfielders normally position according to the game situation, the capabilities of the batter, and wind conditions. The corner outfielders usually stand far enough away from the foul lines that they'll have enough time to get to and catch most fly balls that would land in their section of fair territory. The hang time of balls hit into the air depends on the level of play. Major League outfielders can establish their positions much further from the foul lines than beginning players should because balls in the big leagues are hit higher and thus remain in the air longer, allowing fielders to cover more ground. Outfielders might also make slight adjustments depending on wind conditions, whether the batter is left- or right-handed, and whether the outfielder is left- or right-handed. The batter's tendencies, as exhibited in previous games, are also considered by outfielders as they take their position. Tendency charts on hitters can reveal a lot of useful information for outfielders and the rest of the defense.

The anticipation of where a ball will likely be hit is a key element in getting a good jump. By knowing the type of pitch and its intended location, a fielder can be leaning in a specific direction and get to the ball just a little bit quicker. Some teams like to have their infielders relay the pitch type to the outfielders. All players, even outfielders, can observe the catcher shifting to his target location as the pitch is delivered. The lean of the catcher informs fielders where the ball might likely be hit.

As mentioned, many factors come into play in an outfielder's decision on precisely where to position for each batter and each situation. Does the outfielder need to prevent an extra-base hit? If so, he needs to play deeper than usual, positioning himself in a no-doubles or deep position. Does the batter at the plate represent the tying or winning run? Again, if so, the outfielder must minimize the batter's opportunity to get an extra-base hit. He wants to fill the gaps so that no ball gets past him. Certainly he must not risk making a diving catch. In this scenario, he must play "safety first."

Does the outfielder's team have a large enough lead for him to play shallow? Can he take some chances, such as diving for a ball falling in front of him? In general, outfielders should play shallow when their team has a substantial lead. They should take chances when the decisive game-tying or winning run is not represented by the batter. Go for the tough catch. Trade runs for possible outs late in the game.

How will the wind affect the flight of the ball? Test for this by tossing grass into the air. Adjust position to allow for the effect of the wind on the ball. The wind can influence the outfielder's ability to get to the ball and throwing efficiency, so take wind seriously.

Will the outfielder need to throw to the plate? If so, he needs to play in enough for his throw to reach home before the runner does. Time your outfielders' throws from first touch of the ball to its arrival at the plate. This will let them, and you, know how close they need to be to make a strong throw to the plate.

What is the distance to the fencing in fair territory? Outfielders should play less deep when there's less fair territory to cover.

What is the texture of the warning track? How wide is the track? Outfielders should get a feel for the warning track before the game and calculate how many steps from the grass it takes them to reach the fence or wall. Many unnecessary injuries can be avoided with some simple pregame planning.

Making the Catch

A quick approach to the ball requires a fundamentally correct stance while awaiting the pitch. Outfielders must establish good athletic posture and lean forward with the pitch. From this ready position, an outfielder can execute a forward, crossover, or drop step in any direction. Some outfielders come in better on a ball while others go back more effectively. Adjust communication procedures with each player's unique abilities such as first-step quickness or some other innate ability.

There are a variety of techniques used to catch a fly ball or pop-up; some players prefer one method and others prefer another. These preferences will manifest themselves during practice and games. A routine catch (figure 9.1) is considered one that can be completed with a minimal amount of effort, such as catching the ball about head high. A routine catch usually allows the player to place his feet in a proper throwing position before the catch is made. He must always get his momentum moving for the throw, even if a throw is not needed. This is a good practice and will develop a consistent habit.

An over-the-head catch for a ball hit directly over the head can best be caught by stepping backward with the glove-side foot and moving slightly

Figure 9.1 Routine catch.

away from the anticipated landing spot of the ball, keeping the ball in front and moving in to make the catch with the glove thumb up. If the ball carries over to the opposite shoulder (behind), the player should spin and turn his back to the field. A key point in this move is to keep a straight line after the spin and adjust to the ball. Catch this ball with the glove thumb down.

A backhand catch in which the thumb of the glove points down and the glove-arm is positioned across the body must be practiced as much as the open-hand catch in which the thumb is pointing up and the glove-arm extends away from the body. A good drill to practice these two catches is to have a coach throw football-type passes to the player. As the player runs toward the coach, the coach flips a baseball to his backhand as he goes one direction and to his open hand as he goes the other direction. This gives purpose to a conditioning-type drill (several players taking turns should allow plenty of time for recovery).

A shoestring effort should be executed outside the glove-leg so that the glove and the glove-side knee don't collide (figure 9.2). Trying to catch the ball directly in front is not a sound technique. A coach can create this type of catch by throwing low to the outside of the glove-knee with several players taking turns running at him and making the catch. The fielder makes this catch while remaining on his feet.

A diving catch (figure 9.3) should be attempted as a last resort by "bowing" the chest, extending the glove palm-up (glove side) or thumb down (throwing-hand side). A diving catch is similar to a head-first slide. Sell this catch by raising the glove in the air immediately to convince the umpire the ball has been caught. Practicing this catch at full speed is not recommended, but if a player starts in a kneeling position on both knees (figure 9.4), he can practice diving forward and work on thumb-up and thumb-down catches. Players can pair off. Modifying the drill creates less wear and tear on the body. If practicing indoors, use a mat.

Figure 9.2 Shoestring catch.

Figure 9.3 Diving catch.

Figure 9.4 In practicing the diving catch, the player begins on both knees to reduce wear and tear on the body.

The sliding catch (figure 9.5) has become more popular recently, particularly for fielders approaching a fence or backstop. The slide enables fielders to control their speed and safely make a consistent catch with less risk of injury. One of the highlights of the great Ozzie Smith's career was a catch he made running at full speed toward the left-fielder's position. He performed a high-flying catch while the left fielder executed a bent-leg slide beneath him to avoid a collision. This was a play the two players must have practiced

Figure 9.5 Sliding catch.

often to perfect. Drill this catch by having a coach throw the ball in the air to the sliding player, who attempts to make the catch as the other player goes high to both try to make the catch and avoid a collision.

You might have witnessed Paul Lo Duca, then with the Los Angeles Dodgers, making a catch of a foul pop-up while sliding into the dugout. If you saw it, you must remember it. With practice, players can safely develop the skill to catch while sliding.

A foul pop-up that can be caught in a standing position by a third baseman, first baseman, or catcher is best approached by the player going directly to any fence or dugout and then moving away from the obstruction toward the open field to make the catch. Drifting toward the obstruction can cause uncertainty and possibly injury as the catch is attempted.

The basket catch, made famous by the great Willie Mays, in which the ball comes all the way down to the waist to be caught in the "basket" of the player's palm-up glove, might have worked for Mays but is not the recommended way to catch a fly ball. Only a rare athlete such as Willie Mays can pull off this catch off with any consistency. For all we know, even Mays missed a few!

To catch the ball one- or two-handed is probably a matter of preference, but with today's improved gloves, a one-handed effort is usually very effective and allows for a far greater reach on the part of the outfielder. Some managers (such as Davey Johnson, chapter 1) still believe players should use two hands to make a catch so that the bare hand is right there, ready to grip the ball and throw.

The "bring 'em back" catch (figure 9.6)—that is, the catch over the fence to deny a home run—has become nearly a nightly expectation on sports shows. Watching Jim Edmunds of the St. Louis Cardinals or Torii Hunter of the Minnesota Twins pull back a "sure" home run is always impressive and is

Figure 9.6 Over-the-fence catch.

becoming almost commonplace. In fact, this catch is becoming an accepted fundamental for some outfielders as fielders in general become more daring. Holding a large outfielder's glove in the fingertips adds extended reach, making this catch possible for taller or extremely athletic players. Some outfielders are now working on this "specialty" catch by using their bare hand on the fence to propel themselves higher.

When catching a fly ball, a player should know where he's going to throw it before he makes the catch. This anticipation enables him to get his feet in position to make the most effective throw after catching the ball. The routine of catching the ball and throwing it must be a part of all drills so that it becomes automatic. It's not recommended that players work on catching fly balls without also working on their throws. These skills go hand in hand and should be worked in concert. To get in proper throwing position, a player should try to get his momentum going in the direction he wants to throw prior to catching the ball. A good drill is to have a coach or teammate stand near the top of a stepladder and drop a ball from his highest reach; the fielder moves in, under control, and makes the catch in a throwing position (figure 9.7). Note that the fielder should run in to the ball, under control, with his glove side closest to the ladder and should adjust his move to employ the best timing.

Figure 9.7 This drill gives the fielder practice in catching and throwing the fly ball. A partner drops a ball from the top of a stepladder. The fielder runs under the ball, catches it, and throws it with proper technique.

Communicating on Fly Ball Plays

For the safety of your players (not to mention the strategic importance of catching a fly ball), a communication system must be understood by all involved players and must be practiced frequently so that players develop confidence, skill, and cohesion. Watching two or more players pursue a fly ball or pop-up, with observable fear and uncertainty, is not indicative of a well-prepared team. You might recall the collision in the 2003 playoff game between the Boston Red Sox and the Oakland Athletics when Johnny Damon and Damian Jackson of the Red Sox collided in short center field. That collision resulted in a shook-up Jackson, and Damon being placed on a stretcher and taken to the hospital in an ambulance. During the 2005 season, continual replays of Mets outfielders Carlos Beltran and Mike Cameron running into each other was another reminder of the severity of such collisions. Remember that these accidents are highly publicized Major League incidents that can give only a slight indication of what can happen at lower levels of professional and amateur baseball. With proper communication such incidents can be prevented. Time must be set aside to teach and practice an organized communication system.

An effective system requires complete discipline between all involved players. To maintain a high level of effectiveness, a fly ball communication system must be practiced by the entire team at least twice weekly for 10 minutes. Players gaining familiarity with each other in a variety of fly-ball situations will pay big dividends. This practice is necessary to increase the confidence level of all players. They need to know they won't collide with a teammate when making an all-out effort to catch a ball. Practice is especially important when a new player is inserted into the line-up or a player is making a position switch. Don't assume that a player will automatically perform his role without having practiced the system at a specific position. A player will either make a *first call* as the ball starts down, a *last call* when the ball is halfway down, or a *no call* based on the situation. Nothing else should be allowed.

Communication Between Infielders and the Catcher

Infielders and catchers must use a disciplined form of communication with one another. When a ball is hit in the air and is definitely going to remain in the infield, there are certain rules that help establish the necessary priorities. Note that when a ball is classified as a true pop-up, outfielders should not be involved in the communication process.

The catcher should never call for the ball himself but must honor all calls from any infielder who is calling him off.

The first baseman makes a last call when the ball falls halfway down and he's moving forward or to his left. When moving to his right, he must not make any call but anticipate the possibility of being called off by the second baseman.

The second baseman makes a last call when he's going forward or to his left. He makes no call when going to his right toward the second-base area and listens for the shortstop to possibly call him off.

The third baseman makes a first call when going to his left and forward. He catches balls that will land near the mound. He makes a last call when going to his right and forward, such as in calling off the catcher.

The shortstop makes a last call when going to his left. He also makes a last call when going anywhere forward. He has priority over all pop-ups in the infield.

The pitcher catches only low pop-ups (usually the result of a poor bunt attempt). He makes a first call on these plays. If a pitcher is the best athlete on the team, he might be encouraged to catch pop-ups, but generally he should not participate. He should help by pointing to the ball while remaining silent.

Communication Between Infielders and Outfielders

The depth of the outfielders must be known by all the infielders. If outfielders are in a deep "no-doubles" alignment, infielders will have more space to cover going backward and can be more aggressive. If the infield is playing in, the outfielders will have much more territory in front of them and they can be more aggressive going forward. If the outfielders are in a throwing position (shallow), they'll have a better chance of catching balls closer to the infield. Plan ahead.

Never call for the ball until it has just started its downward flight. This is the first call. Use the call "I got it!" loud and clear only once. (Yes, it's poor English, but it's what players are used to hearing.) Verbal communication should be held to a minimum as established by priorities. All calls are made only once. Once you're called off, don't watch the ball anymore; instead, turn your eyes to the face of the fielder making the catch to read his confidence level. If he looks at all unsure of the catch, be prepared to help him out.

Make slight adjustments in the system to accommodate differences in athletic ability and range. Know the relative abilities of all players. For example, Derek Jeter of the Yankees covers more ground than teammate Hideki Matsui because of his superior defensive ability. However, disciplined priority rules must always be followed.

Again, practice at least twice per week for 10 minutes. Start slow by walking through the system before going full speed. Learn at a controlled pace and practice at game speed once all players understand their roles. Gaining an understanding of priorities by looking at a diagram isn't enough. The system must be practiced and adjusted on the field.

Again: first call when the ball starts down, last call when the ball is halfway down. The only verbal communication is "I got it," which is said one time. Don't help a teammate by calling "plenty of room." Let him make his own decision when approaching a fence or dugout.

If an infielder is going back on a ball toward an outfielder and can turn around so that he's facing home plate, he should wave his arms overhead to signify the catch is easy for him, and the outfielder should let him take it. In such a case, however, he can still be called off by the outfielder.

The third baseman makes no call when going back but listens for the shortstop's first call or the left fielder's last call.

The shortstop makes the first call going to his right rear toward the foul line and listens for the left fielder's last call, so he can give way to him. He makes no call when going toward the center fielder. He makes the last call when going to the area around second base. He must know the depth of the center fielder. This priority is the most difficult to master.

The second baseman makes the first call when going to his left rear but makes no call when going to his right or straight back.

The first baseman never calls when he's going backward or toward the second-base area.

Communication Between Outfielders

When a fly ball is being contested between two outfielders, the center fielder is the only one who should make a call. Eliminating unnecessary verbal calls prevents confusion, and all three outfielders will feel confident that they can attempt difficult catches while going full speed.

The left fielder never calls when going to his left toward the center fielder. He makes the first call when going toward second base. He makes the last call when going straight in or toward the left-field foul line.

The right fielder never calls when going to his right toward the center fielder. He makes the first call when going toward second base. He makes the last call when going straight in or toward the right-field foul line.

The center fielder makes the last call at all times.

Total Team Communication

Disciplined team communication is a must for an effective strategy to allow a team to catch as many balls in the air as possible. From a safety standpoint, disciplined communication is a high priority. How many players have been lost to injury for a season because of a collision on a pop-up or fly ball? Most collisions do not have to happen.

Figure 9.8 condenses the entire communication system into the team effort required to make the system work effectively. To interpret the illustration, simply follow the basic principles of the system.

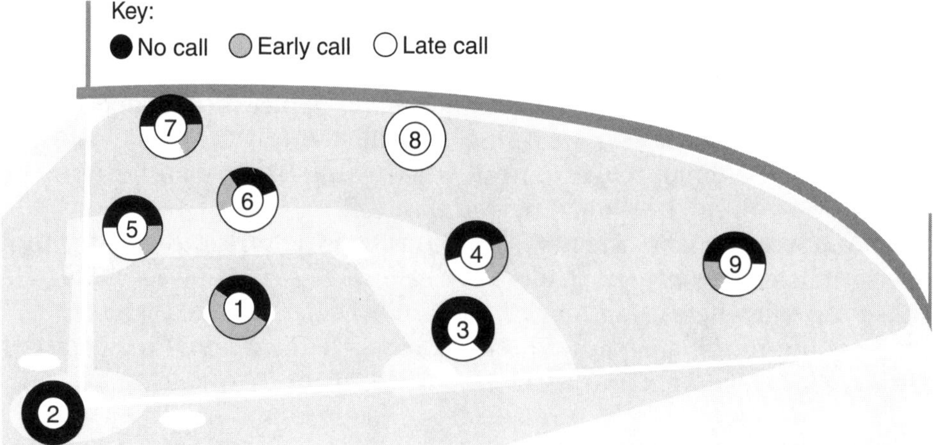

Figure 9.8 Communication system for fielding pop-ups and fly balls.

When a player approaches the ball while running through the area in his circle that's solid black, he makes no call. When running through a gray area, he makes a first call. In a white area, with no shading or markings, he makes the last call. There are no other options. The required discipline for this system to work must be developed through full-intensity practice, involving a player at each position, conducted at least twice a week.

Practice Organization

During a regular or pregame practice, time should be allotted for fly ball communication practice, occasionally replacing an infield drill. Infielders traditionally field ground balls during batting practice, and an occasional break with tradition to work on fly balls and pop-ups would be a welcome diversion. Increased familiarity at any phase of the game produces positive results, and fly ball coverage is no exception.

Skills can't be stored in spring training or preseason practice but must be refined as part of a team's pregame program. Fly ball communication is a vital part of game preparation, especially during a lengthy schedule when pregame preparation might not remain a high priority.

Single-line, take-a-turn kinds of drills are effective when learning any isolated part of the communication system. When introducing a system, it must be taught and practiced at a slow pace. This can be accomplished by having players walk through their assignments, at first throwing them fly balls, and afterward using a machine to simulate a particular situation. As players gain confidence through successful repetitions, the drills can proceed to gamelike intensity. When each isolated aspect of the system has been worked on at full speed, then balls can be hit to all possible locations. Fielders will need to adapt and follow the various rules of priority that require them to make decisions. A fungo hitter is preferred at this point, because fielders won't always know or be able to predict where a ball will land. This phase serves as an exam or quiz and should be repeated periodically. If any isolated part of a priority situation proves troublesome, then that part should be worked on until it's mastered. Building strong parts leads to an effective overall system. Players must have complete confidence in the total system for the system to work. When first learning and practicing the system, players should always pull up short and let the ball drop if there's even a remote chance of a collision.

Isolated parts of the system can include communication between two or more players and should be practiced in separate units at first:

1. Left fielder, shortstop, and third baseman
2. Center fielder, left fielder, and shortstop
3. Center fielder, shortstop, and second baseman
4. Center fielder, right fielder, and second baseman

5. Third baseman and catcher
6. First baseman and catcher
7. Right fielder, second baseman, and first baseman

Every team needs to practice this communication system and work out the details within a variety of individual skills. Adjustments can be made, and you'll soon realize that the system really works! Injuries will be reduced, and collisions on fly balls can be completely prevented.

Having the right type of equipment available also helps players in practicing the communication system. A player's glove should be flexible enough to allow him to catch the ball one-handed. To provide maximum reach, outfielders' gloves should be as long as the rules allow. Flip-type sunglasses are recommended and should be used in practice whenever the sun is bright. Nonflip glasses, while fashionable, don't provide the best relief from the sun.

The Hummer pitching machine allows for quick adjustments to create a variety of fly ball and pop-up situations. The Accubat is a racket-type teaching aid that allows even the most inexperienced parent or coach to hit pop-ups with accuracy and consistency. All that's required is hitting the ball from underneath, into the air, in the desired direction. The traditional fungo bat is still baseball's greatest teaching aid but requires skill and experience. A good fungo hitter is an asset to any team.

Review of Last Calls

- The center fielder (8) always calls for the ball last and has the final say.
- The left fielder (7) makes the last call over the shortstop and third baseman when he's moving straight in or to his right.
- The right fielder (9) makes the last call over the second baseman and first baseman when he's moving straight in or to his left.
- The third baseman (5) makes the last call over the catcher. It's also recommended that the third baseman catch all balls that might land near the mound because he's less likely to be looking into the sun. Plus, giving him sole responsibility makes for less confusion.
- The shortstop (6) makes the last call over all infielders.
- The second baseman (4) makes the last call over the first baseman.
- The first baseman (3) makes the last call over the catcher.
- The catcher (2) gives way to all calls. He only has to be a good listener.

All involved players must understand the rules of priorities and review them as often as necessary. When these priorities become second nature, the system will flourish and collisions will become a thing of the past.

Understanding Rules and Situations

Don't rely on the scoreboard to always be accurate. On many occasions, erroneous information on the scoreboard has caused team confusion. Knowing the number of outs as well as the ball and strike count is obviously critical. Teammates should always remind each other of the game situation, especially the number of outs. Catching a fly ball when you think there are already two outs can lead to a major embarrassment when men are on base.

If you're the visiting team playing defense, and if a runner is on third late in the game, don't catch a long fly ball that's close to the foul line. Let the ball drop and hope it falls foul. If you catch it, the runner from third surely scores on a tag-up. If you're the home team, catch the ball. Whenever possible, the better thrower should try to take the ball in a tag-up situation.

When a fielder makes a sliding catch under control, his slide is considered a voluntary movement, so he can recover and throw out an advancing runner even if his slide takes him into a dead-ball area, such as the dugout or bullpen. An involuntary fall creates a dead-ball situation.

All players need to understand the infield fly rule. On an infield fly, even though the batter is automatically out, runners can advance at their own risk.

A catch is legal when a fielder has completed "a baseball move" with the ball in his possession. If the ball comes loose after he hits the ground or a fence, his "catch" is not a legal catch.

Catching pop-ups and fly-balls in a safe and efficient manner must be a high priority in the game. The system outlined in this chapter should be adapted to suit the individuals of each team. The system, if implemented as described, will improve game performance and prevent many needless injuries.

10

Making Cutoff and Relay Plays

Ed Flaherty

Baseball games are more often lost than won. Errors, walks, hit batsmen, passed balls and wild pitches, and poor communication in the outfield eventually lead to big innings and subsequent loss of games. Add cutoffs and relays to the list. Breakdowns in routine defensive plays give opponents extra chances to score.

Once the ball is put in play, a perfectly executed defense allows the offense only what they have earned and nothing more. As much as baseball is an individual sport, excellent team defense is the result of the strategic movement of all nine players. All players must realize that no one player's role is more important than any of his teammates.

During big innings by an offensive team, there's often an incorrectly executed cutoff or relay that lengthens the inning. An effective cutoff and relay system gives the defense confidence and takes away the opponent's aggressiveness on the bases. A properly executed cutoff or relay that results in an out is a morale booster for the defense and kills the momentum of an offensive rally.

To illustrate the importance of all nine players on defense, consider the following play. A batter hits a single to right field with a runner on first base (figure 10.1). This seems like a simple play, but it involves many little things. For example, the second baseman positions on the inside of second base while watching the runner tag the bag. This could cause the runner to take a wider turn and force him to take a longer time getting to third base. The shortstop's job is to be in a direct line to third base between the outfielder and the third baseman. The third baseman makes sure that the

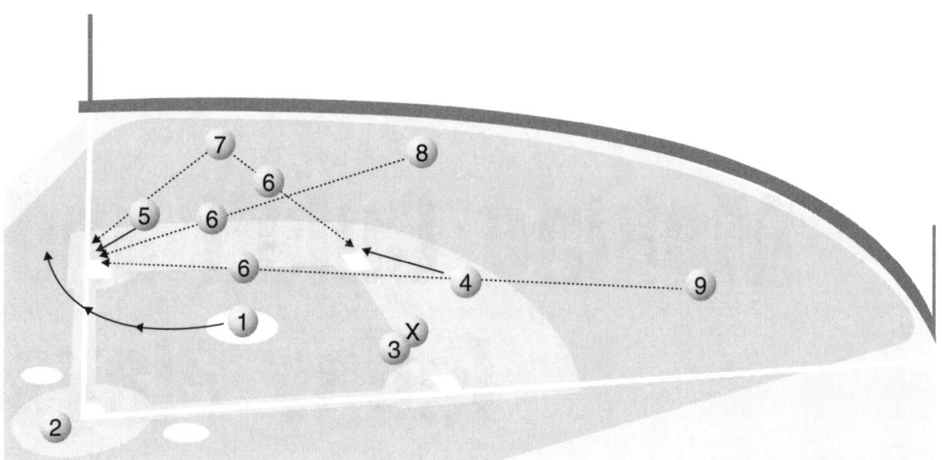

Figure 10.1 Runner on first base; single hit to each field.

shortstop is lined up correctly. If the shortstop is positioned correctly he will be no more than 45 feet from third base. By doing this, the shortstop has made it difficult for the runner to decide whether to advance to second base. If the shortstop were farther out toward the outfielder, the runner could easily read the throw. The first baseman will watch the runner tag first base and position himself, without causing an obstruction, so that the runner makes a wider than normal turn. These little positioning ploys could allow the defense to retire the runner at third and still keep the other runner at first base.

Championships are won by teams that have talent and desire and play a fundamentally sound game. An effective cutoff and relay system is a staple for every good team. Making an out without having to pitch a ball is a great morale booster for a team and can break the momentum of an offensive rally. Coaches and teams should take tremendous pride in their cutoff and relay system and be diligent in how they practice each day. It starts with a sound long-toss program so that each player develops a strong arm. The team should spend some time during each practice on cutoff and relay positioning and communication. During live scrimmages, coaches should demand that cutoffs and relays are executed correctly.

Many people feel that the most exciting 12 seconds in baseball is a triple. But for a coach, the most exciting play is a perfectly executed cutoff or relay that results in a runner being cut down at the plate or third base. These plays are the result of sound technique in positioning, throwing, and receiving the ball. Communication during these plays is of utmost importance. Cutoff and relay drills should be practiced daily so that the execution becomes second nature.

Planning and Reviewing Terminology

The coach must first explain common terminology so that all players understand the terms used in teaching cutoffs and relays. They must understand the difference between a cutoff man and a relay man. Usually, the shortstop is the cutoff man on throws to third base from the outfield; the third baseman is the cutoff man on throws to home plate from left field; and the first baseman is the cutoff man on throws to home plate from center field and right field. The first baseman is also a cutoff man on an extra-base hit with a runner on first base who has a chance to score on the hit. Cutoff men are positioned in the infield and are the last men to throw the ball to the intended base or to cut off the throw.

The relay men are usually the shortstop and the second baseman, who go into the outfield to receive the throw from an outfielder who has chased down a ball that has gone beyond him. Relay men are the link between the outfielder and the intended base or a cutoff player stationed between the relay man and the intended base. The shortstop and second baseman make up a tandem relay; together they go into the outfield and line up behind one another.

Backups are the players responsible for getting behind the intended base in case of an overthrow. A crow hop is a technique executed by an outfielder that allows him to gain enough momentum to make a strong and long throw to his intended target.

All nine players are instructed to be prepared on every play. Coaches assume that players are always ready, but the truth is that many are not. During practice drills and scrimmage games, coaches should question players on their responsibilities if the ball is hit to them. Before each pitch, players should run down a mental checklist, reviewing the information they'll need to make the play:

1. How is the ball hit—on the ground or in the air?
2. How deep is the hit?
3. How fast is the ball traveling?
4. What are the field conditions?
5. What is the game situation?
6. How strong is my arm?
7. How fast is the base runner?

By reviewing any situation that might arise in a game, players can react more quickly to an impending play.

Cutoff and Relay Throws

Throws made during cutoff plays or relays should always be on target. Throws should never be rushed because if a ball is mishandled or overthrown, a play won't be possible on the runners, which many times results in the offense getting extra bases. Throws must be made under control and on target. Accuracy is more important than the strength of the throw because a ball traveling in the air covers much more distance than the runner can cover in the same amount of time. Teach your outfielders and relay infielders not to max out their throws but to always throw under control. Many times a throw made with a smooth motion has greater velocity than a ball that has been thrown from the tight grip and tense muscles of a player trying to throw too hard.

Throws should be made with an overhand motion so that the ball stays on a direct line during its flight. Throws from outfielders to cutoff players should aim for the cutoff man's head. Throws from outfielders to relay men should be chest to head high. When a throw is made at chest or head height, it's easier to fake a cutoff and easier to catch if making a cutoff or relay throw. When a throw is too high, a player running to first can read it more easily and might advance to second base, removing the double-play possibility. A good rule of thumb is to teach outfielders and relay men to throw the ball at about 85 percent effort. This ensures greater accuracy and provides the best chance for a good bounce to the base. Throws from cutoff men to the intended base should be aimed at the belt so that a quick tag can be applied to the runner. Throws from relay men in the outfield to the intended base must be accurate.

As a coach, you should *never* allow throws that are made over the cutoff or relay man's head. Be persistent. Engrain this fact in the defensive player's mind at all times. It's quite common to go to a game, observe pregame infield warm-up, and watch many rainbow-like throws go over the head of cutoff players. Allowing this only encourages your players to be lazy and to develop poor habits.

Outfielder Techniques

The outfielder should charge all ground balls aggressively but under control to make sure that he catches the ball. Depending on the situation in the game and field conditions, the techniques the outfielder uses to catch a ground ball will vary. In any case, outfielders should gain momentum as they catch the ball and use a small crow hop as they begin their throw. Obviously, it's important to field the ball under control or else the runners will advance to the next base or beyond.

An outfielder is often in a rush to catch the ball and takes his eyes off it. The result is the ball gets by the fielder and rolls for some distance. The outfielder should get behind all fly balls and have momentum moving toward his target as the catch is made. This will give him the best chance to make the strongest, most accurate throw to his intended target.

An outfielder should catch the ball with his glove-side foot forward so that he can execute a controlled crow hop as he throws the ball to the cutoff man. This technique allows for the quickest and strongest release of the ball.

All of the outfielders' throws to the cutoff and relay men should be chest high with as much carry on the throw as possible. Throws should be made overhand, not sidearm, so the ball stays on a direct line. Outfielders should also finish the throw by staying in a direct line to the target rather than spinning to the glove side. This makes for better carry on the throw and keeps the ball straight.

Relay men should allow outfielders to make as long a throw as they're capable of making. This will cut down on the distance of the following throw. On throws to cutoff men inside the diamond, accuracy is of utmost importance because if a throw is off line, the throw will have to be cut off, resulting in a slower time getting the ball to third base or home.

If two outfielders are going after a ball and both have an equal chance to make a play, the outfielder with the strongest arm should make the catch. Likewise, if the momentum of an outfielder is more advantageous for one over the other, the outfielder with the best angle to the target should make the play. For example, on a fly ball to right center field with a runner tagging at second, the right fielder should make the play.

Communication During Cutoffs and Relays

Communication is vital on all cutoff and relay plays. Simple verbal cues are yelled out to cutoff men to explain where they should be stationed and what to do with the ball after catching it. The player at the intended base communicates to the cutoff man whether he should move to his right or left to be in a direct line between the outfielder and the base. He yells, "Right!" if he wants the cutoff man to move one step to his right or "Left!" if he wants the cutoff man to move one step to his left. The player at the base yells, "Right! Right!" if he wants the cutoff man to move two steps to his right, and so on.

Once the outfielder releases the ball and the ball is on its way to the cutoff man, the player covering the base should communicate to the cutoff man what should be done with the ball. One option is to let the ball continue to the base. If the player at the intended base chooses this option, he'll call out, "Go, go, go," so that the cutoff man will let the ball go through. If the ball is off line and should be cut off, he'll yell, "Cut!" If he would like the ball cut off and thrown to another base, he'll call out, "One," "two," "three," or "four," depending on which base he wants the throw to go to.

Only the players involved in the play should communicate cutoff instructions. Other players should stay quiet because confusion will result if opposite calls take place. On singles to the outfield, there should be no calls on where to throw the ball. Outfielders are trained where to throw the ball on singles and don't need instruction. For instance, with a man on first and second and a single to right field, the right fielder has a choice of throwing to home plate (first baseman is the cutoff man) or to third base (shortstop is the cutoff man). He'll decide where to throw the ball based on the factors discussed earlier.

Players should practice allowing throws to go through to the base as much as possible and to cut throws off only when they're extremely off line. If players can do this, coaches will find that stronger throws become more commonplace, which allows cutoff men to position closer to the intended base.

A good rule of thumb is for the ball to be cut off only when the throw is well off line. If the throw is only 5 feet off line to home plate, for instance, it's quicker for the catcher to go get the ball and hustle back for the tag than it is for the ball to be cut off and then relayed to home plate.

Cutoff Player Positioning and Techniques

Positioning for the cutoff man is important because positioning affects how the ball will travel to the intended base and whether or not the runner will be able to advance. A good strong throw from the outfielder through the cutoff man's chest will result in a nice clean hop to the intended base. Occasionally, a great outfield arm will carry the throw right through to the base. For this to happen, the cutoff man should position no further than 45 feet from the intended base. At this position, the ball should take one hop to the base if thrown on line and through the cutoff man's head. This position also allows the cutoff man to freeze the runner by faking a cut. Sometimes, an outfielder's arm strength won't allow the cutoff man to position 45 feet from the base, so he must move as close to the outfielder as necessary.

The depth of the hit ball is also a factor in the positioning of the cutoff man. Again, he must adjust according to the particular circumstance. Cutoff men should not go out too far for two reasons. First, if he goes out too far, the ball will have to be cut or the result will be a ball rolling at a very slow pace. Second, the runner will have a very easy time reading whether he can safely take another base. By positioning about 45 feet from the base, the cutoff man can move forward on a throw that's short of its target.

All throws must be caught in the air. The cutoff man should give the outfielder a good target on every throw. His chest should be squared to the outfielder, his hands should be raised, and he should call the outfielder's name to reinforce where the outfielder should throw the ball. The cutoff man's feet should be moving, not stationary, much like an infielder in his setup position. The ball should be caught on his glove-hand side, and as he's about to receive the ball he should position his feet in a way that allows him to make the quickest throw to the intended base.

As the ball is arriving from the outfielder, the cutoff man will hear what the ensuing call will be—either "Go, go, go" or one of the "cut" calls. If the cutoff man is instructed to cut the throw and throw it to the intended base, he'll drop-step his left foot so that his feet are in a good position to relay the throw. If there's an anticipated cut call and possible throw to second, the cutoff man will place his left foot forward to be in a good position to throw to second. This happens many times on a base hit to left field with a runner on second with the third baseman as the cutoff man (figure 10.2). Seldom will the runner be out at the plate if the throw is cut. Thus, many third basemen line up with their left feet toward the outfield. If the call is "Go, go, go," he fakes a cut. This footwork is vital in making the quickest transfer to the intended base. Most plays at the plate or third base are very close so an extra step could make a difference in the call.

Players should practice allowing throws to go through to the base and cutting them off only when they're off line. Again, it's quicker for the player at the intended base to move a few steps, receive the throw, and then go and tag the runner than it is for the ball to be cut off and relayed to the base.

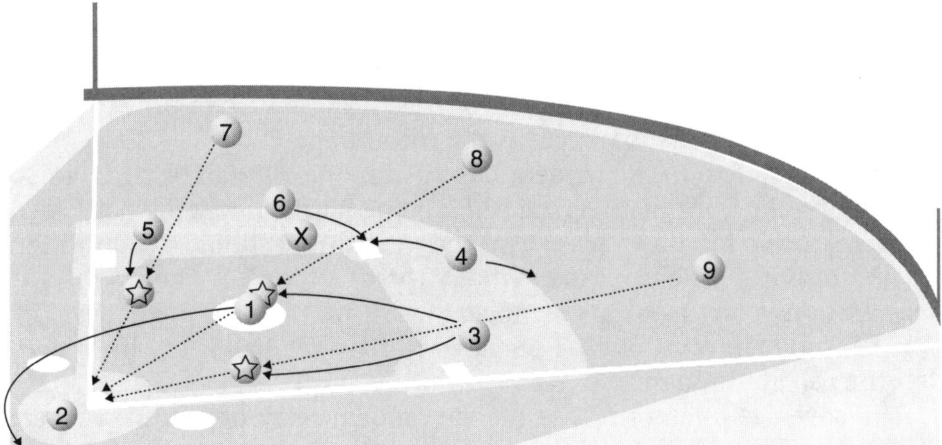

Figure 10.2 Runner on second base; single hit to each field.

Tandem Relay

For batted balls that get by an outfielder, use a relay system that involves both the second baseman and shortstop, who go into the outfield and make a relay throw to either third base or home plate. This is called a tandem or piggyback relay.

The tandem is set up once the ball gets by the outfielder and becomes a potential extra-base hit. Depending on the side of the field the ball is hit to, the middle infielder on that side of the field (front man) sprints toward the outfielder retrieving the ball and allows the outfielder to throw the ball from 100 to 120 feet. If the outfielder has an exceptional arm he can throw further, but 150 feet should be the maximum because the accuracy of this first throw is important. The backside middle infielder (backup man) sprints to a position 20 to 30 feet behind the front man.

The tandem allows the defense to still have a play even if the first throw is over- or underthrown. It also allows for a verbal call from the backup man to the front man on where to throw the ball. The front man in the tandem tries to line himself up with third base or home plate as much as possible, although it's not as important for him to be in a direct line as it is for a cutoff man. He'll put his hands in the air and yell, "Hit me!" to the outfielder so that the outfielder knows where the front man is as he picks up the ball.

As the ball is in the air from the outfielder, and if the throw is a strong one that comes on the glove side, the front man will backpedal to cut down the distance on the next throw. The relay man must always be working to get into position to catch the ball on his glove side. If the throw is bad, he must move to try to catch the ball in the air. Sometimes for the front man to catch the ball, he must jump for it or field it on a short hop. If this happens, he should allow the ball to go through to the back man in the tandem. The next throw will be to either third base or home plate. There will be no cutoff man to third base for this throw, but the throw to home plate will have the first baseman as the cutoff man.

The backup man in the tandem has the responsibility of being 20 to 30 feet behind the front man. As the ball is being picked up by the outfielder, he looks to the infield to see where the next throw should go, and then communicates to the front man either "three," "four," or "hold." "Hold" tells the front man to look to the infield to see if another play might develop. The backup man must also be prepared to field the ball if the front man lets the ball go through.

The coverage of second base on the tandem relay depends on where runners are located. If the bases are empty or runners are on second and third and an extra-base hit develops, the first baseman watches the batter touch first base and then follows him to second base. If a runner is on first base, the first baseman has the responsibility of being the cutoff to home plate. The outfielder to the side opposite of where the ball is hit should cover second base. For instance, if an extra-base hit goes to right-center field with a man on first, the left fielder is responsible for covering second base (figure 10.3).

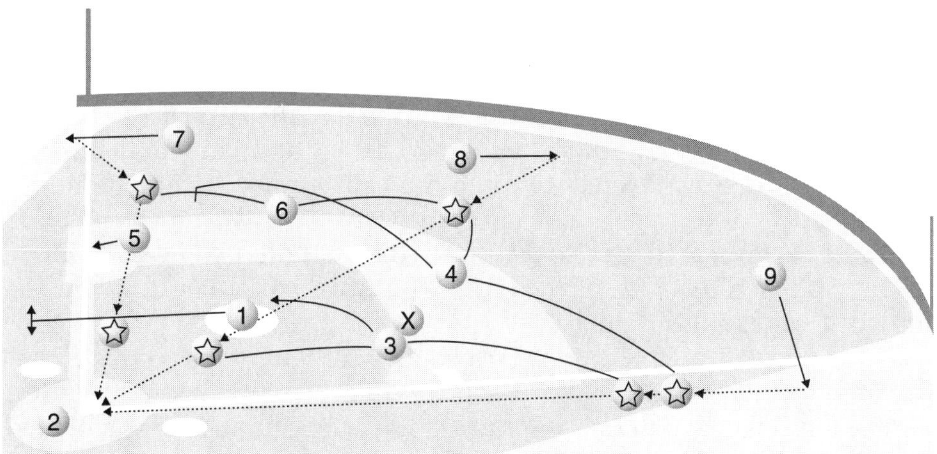

Figure 10.3 Runner on first base; extra-base hit to each field.

Extra-base hits hit down the left-field or right-field line require a slight variation of the tandem relay. On a ball down in the left-field foul area with a man on first, the first option is to try to cut down the first runner at home plate. The shortstop won't be able to go all the way to the foul line because the second baseman will have too far to travel to line up behind the shortstop. Thus, the shortstop lines up in fair territory so the second baseman can line up behind. This requires a throw back toward the middle of the field but allows for the tandem to be set up. With the shortstop remaining in fair territory, his throw home is less likely to hit the runner trying to score.

On a ball hit to the right-field foul area with a man on first base, the second baseman moves to a relay position on the foul line, and the first baseman becomes the backup man in the tandem because first base needs no cover on this play. The shortstop can now maneuver as either a cutoff man to third base or a cutoff to home plate, if needed. Recall this critical tandem play by shortstop Derek Jeter during a pivotal New York–Oakland playoff series? From outside the first-base foul line, Jeter flipped the ball to catcher Jorge Posada, who tagged Jeremy Giambi in a very close play at the plate. That play hit the highlight reel for the rest of the week. The tandem relay is a safety mechanism that sometimes pays off with big dividends. If Jeter had not been in position, that series might have gone Oakland's way.

Verbal and Visual Communication

Depending on the level of play, the experience of the players, and the length of time a group of players have played together, visual communication is an option a defense can use on cutoffs. This would take the place of the "go" or "cut" calls, which can create confusion if more than one person is yelling or if the stadium is very noisy.

Visual communication on cutoffs simply requires the cutoff man to understand the type of throw being made, the direction of the throw, the score, and the position of the runners. Once the outfielder releases the ball and the ball is traveling toward its target, the cutoff man will determine if he'll need to move his feet to catch the ball. If the cutoff man doesn't have to move his feet, he won't cut off the throw and will allow the ball to continue to the base. He'll also fake a cut. If the cutoff man needs to move his feet to reach the ball, he'll cut off the throw and either throw to the intended target or hold the ball.

Cutoff players need to be drilled over and over on different scenarios that can arise in this cutoff system. At the youth level, visual communication may be too advanced. Visual communication can begin to be implemented at the high school level, at which infielders have a better understanding of the strategy of the game.

Backup Techniques

Backing up bases is another major component of cutoffs and relays. Backup players need to go full speed to their proper position. For pitchers who are backing up third base or home plate, the backup position is well behind the base, as close to dead-ball areas as possible. The backup player should be able to keep the ball in front of him. Sometimes backup players get too close to the base and when the player at the base misses the ball it also skips by the backup man. The left fielder, if he doesn't have another assignment, should be moving to back up third base on balls hit to right field. Backing up is all about taking pride in a team concept. A good way to practice backing up is simply to let the throws go by the intended target in practice, creating a game situation. Backups should position as deep as possible to have the best chance of catching the errant throw before runners can advance or before allowing the ball to go out of play.

Special Situations

Certain situations arise in games that create a change in a cutoff setup. The importance of preventing a runner from advancing to second base and thus keeping the possibility for the double play alive should be stressed at every practice. One play you see a lot is when a runner is on first and a single is hit down the left-field line. Many times, the left fielder comes up with the ball and throws to third with the intent of retiring the runner from first who's trying to advance two bases. However, many times the runner is safe at third, and the batter who has hit the single advances to second base on the left fielder's throw. On this play, the shortstop needs to line up as a cutoff man to second base so that the left fielder knows it's important that the batter be forced to stay at first base. The only time the left fielder will throw to third base is when he has a 100 percent chance of retiring the runner.

Another situation that must be reinforced for young players is when a runner is on second base and a batter hits a single to left field. Here, the third baseman lines up as the cutoff man to home plate, requiring the shortstop to cover third base.

The size and dimensions of the ballpark should be considered when setting up or adapting your cutoff and relay systems. For instance, on a field that's very deep, the tandem relay players might need to go deep into the outfield to meet the throw. The throw from the front man in the tandem to home plate is now very long and might require a cutoff man to home. The first baseman is always the cutoff man on an extra-base hit with a runner on first base. Some parks are very shallow in certain areas and might be too short for an effective tandem relay to be employed. Coaches will sometimes need to adapt their cutoff and relay system to match the ball field.

The score of the game and the inning are also factors in cutoffs. With a 2-run lead in the ninth inning with a man on second, it might be a mistake to even attempt a throw to home plate. The shortstop or the second baseman is instructed to assume a cutoff position for a throw to second and ensure that there's no chance for the runner who hit the single to advance to second. This is what's called a "no-doubles" situation—that is, every defensive move related to this play should be with the idea of keeping the runner at first base.

One particularly tough play goes as follows: The offensive team has a runner on second or on first and second, and a ground ball is hit to the second baseman's right in a spot where the second baseman could make a great play, or the ball could get by him and go for a single to center. Situations have occurred in which the first baseman has moved to his cutoff position, when suddenly the second baseman makes a great play and either has no one to throw to at first or else the shortstop can't complete the double play. This happens because the first baseman makes his route directly to the cutoff position on the mound. Instead of heading directly to the mound, the first baseman should first move toward the plate, watch the batter touch first base, and then angle to the mound for the cutoff. If the first baseman takes this route, by the time he takes his first couple of steps he'll be able to read whether the second baseman has made the play or if the ball has gone into center field.

Drills

A well-structured relay from an outfielder fielding a ball against the fence, making a throw to the front man in a tandem relay, who then relays a perfect throw to home plate is not a play that just happens by chance. This play is the result of a diagrammed chalk session given by the coach and followed by drills that improve the skills required in cutoffs and relays. The following drills are useful in building an effective cutoff and relay system.

Square Drill

The square drill is a great drill for infielders to work on transferring the ball quickly. First basemen are incorporated into this drill so they can also improve their transfer of the ball.

Players are positioned in a square anywhere from 45 to 60 feet apart. The ball is thrown clockwise and is moved rapidly from player to player. When the ball reaches the last player on the square, it is thrown counterclockwise, with the receiver now spinning to throw to the next player. Diagonal throws can be incorporated. Reversing the ball, as occurs in a cutoff, can also be included as a player's choice. Good footwork is emphasized to attain the quickest possible transfer of the ball, much like the footwork of a cutoff man. Receiving the ball in the palm of the glove is emphasized so that little time is wasted in the transfer.

A variation of this drill is to have players throw bad throws so that the receiver has to work to catch the ball on his glove side.

Rapid-Relay Drill

Three or more infielders line up 45 feet apart. The player on the end throws the ball to the next player in line, who continues to throw the ball down the line to the following player. Then the ball is thrown back up the line. Players position themselves like cutoff men and turn glove side when throwing to the next player. Outfielders can be incorporated into this drill at the ends of the lines.

You can make this drill competitive by forming two or three groups and lining them up over the outfield. Each line begins throwing at the same time. The first team to throw the ball all the way down the line and back without dropping it wins.

Timed Cutoff Drill

Outfielders station 200 to 250 feet away from home plate. Cutoff men station in the cutoff position with catchers at the plate. The coach hits balls to the outfielders at a predetermined distance. The outfielders make throws to the plate while another coach times the throw from the time the ball hits the outfielder's glove to the time it reaches the catcher's glove.

This is a great teaching drill with immediate feedback to the players on a variety of techniques: effort of the throw, when to cut the ball off, when to let the ball go through, and the cutoff and transfer throw. Players will learn from their times the importance of accuracy and throwing the ball through the cutoff man's head.

Like the rapid-relay drill, this drill can become a competitive game between different sets of outfielders and infielders.

Six-Out Game

This is one of the best drills I know of and is best saved for the end of practice. This drill incorporates hitting, base running, and both individual and team defensive skills. Because of the nature of the drill and the amount of base hits and extra-base hits, cutoffs and relays are practiced in a live competitive atmosphere.

Teams are divided into four players per team. One team is the hitting team, two other teams make up the team in the field, and the fourth team works in the hitting tunnels or on batting tees. A coach pitches from 45 feet away from behind a protective screen. Pitchers can stand behind the protective screen and come out to back up bases. The drill progresses just like a real game except that the coach is pitching. Each team gets six outs, with the bases being cleared after the first three outs. After six outs, the teams rotate. Runners can be placed on the bases before the inning starts if the coach wants to work on specific situations.

This drill is highly competitive, and because the coach rather than a pitcher is throwing, challenging balls are hit all over the field. Many cutoff and relay situations occur, making this drill gamelike. Play can be stopped at any time for the coach to review a particular situation.

11

Choosing Defensive Tactics in Games

Ken Knutson

Despite the title of this chapter, the strategies covered in this section have as much to do with offense as they do with defense—in some cases, maybe more so. That's because you need to get into the head of offensive opponents to anticipate the tactics they'll employ if you're going to make the best decisions on how to counter them defensively.

A simplistic view of defensive game management is to try to shut out the other team, keeping the opponent from scoring at all costs. But to be consistently successful as a manager, you need to forget about keeping the opponent to zero. The real key is ensuring that the other team scores fewer runs than you do.

A critical part of my philosophy on good defensive coaching is that some runs are worth conceding. This is an organizing principle I'll expand on throughout the chapter. I believe that certain runs at certain points in a game have essentially no negative impact on your team's chances of winning. These runs (a late run tacked on during a blowout, for example) are almost always inconsequential. I would add that in some cases giving up a run can actually be considered a positive. Just think back to the last time you faced bases loaded, no outs, and you got out of the inning and gave up only one run.

By contrast, some runs are devastating. Allowing the offense a big inning when you have a comfortable lead late in a game, for example, is particularly hard to accept. And it's even harder to swallow when errors in the field contribute to the offensive barrage. Such situations are killers and can be shocking blows to a team's morale.

Although it's true that each time an opponent touches the plate safely it scores another run, the value of each score differs depending on when and under what circumstances it occurs and its significance to the game's outcome. The defensive tactics you consider and employ should be based on their potential costs, in terms of game-determining runs that might be scored by the offense.

When it comes to defensive strategy, I've found the best place to start is with "the book," as in, "I'm going by the book." Going by the book is probably more common on the defensive side of the game than on the offensive. A defense needs to be conservative so that the ball club doesn't beat itself. At the same time, sound strategy enables a defense to win games. The hope is that a good defense makes plays that help win ballgames, but more important is that a good defense never beats itself by losing a game on the field. Going by the book helps us to make reasonable and consistent defensive decisions by putting parameters on what defenses can, should, and (in some cases) must do.

A cardinal rule in the book is to play for the win on the road and the tie at home. The home team has the advantage in extra innings. In fact, being the home team in an extra-inning ball game is the biggest plus in all of sports. The sudden death of the home team scoring, coupled with the pressure of the "what might happen if we don't score?" mentality of the visitor, puts a lot of pressure on the visiting team in extra innings. They know that to win they must first score themselves and then also hold the home team from scoring—this makes winning on the road in extra innings a doubly hard task. This is why I do everything I can strategically, on both defense and offense, to avoid being the visitor in the tenth. The only thing worse than being the visitor in the tenth is being the loser after nine!

Anyway, I mention going by the book only to note that knowing what to do in an isolated game situation is never enough. You have to see the forest as well as the trees. Following the rules by referring to the book allows us to get the big picture, giving us a framework to understand why we do what we do as managers.

As I discuss defensive game strategies, rules from the book will pop up from time to time, providing a philosophical foundation to help us decide what choices we should make as coaches. Whether it's how we position our defense, manage our pitching staffs, opt to bunt, and so forth, we must understand to what end we're doing what we choose to do. In short, as baseball managers, we need to understand both the "when" and "why" of what we do. Rules from the book can help us out with that.

While we're at it, here are some other rules of note from the book:

- If you see a bunt, get an out. Any out is great.

- Don't try to win the game on defense. Control the damage, and don't jeopardize your team's chances for success. It's far easier to come back from down 1 run than to climb back from being down 3.
- In a tie or 1-run game, try to defend the double when it makes sense.
- Don't get beat with an open base. Pitching around a guy is a great way to get an out or to avoid a good hitter.
- Get your best guys in the game when you have the lead. Win with your closer, get beat with your closer.

Getting beat late is the most devastating way to lose a ball game. To lose a game that you had been winning throughout is extremely hard on your club. Teams might lose confidence and question their ability to close out games; they might question how they play and begin to press both defensively and offensively. In the long run, they might become aware of their inability to hold leads, which erodes their ability to play sound, fundamental baseball.

Once you get the lead, you can't give it back.

Every year I've been a college coach, the teams I have managed have averaged 5 to 8 runs per game. I doubt my team's experiences are much different from those of other college clubs. Knowing this, you can be pretty sure that if you give up 3 or 4 runs early, you do have time to come back. You also have the confidence to recognize that all things being equal, if you can stop the bleeding and hold your opponent scoreless from here on out, you have a real shot at winning.

Giving up runs late, by contrast, means that you might have only a few outs or at best a few innings to work with. My feeling has always been that it's more of a priority to be good late on the mound than to be good early. This philosophy has dictated how I manage a game and how I set up my pitching staff.

Don't get me wrong: I'm not implying that starting pitching isn't important. Starting pitching is very important. Without good starting pitching, you can't get to your plus bullpen. But it's important to take a look at the facts and to take into account the realities of modern-day baseball. In some years, for instance, pitchers on my college teams have had as few as two or three complete games, and never more than a dozen in a season. The aluminum bat has created an offensive game in which you see pitch counts routinely fall between 135 and 150 pitches in a nine-inning game. In some games, your club's pitch counts are going to be significantly higher than that. Starting pitchers can't be expected to be around for the end of the game when pitch counts hover at these high numbers. Someone needs to throw the final 20 to 30 pitches of a ballgame. And how you organize your pitching staff will determine whether the guy throwing the last couple of dozen pitches can get your team the win.

Pitching Staff Organization

The key element to any defensive management strategy is the use of the pitching staff. And I say this not only because I was a college pitcher and am the pitching guy (along with being the head coach) at the University of Washington. Many factors influence score- and inning-based decisions, but all of these ultimately connect back to how well your team pitches and how well you manage your pitchers. More on this later.

In setting up my pitching staff, my first intention is to have one of my very best guys on the mound late as my closer. Ideally, my closer will be one of the top pitchers on my staff. In fact, I'd even say that I'm fine if he's my *best* guy. Do the math—your closer has a chance to appear in significantly more games, and have more of a direct impact on your ability to win, than any starter, even one of your top guys. At the University of Washington, our school record for wins for a pitcher is 12, and our school record for saves is 20. Given these numbers, it's an easy decision to give one of your top pitchers the role of closer because that's where he'll have the greatest impact.

Will Fenton, All-American closer at the University of Washington, did not give up an earned or unearned run during the 2003 season.

A strong bullpen with a dominant closer affects the way the other team plays. Having a solid closer shortens the game for the opponent. The other manager knows he might have only seven or eight innings to beat you. A case in point: In the mid 1990s, my University of Washington Huskies had a streak of over 90 consecutive games in which when we led in the ninth inning, we won the game. Some years later, in 2003, Will Fenton, All-American closer for UW, did not give up a single run (earned or unearned) the entire year. My point? Your closer is one of the more important members of your squad. And that might be an understatement.

Several factors come into play when you're deciding whom to use in the closer role: a pitcher's pitchability, resiliency, and poise, as well as the abilities of your other pitchers. Poise, resiliency, and pitchability mean nothing if you do not have strong starting pitchers available. As I've said, without good starting pitching, you can't get to your plus bullpen and to your quality closer. If you can't give the lead to your closer on a consistent basis, it might be better to use your closer as a starter, especially if he has pitchability.

Pitchability is the ability of a pitcher to pitch, not simply throw. Effective pitching starts with command, so the greater a pitcher's pitchability, the more pitches he'll be able to throw and, more important, to control. If a pitcher doesn't have great pitchability, he can still be a great closer or part of your plus bullpen, as long as whatever pitch he can throw for a strike is dominant. In fact, many times you'll see a pitcher with one dominant pitch become a very good closer. Because your opponent's lineup won't see your closer more than once a game (one hopes!), that one pitch can be very effective.

If you have a guy with one great pitch and a pitcher with tremendous pitchability, I would probably make the pitcher with the better pitchability a starter or long reliever, and use the one-pitch guy as a closer. Of course, this assumes all other things—namely, resiliency and poise—are equal.

Resiliency refers to a player's ability to pitch at least two or three games in succession, throwing 10 to 25 pitches each game. Players with resiliency can pitch in back-to-back games as long as their pitch count is reasonable. A closer with this ability is a great asset to any staff.

My rule of thumb is to keep the pitch count under 25 pitches if I want to bring a pitcher back the next day. This rule, however, depends on the types of pitches thrown, the recent workload or days thrown in succession, and any idiosyncrasies the player has. Remember that each guy is different. Based on circumstances, you might have to adjust the 25-pitch limit. What I've found is that my most resilient guys can throw three days in a row provided they have moderate pitch counts.

Poise is the ability to throw under pressure, to perform when there's no room for a poor performance. Your team must feel that they have the best chance to win when their closer is out there. Players as well as managers need to trust their closer. And, frankly, as far as I'm concerned, once I hand the ball to my closer late in the game, my job is done (well, at least as far as pitching goes). The last three outs of the game are difficult to get, and the game's outcome always rests on the closer's shoulders. That's why he needs to have poise.

So, where do you start in sorting this all out? First, rank your pitching staff from 1 to 10, with 1 being your most effective pitcher and 10 being your least. If you have a three-man rotation, you probably want pitchers 1 through 4 to be your three starters and your closer. Which one of the four becomes your closer should depend on the factors just discussed: pitchability, resiliency, and poise. The other three will be your top three starters.

The late inning setup or back-end guys (pitchers 5 through 7) should generally be rated ahead of your long relievers. These three setup pitchers are considered part of your plus bullpen. Your long relievers might also be swing guys used late in games when you're ahead; this will give your plus bullpen some rest. On the college teams I've coached, it's usually the younger guys or those who haven't pitched as well who fill the role of long or swing relievers.

Unfortunately, sometimes everyone in your pen looks pretty much the same, especially those guys in the last slots of your pitching staff. This is when you need to know your pitchers well enough to create roles for each guy. They need spots in the pitching plan that they can master and find success in. They're on the roster, so you need to find ways for them to help the team have the best chance of winning.

What I'm advocating is a commitment by the manager to a plan. Again, it's all about pitchability, resiliency, poise, and knowing the strengths and limitations of the starters on your staff. Focusing on these criteria will help you create a functional bullpen and allow you to map out a strategy of how to most effectively use your arms depending on the score and inning of the game.

Bullpen Management

There are many schools of thought regarding how to best use a bullpen, ranging from the traditional to the not so traditional to the downright bizarre. Let's take a look at some of these.

Traditional Pro Bullpen Management

Traditional pro bullpen management is based on established roles. After the starters, you have a set of long relievers. How you use these pitchers depends on the score and the opponent's make-up—that is, their mix of left-handed and right-handed hitters. The ability to flip a lineup by using a long reliever who pitches with an opposite arm of your starter is a great tool for stopping an opponent. This is especially effective when you bring in a left-handed reliever following a right-handed starter. A left-handed long reliever coming into a game against a bunch of left-handed batters forces the opposing manager to pick one of two unattractive options. First, he can let his left-handed batters bat, giving up best hitting match-ups by staying lefty on lefty for at least part of the game, or he can decide to make lineup changes now, exposing his club to less favorable match-ups or a weaker defensive setup in later innings.

Situational guys, the backend guys in the bullpen, get you to the closer. Strikeout pitchers work well in this role because in traditional pro bullpen management, the closer usually starts innings, and the situational guys come into the middle of innings to put out late rallies.

The guys who pitch in the seventh and the eighth innings can be either left-handed or right-handed and may be interchangeable based on the opponent's mix of hitters and where you are in their lineup. Remember that it's always a race to the closer. The first team to get to its closer usually wins the game.

Everyone in baseball knows this strategy. The unknown is when the opposing manager will pull the trigger and bring in his closing guy. Following traditional pro-style bullpen management, it's usually at the beginning of the ninth inning, sometimes at the beginning of the eighth, and very rarely any earlier than that. However, in college baseball, I have seen (and used) what I call the silver bullet.

Silver Bullet Plan

Your silver bullet is one of your team's top three pitchers, the go-to guy you turn to when the game gets tough. It doesn't matter if you're in the first inning or the ninth. What's most important is pitchability.

Because he'll have some long outings, the bullet must have at least two very good pitches. Also, you want to have the lead before using this weapon; you don't want to use up your guy in a losing cause. Finally, understand that if you're planning on using a silver bullet, you still need another closer for when your bullet's unavailable in late innings. For these reasons, this system tends to work best with deep pitching staffs with good offenses: teams that can come back from early deficits.

Next Best Guy

A third option is very simple: When you have decided to make a move, try to keep the opponent from scoring by bringing in your next best guy.

This strategy is not dictated by score or match-ups, but more by necessity, such as in the case of a must-win game or when you don't have an effective bullpen. In this system, no roles are established in your pen, so you go with the guy who seems to have the best chance of doing the job.

Reliever Scheme

When the bullpen isn't as good as you want it to be, try to get through the first few innings with a reliever, then bring in a starter to finish! Instead of getting beat late because the starter can't go nine, limp through the early frames, hoping to get enough runs that your starter-turned-reliever can finish. This is an unorthodox strategy but sometimes worth considering. When your bullpen is tired or parts aren't available, this approach might keep you from getting beat late.

If you want a good bullpen, you have to give it work. Script your plan ahead of time and stick to it. Find something that you can believe in—be it pitch counts, number of walks, good pitch evaluations, assessments of the number and types of hits and outs pitchers are giving up, or something else that you can track and measure—and rely on it. In shutouts, I'll keep sending my starters out there, particularly if pitch counts are good or if they have retired a lot of batters or if match-ups favor us winning. But if it's a normal, regular ballgame, stick to your strategies. Have a plan and work it!

Game-Day Management of the Pitching Staff

In most games, the coach will have an idea, based on a bunch of factors, as to how many runs his team will likely score. In college baseball, you can figure that on most days a club will score 5 to 8 runs. Knowing this, you can give your starter more room and allow him to give up a few runs, knowing that your team is likely to score as well.

Your offense's strengths, the ability of your club's bullpen, the history of your starter to persevere through difficult at-bats or innings, game schedule (whether it's the first game of a series or the last, when your next game will be played, and so forth)—all of these factors go into your decision on if and when to make a pitching change.

I mentioned that a college team can usually expect to score at least 5 runs in most games, but if you're facing a tough pitcher with a low ERA, you can't count on those 5 runs. In this case, you can't let your starter give up many runs early. If the other team is hitting your starter, you'll need to go to your pen earlier than usual. Similarly, if you're in a must-win situation, you might also need to pull your starter early, especially if your pen is well rested. As your starter's pitch count gets higher, and as the other team's batters start coming around for the third time, you usually need to start thinking pitching change.

Your opponent's ability to shut you down late will also dictate game-day management of the bullpen. Some opponents are so good late because of their bullpen's ability, particularly the skills of a solid closer. In this case, you must do everything possible to keep their closer or plus bullpen out of the game. Under these circumstances, you're playing a much shorter game—you need to be ahead by the sixth or seventh inning. A team can't give up late runs and expect to come back in the last couple of innings against a quality bullpen and its closer. Remember Will Fenton and the Husky teams of the '90s!

The important decision then is when to go to the closer. This is an especially consequential decision if the closer is significantly better than the rest of the plus bullpen or if the plus bullpen isn't available. All of the factors discussed earlier—the day of the series, whether you're in a tie or a 1-run game, being home or away, the scope or importance of the game, the resiliency and endurance of the closer, the possibility of having to pitch through multiple innings—need to be weighed and taken into account when making the decision to bring in the closer.

Using a Quality Closer

- If the setup guys are good, use your closer exclusively in the ninth. If the setup guys are not so strong, use your closer sooner.
- At the end of a series, if your closer is well rested, or if you have days off before the next game, go to your closer as early as his abilities allow.
- In tie games at home, go to the closer in the ninth with the idea that he'll go two or three innings; this means your opponent's guy has to go three or four innings.
- In tie games on the road, give yourself one or two innings to win the game, then make a move—unless the game dictates that you have to use up your closer.

When all else fails, remember that it's your job to slow down the game when things go poorly. You should be able to get a relief pitcher in the game in one to two hitters, if you do it properly. Have the catcher and infielders visit the mound. Slow down your signs to the catcher. Stall. Talk with an umpire. Do whatever it takes.

Remember, also, to use your trips to the mound effectively. Get pitchers concentrating on the next pitch and the plan. Relate positive ideas. At the same time, get your bullpen ready. After one trip, the next relief pitcher should be ready. Never leave the dugout without getting the next guy up, particularly if you're likely to make a pitching change soon.

I hope what I've talked about will help you use your bullpen wisely. Most pitchers don't understand or appreciate the importance of bullpen management, regardless of how clear it is to the manager, unless of course it's clearly communicated to them. When roles are defined, it's easier for guys to anticipate when they'll be throwing and how they can be more effective pitchers. Great bullpens make great managers. It's easier to manage a 4-2 game than it is to suffer through an 18-15 slugfest. And, remember—everybody wants to be a starter until they become a reliever!

Defensive Positioning Based on Game Situation

Defensive positioning in baseball is based on a variety of factors, including the score, inning, number of outs, field conditions, batter at the plate, and how many men are on base. Many defenses are considered standard, so we won't discuss those here. Instead, let's look at some interesting considerations based on game situations in which what to do is debatable and worth discussing.

Early in the Game

Early in the game, you want to avoid big innings with defensive decisions and to save runs when appropriate.

With runners on first or first and second with no outs, anticipate the bunt (figure 11.1). The main objective in this situation is to get an out. Any out is a good out. To determine if the bunt is in order, hold the ball on the mound, step off hard from the mound, pick, hold and pick, and so on. These are ways to find out if the batter is intending to bunt. Once you know the batter is bunting, get your defense into the appropriate positions to get an out. The pitcher must throw strikes. You don't want to put the hitter in a good fastball count when the hitter might be turned loose, creating a big inning. Throw a strike, field the bunt, and take the out!

With a runner on third with fewer than two outs when should you play your infield in to try to save a run? If the run is not the go-ahead or tying run, don't play in under any circumstances, especially if other runners are on base. Often the best strategy is for the defense to trade a run for an out. In general, concede the run and opt for getting a ground out at first

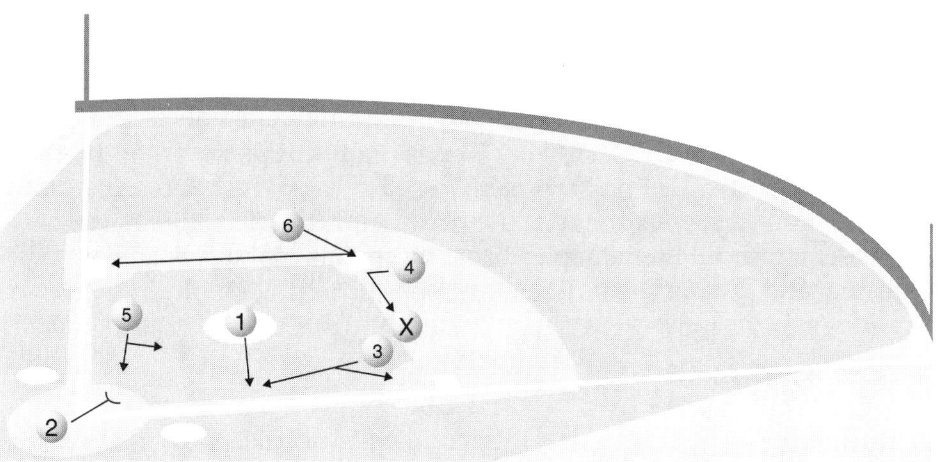

Figure 11.1 Runner on first, no outs, bunt defense.

when the costs of the run are low—you have the lead, there are no outs, the runner and hitter can really run, the defense is a good offensive team, your pitcher isn't very good, their pitcher isn't very good, the hitter can hit, or you're in the middle of their lineup.

Early in the game, many teams won't play their infield in because they feel they'll have a chance to score many runs and want to stop the opponent's chances for a big inning. Staying close and minimizing the damage allows them to rally in the later innings. However, late in the game there are fewer outs to work with, and playing in could be the best course of action. Consider playing in and cutting off the run under any of these circumstances—your team is behind a few runs, there's one out, slow runners are at the plate and at third, good pitchers are in the game, your team has had a hard time scoring, you're down in the order, a good bunter is at the plate (you need to defend the safety squeeze or push bunt), the hitter has two strikes on him, or it looks like rain.

With a runner on second and no outs, trying too hard to keep the runner from advancing to third can create a big inning. Be aware of the offense's intent. Getting the first out is important. Many offenses are willing to execute their offense and give up the out with a ground ball to the right side. Accept their generosity and take the out.

With runners on second and third and fewer than two outs, should you still play in and cut off the run? A routine ground ball out might cost you two runs and a runner on first. This is a heavy tradeoff for saving one run early. Early in the game, playing back is nearly always the correct defensive choice. Don't try to win the game on defense; control the damage and stay close. Early in the game, play back and concede the run. Don't gamble by increasing the potential for a big inning. Don't get blown out early. It's far easier to come back when you're down 1 run than when you're down 3.

With bases loaded and no outs, playing the first baseman inside the baseline versus a right-handed hitter is standard defense. This defense speeds up the play on a ground ball to the first baseman and protects against the push bunt. Because he's playing on the opposite-field side of the hitter, the first baseman is also not likely to get a hard-hit ball, as might be the case with a left-handed pull swinger. Also, a slow-hit ball to the right side might result in getting an out at the plate. Versus a left-handed hitter the first baseman should usually play back (more than in), so he can cover the four hole and protect the pull side in hopes of getting an out.

Late in a Close Game

With runners on first or first and second with no outs (figure 11.2), the bunt is on unless you're in the middle of the order or facing their best hitters. You must get an out. Any out is good, and it's critical that your pitcher work ahead of the hitter in a bunt situation. This is the only way your bunt defenses will be able to function. Don't try to win the game on defense. Do try your best to minimize runs. It's much easier to come back after being down by 1 run than after being down by 2 or 3. The book makes a lot of sense late in the game. Play for the tie at home and the win on the road, especially on defense! This rule must dictate your defensive strategy.

With runners on first and third and no outs, get an out on any play (runners stealing, leaving early, and so on). Trading a run early for an out when you have no outs is generally okay; with one out, you need to work hard not to give up a run. With two outs, don't give up a run. Run the appropriate defenses based on the situation and abilities of the offensive team.

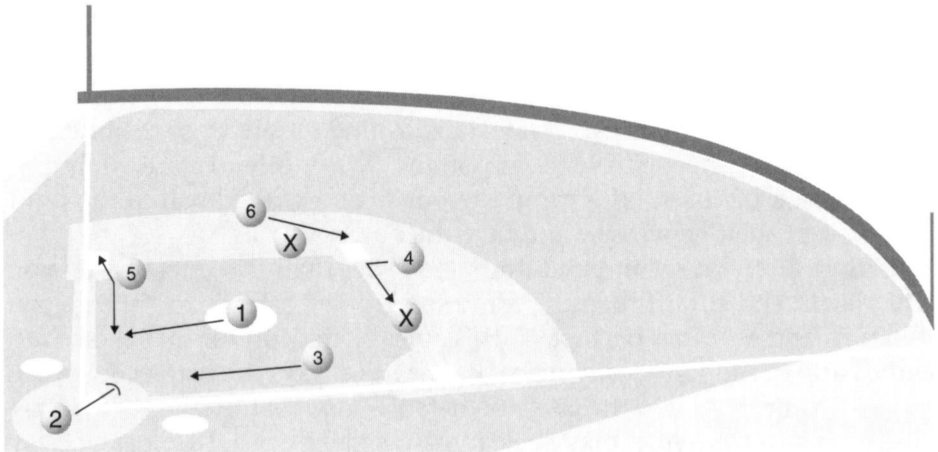

Figure 11.2 Runners on first and second, no outs, bunt defense.

With bases loaded and no outs (ouch!), go by the book. The score will dictate if everyone is going to the plate or if you're playing for two in the middle.

Runners on first and third late in the game is the situation with all the decisions. With no outs, you generally have to play as if you're going to give up one run unless it's very late in the game (bottom of the eighth or later) and it's the game-winning run. On a ground ball, the decision is whether to give up a run and try to turn a double play with no outs or look the runner back and get one out at first or second. Some teams try to look the runner back and then turn two. But this is a risky situation for the defense. The offense would have to make a mistake for the defense to get two without a run scoring (that is, after looking back the runner at third on the ground ball). This play shouldn't be an option.

When the game is late (bottom of eighth or later), defend the game-winning run with no outs by bringing all your infielders in. Look the runner back and get one with a ground ball out at first. Disregard the runner at first when he advances to second on the out. Get ready to play the situation, runner on second and third with one out.

31 Defenses

Runners on first and third base have always provided a challenge for the defense. The coach needs to decide which runner to pursue and where the team should try to get the out. The number of outs and the inning will determine which base runner is important. Also consider the principles in the book: win on the road, tie at home. The pitchers, the bullpens, the ballpark, and your team's position in the batting order will also influence your decision.

There are many 31 defenses to combat the many 31 offenses run in college games. I am not going to delve too deeply into all the defenses you might use to defend against the straight or double steal. In a nutshell, your choices are these: no throw, throw through to second base, throw to third to pick off the lead runner, employ some type of cutoff play by throwing to the shortstop or second baseman inside the diamond, or make a fake throw to second followed by a pickoff throw to third. The inning, number of outs, and score dictate which of these defenses is most appropriate. Determine the importance of each runner or run as well as the potential match-ups between your pitcher and their hitters, and make your decisions accordingly.

A few rules based on a sound defensive philosophy can defend against any trick play or offense that might be executed in a 31 situation. Most of these situations happen quite quickly, created by a cutoff play by a middle infielder or after a pickoff move to first base with the runner stealing. So it's important to anticipate what might happen and follow what you've trained for in practice.

We practice defending against three standard 31 plays: the steal and stop play, the early steal, and the delayed steal. All of these plays are initiated on steal attempts by the runner on first base. Regardless of the situation, our first goal is to check or stop the advancement of the third-base runner. If we have no play at third, our goal is to get the ball into the middle of the infield, throwing to the shortstop or second baseman accordingly. Once the ball is in his hands, we again check the runner at third base to see if we have a possible play. If we're confident that the runner at third base is not a threat to score or if we have no play at third, we turn our attention to the runner at first base, attempting to get an out with an aggressive rundown.

Fake throw plays can be used to good effect against the early steal. For example, have the pitcher check the runner at third, fake a throw to the middle, and then turn back to the runner at third base. At a minimum, this keeps the runner at third base from leaving on the throw to the middle infielder.

Fake plays can also be initiated by the first baseman. For instance, when a 31 offense kicks in on a pick to first with a straight steal by the runner at first base, prevent the third-base runner from taking home by having the first baseman fake to second. Although this play always gives up second base, you again have a very good shot at getting the lead runner out on a play at the plate.

Delayed Steal

The most important aspect of defending the delay steal in a 31 situation is to anticipate the play. Be disciplined. A middle infielder must cover second base, and catchers can't be surprised. They need to act and react, throwing to the appropriate base in rhythm. Getting help from the bench is a must; developing a delay call for the team is a necessity. Face it: This play is hard for defenders to see. Do anything you can to communicate to your players what's happening on the field. Last, all of this strategy is moot if we can't implement the basic mechanics of the play. Emphasize to players the importance of catching and handling the ball cleanly.

When faced with the delayed steal, we execute whatever 31 defense is on for that particular pitch. Our standard defense is to check the runner at third and throw through to second if he's not a threat to score. Despite the broken nature of the delayed steal, the catcher does have time to peek at third and check the runner. Because the play develops significantly slower than standard 31 plays, he often has time to throw out a runner at second. In fact, this play often leads to runners being hung up halfway between first and second, triggering a routine 31 defensive response. The good news is that if the play is executed properly, the ball will be in the middle infield, setting the team up for a standard 31 defense. For an alert defense, the delayed steal should always result in an out.

The other play we use is the push or walk-back. We use this play when we absolutely can't give up the run or second base because of the game situation. This play occurs when the middle infielder receives the ball from either the catcher or pitcher with the first-base runner stopping halfway between first and second in an early or straight steal play. The middle infielder immediately checks the runner at third, ensuring he's not a threat to score. He then pushes the runner back to first by running or walking him back toward the bag, always checking the runner at third in case he tries to take home. If the first-base runner allows the middle infielder to tag him, take the out. Again, however, our philosophy and top priority is that under no circumstances will we allow the run to score.

These types of 31 offenses are designed to create rundowns and mistakes. Most 31 offenses are only successful, however, when a coach makes a bad decision or the defense fails to throw and handle the ball effectively. They can happen accidentally, from balls cut off from the outfield, through picks or well-defended delays, after base-running mistakes, and so on. They happen intentionally, as well, as 31 offenses. No matter how they happen, you need to defend them with strategy and execution. In the end, it's the game situation that dictates your defense.

31 Bunts

The safety drag or push bunt to the first-base side in a 31 situation is a very difficult play to defend (figure 11.3). When properly executed, it will result in a run and a base runner advancing to second. It might even result in a base hit. Remember that your goal is to get an out.

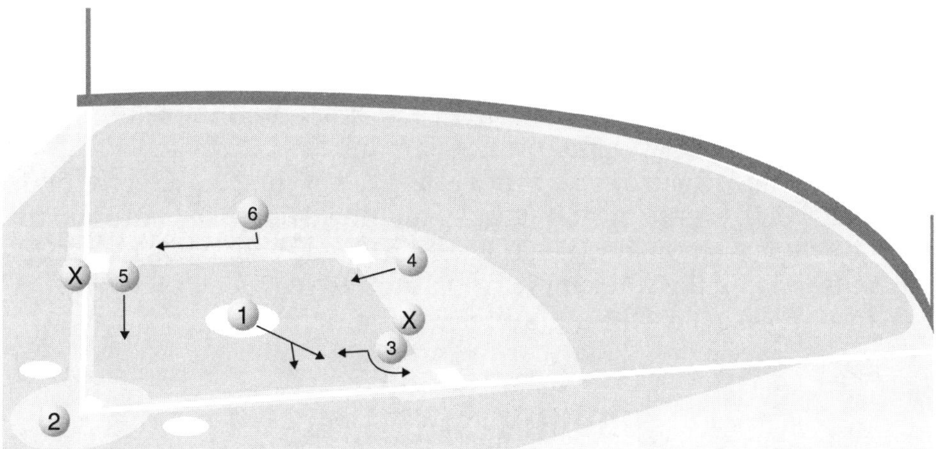

Figure 11.3 31 defense against a push or drag bunt down the right side. The pitcher and first baseman communicate on ball and bag responsibility. The second baseman plays the ball.

The first baseman can beat the play on an average to poor bunt by being very aggressive, throwing out the third-base runner at the plate or, on a good bunt, getting an out at first. The common right-side drag or push defense, with no runners on base, is for the second baseman to cover first. The second baseman has the primary base responsibilities. The pitcher and the first baseman have primary ball responsibilities (figure 11.4). This doesn't work, however, in a standard 31 situation because the second baseman is at double-play depth. He can't get to first base in time to cover the bag. The only solution to beating the bunt is to have the pitcher and first baseman communicate ball or bag. The second baseman will have the ball as his primary responsibility if the ball is pushed past the pitcher. The third baseman in this situation must honor the bunt and leave his position to field the ball if it's bunted toward third.

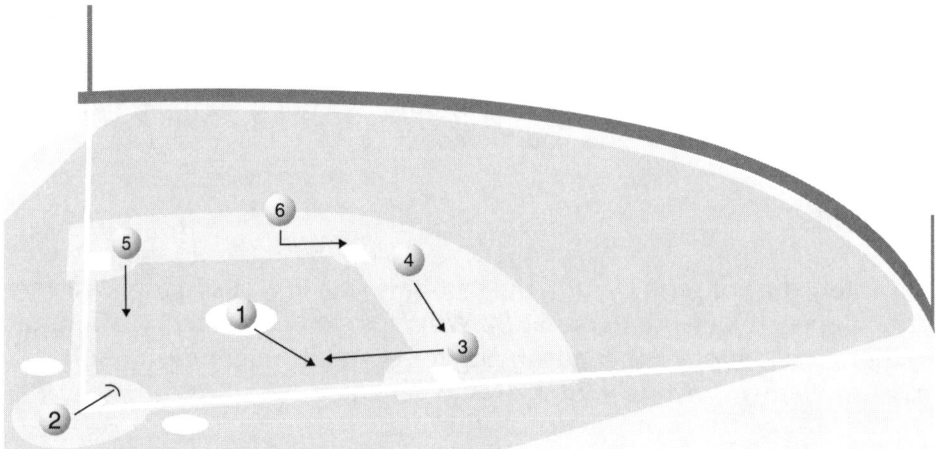

Figure 11.4 Bases empty, push or drag bunt hit to the right side.

Finally, a defensive play can be run in a 31 situation with the third baseman. If the batter shows bunt, plan to have the catcher back-pick to third with the third baseman covering the bag instead of charging after the bunt. Although you'll expose the left side of your infield on a ball bunted up the third-base line, you can mitigate this risk by having your pitcher locate his pitch up or out of the strike zone. When executed well, this play gives you a chance at picking off the lead runner.

Nonbunt Situations

With a runner on second with one out, play the book in a 1-run game. Play for the tie at home and the win on the road. In a tie game, go hard after the hitter, especially in a regular game situation when anyone but their best hitter is at the plate. Everything must be an out pitch. You are trying to get the hitter to swing at balls or borderline strikes. Remember that a walk won't hurt you too much and the double play is set up for the next batter.

If your opponent's best hitter is at the plate, don't throw him a strike. Try to get him to chase a bad pitch by throwing him balls off the edges, not strikes on the edges. Command, a good catcher, and out pitches are essential in executing this strategy. If you don't have these three pieces working for you, then you're probably forced to intentionally walk the hitter.

When facing runners on second and third with one out, teams decide to intentionally walk the hitter more often than they do when there's only a runner on second. Heck, the same ground ball that scores a run might be the perfect double-play ball. The problem with any intentional walk in this case is that now the next hitter knows he has to see strikes—you can't walk him. It's always easier to get a hitter out when you don't have to throw him strikes than when you do. This philosophy dictates the strategy and discourages the use of the intentional walk. However, the argument that one ground ball ends the inning and keeps two runners in scoring position from scoring makes sense as well. Is it easier to get one ground ball and turn a double play than it is to get two hitters out with no runners advancing? The score, where you are in the lineup, and your defense's and pitcher's abilities should dictate the call.

Defensive Alignment

The most important defensive data you can gather is where the opponent's hitters tend to hit the baseball. Keep a spray chart that shows the location of hit balls. A good spray chart will also show the types of pitches thrown, the types of hits, counts on the batter, whether the pitcher was right-handed or left-handed, and first-pitch tendencies. Keep it simple, and keep it accurate. Plan on playing a hitter defensively the same way you plan on pitching to him. If you intend to pitch him in, play your defense for the pull; if your strategy is to pitch away, play your defense away as well. Your goal is pitch into your defense, not against it. In short, set your defense to your pitch plan.

Although defenders should always move with the count, the shifts must have merit. Batters ahead in the pitch count (1-0, 2-0, 2-1, 3-1) have a greater chance to pull the ball. Shift and play them accordingly. Batters who hit the ball consistently where it's pitched are less likely to be defended by any shift.

Here are a few defensive alignment observations:

- Breaking balls and change-ups get pulled or are swung through.
- Many more balls get hit in the four hole and six hole than down the lines.

- Hitters like to pull when ahead in the count.
- Some hitters adjust with two strikes.
- Two-thirds of all pitches are middle away.
- In a no-doubles defense, any fly ball that stays in the park should be caught.
- A base hit in the four hole, followed by a home run, is worse than a double down the line.
- Most hitters try to go the opposite way on a hit and run.
- Coaches are better on spray charts than players.
- The best indicator of where a hitter will hit a baseball is his swing against a particular pitch.
- Pay attention to swings on fastball counts.
- A properly aligned defense catches lots of line drives.

Defensive alignments are a part of your strategy and should be a constant point of emphasis during a game. In fact, I might even argue that every defender should change his defensive alignment on every pitch.

Defensive Replacements

When leading late in the game, you need to get the poor defenders off the field. However, you also need to gain a significant defensive advantage when you make these changes. An inexperienced replacement, based on his age or amount of recent playing time, might not be an advantage even if he's on paper a better defender. When a player hasn't been out on the field the entire game, it's not enough simply to look at his defensive skills. The sun, wind, lights, rain, or other field conditions are all factors that make it difficult to bring someone in late. So if you're contemplating a defensive change in the later innings, make sure it provides a significant boost to your defense.

Tie Games

The book gives you some insights. When playing for the tie at home, make the defensive move. When playing for the win on the road, keep your offense in the game. Also, where you are in the lineup (an average or below-average defender won't be up for a couple of innings), the strength of your bullpen, and the abilities of the lineup (especially compared to those of your opposition) should all influence the moves you make, if any.

Take care not to lose all of your offense with your defensive moves because you might need to score again if you lose the lead. You need to gain an advantage with the moves you make so that you can win with your top players. At the end of the game, you need to have your best team on the field based on the game situation. Period.

Shortened Games

When bad weather is coming or if there's a time limit because of travel or a tournament, the manager must consider shortening the game. In such cases, manage the game from the very first pitch assuming that you're in the fourth inning. Manage your pitching staff aggressively to avoid giving up the lead. Plan on skipping your middle-relief guys if rain, delays, or shortened games are strong possibilities.

Don't be sitting on the bus, beaten, with your plus bullpen and closer ready to pitch. If the game goes nine innings and you have used up your bullpen, then you need to work backward and piece together the rest of the game. When in doubt regarding the length of the game, stop any rally.

I hope this chapter has given you some insights on how to manage the defensive side of the game; use the ideas suggested to help your team maintain that 1-run advantage. Managing a pitching staff, especially a bullpen, is the key to creating a great defensive ball club. The book, or at least an understanding of its contents, gives you the ability to develop a strategy, organize a plan, and make good decisions. The fundamental philosophy that you don't lose games on defense and that you control damage, making opponents earn their runs, dictates the defenses you run. Awareness of game situations, defensive alignments, offensive threats, pitch plans, field and weather conditions, and so forth all lead to better defensive choices and more successful teams. Finally, remember that most runs are important, but some runs are much more significant than others. The axiom "You never know what run will beat you" is true. Work hard to not give up runs. From our perspective, we need to believe that the run we saved by executing sound defensive baseball strategy is the run that *didn't* beat us.

12

Communicating Tactics in the Field

Bob Bennett

A successful team defense is made up of the bits and pieces of valuable information transferred from player to player, coach to player, and player to coach. Accurate, consistent communication weaves the fabric of a team's defense. The team that communicates well is generally a sound defensive unit.

On the baseball field, players and coaches talk to one another in team-, position-, and situation-specific baseball languages. Players translate body language and verbal and physical signals sent to one another and employ priorities, territories, timing, and positioning to convey important messages. From fielding a simple pop-up to executing an intricate bunt defense, communication is essential to a successful and safe result.

Effects of Good Communication

Communication is the key to teamwork, the difference between success and failure. Players must learn to take advantage of all the information available to them. Tough decisions are easier to make when players know exactly what they're facing. They gain this knowledge through listening to their teammates and through sharing their own observations and experiences.

Good communication helps to ensure player safety, create an efficient defense, and develop trust and confidence among teammates. The defensive unit that learns to communicate well can play with minimal risk and maximum strength. Create a winning combination by developing responsibility, exhibiting leadership, and fostering teamwork.

Ensure Safety

Perhaps the most important role communication plays on the practice or game field involves safety. When two or more players are aggressively pursuing a fly ball, pop fly, or ground ball, hazardous situations can arise. With proper cooperation and communication, players can operate at full speed with minimal risk.

People tend to think of football and basketball as contact sports that are more dangerous than baseball. That may or may not be true, but baseball is *not* an inherently safe sport. Whenever several players are involved in a play, the risk for collisions is high. Cooperation and proper teamwork dramatically reduce the risk of mishaps. Every defense should find ways to maximize the potential of each player within the safest environment possible.

When it comes to safety, baseball teams regularly encounter a multitude of unusual conditions and challenges. Dugouts, side fences, gates, poles, outfield fences, and unnatural surfaces are all potentially hazardous and dangerous to a player's health. Weather conditions such as rain, sun, and wind can also render the baseball environment more perilous than it appears to be. Only through cooperation and proactive communication can ball players make their setting relatively safe for all involved.

Obstructions, pitfalls, and severe weather conditions can be endured and worked around if leadership and cooperation prevail. Any potential problems need to be recognized, prioritized, and dealt with in the pregame preparation as well as during the game itself.

During pregame preparation, or earlier when possible, each player should survey the facility and check the weather conditions to ascertain their impact on the game. Here are some suggestions for each position.

The catcher should check the turf, the cut of the grass, and the dirt area in front of home plate to prepare for bunts, bad hops, and other situations. Checking the way the ball rolls on bunts prepares the catcher for slow-hit balls and bunts. The catcher needs to remember that he may not be the only one fielding bunts; he needs to talk to the pitcher and infielders as well. A survey of the backstop—its surface and its distance from home plate—provides additional information for making decisions. The catcher should note the sun and wind conditions and their possible effect on pop flies and then share that information with the pitcher and corner infielders. If the sun or wind affects a particular position more than others, the priority area of that position should be reduced. The other positions will increase the ground they normally cover to make up the difference. The catcher should examine the dugouts and the pads on or near the backstop and take note of any other facility issues. As necessary, he needs to deal with these issues before the game starts.

The pitcher should make a similar evaluation, going over the priorities of each position. Because the pitcher can be a major communicator on pop flies, his knowledge of the playing surface in front of and around the mound is particularly valuable. This is not so much a safety issue, but the pitcher should also assess how bunted balls behave down each baseline.

Infielders should examine the playing surface and note any unusual features. They should evaluate the dugout's distance from the playing field. This information will help them back up bases and make decisions on pop flies and special plays. Checking side fences, dugout structure, and any other possible trouble spots helps the infielder plan to deal with plays in those areas. Anything worth noting should be shared with teammates. The infielders should also observe the sun and wind conditions and discuss their findings with teammates.

The outfielders first assess the warning track. If the warning track is less than 20 feet, they should treat the field as though there is no warning track. Next, they should evaluate the structure of the fences and determine if the fences offer advantages or disadvantage for fielding balls. How does the ball bounce off the fence? They examine the surface of the outfield and warning track and consider the amount of foul territory. Finally they, too, examine the weather conditions (such as sun and wind) and prepare to make necessary adjustments.

Create Efficiency

An outfielder chasing a fly ball on or near the warning track is more apt to make a great play if he knows his surroundings. This is a part of home-field advantage and why all players, to the extent possible, should do whatever they can to make *every* field feel like their home field. Through good communication, the off outfielders can make an environment on a particular play much safer for the player involved in the play. An outfielder who can rely on his teammates will be able to chase balls with maximum effort, confident he won't run into a fence or collide with a teammate.

On bunt defenses, double-play balls, rundowns, pop flies, ground balls, passed balls, wild pitches and wild throws, the need for cooperation is paramount. With proper cooperation and teamwork, a team can cover more territory. Players feel free to go all-out for plays in their areas when good communication is at work.

Develop Trust and Confidence

Trust is essential in developing a formidable defensive team. The best defensive units believe that each player on the field will be in the correct position, respond promptly, and give maximum effort on each play.

Actions and words either develop trust or create insecurity. An outfielder running full speed toward a fence reacts positively to a teammate he trusts but hesitates if a teammate is tentative or erratic with information.

Trust is important whether you're warning a player about an obstacle, assuring him that he has room to make the play, directing him to a proper throwing target, deciding who should field the ball or cover a base, reminding a player of an upcoming situation, or signaling the duties of a potential play. Without trust, the information being relayed has little meaning.

Player credibility is also vital to good communication. When credibility and communication flow, confidence grows. Players who care about each other and share daily challenges begin to feel confident in each other. When the second baseman and shortstop realize how important the other is to solid defensive play, communication becomes a staple. Likewise, a group of outfielders who trust each other recognize the importance and value of each outfielder to the defensive unit. Each outfielder is an important leader. Having confidence in one another helps each outfielder play to his maximum potential.

A sound catcher provides essential leadership through pitch selection and play direction. An unassertive catcher creates chaos and destroys timing and aggressive play. A free flow of information between catcher and pitcher gives wings to the game plan. Pitchers develop confidence in catchers who call the right pitch at the right time in the right situation.

Ground Rules for Good Communication

Communication is an ongoing, two-way transaction. Start by simply paying attention. Players must make a constant and diligent effort to find the best way to relay information to each other.

Much of the communication that takes place on the baseball diamond is done in tense situations and must be delivered and received under stressful conditions. The information sent and received may be important enough to change the outcome of the game or turn a dangerous play into a safe one. Thus, the message should be clear, precise, and direct. It should be given with both the receiver and the situation in mind. The receiver should be alert and receptive to the sender.

Establish a few simple ground rules for all players:

- Pay attention.
- Be aware of situations.
- Be direct and to the point.
- Be assertive.
- Be clear.

- Ask for clarification if a message isn't understood.
- Be cooperative.
- Be consistent.
- Be sure.

Where the communication takes place determines how to deliver the message and the level of need. Much of developing cooperative relationships occurs in the locker room, at practice, and prior to the game. Much is also done off the field. Preparation for heated game situations is aided by position and team meetings and by simple discussions among teammates.

Plant the seeds of good decision making in less tense settings such as the clubhouse or the practice field. Players need to use this time to learn the strengths and weaknesses of their teammates. In these settings, players can study the tones and inflections of their teammates' voices for use under pressure. The better practiced, the better the message will be understood. Practice and polish communication skills in all situations.

Methods of Communication

Players can communicate with physical gestures or signals or with verbal signals, tones, and inflections. Through either verbal or physical messages, the range of success in getting important details transmitted runs from dismal failure to amazing achievement.

The clarity of the signal or message is important, but the setting makes even more of a difference. Eye contact, acknowledgment, and a positive delivery and reception improve the message. Consider how, when, why, and where when you're sending or receiving information.

How the communication is carried out should match the setting and situation. An urgent message calls for a serious and deliberate delivery and a serious and deliberate response. For example, when two or more players are in the vicinity and capable of making a play on a bunt, one should loudly call for the ball, and the others should remain silent to acknowledge the call and assure the player calling for the ball that he has the freedom to make the play.

Some communication occurs calmly and with little stress attached. A lot of information can be exchanged in a straightforward manner. At other times the vital information must be transmitted and understood under dire circumstances. Crowd noise, heated competition, imminent obstructions, opposition's involvement, and highly difficult plays often make an urgent message necessary.

An urgent message should be delivered without panic. Deliberate signals and forceful gestures with urgent voice inflections are in order when dynamic attention should be given to that situation. It's often necessary to use both hand signals and vocal signals, which is why all players should become familiar with the body language and voice of each teammate.

Verbal Communication

Players need to understand and speak a common language. The words and terms need to be game- and sport-specific as well as team- and position-specific. Terms, words, and shortcuts are used to describe defensive coverage and player duties.

Different coaches and players use different terms and descriptive words to describe similar plays. Whatever terms are used should be specific to the team and should be used only by that team. For example, there are several phrases to use when directing a player to cut the ball on a relay throw—"cut," "cut it," and "relay" are a few. A team should pick a single phrase and use it consistently.

Here are some potentially team-specific terms for use in common situations:

"Ball! Ball!"—accept responsibility to field the ball.

"Take it!"—recognize that a teammate has called for the ball.

"A lot of room!"—assure the receiver that he has the space and unobstructed opportunity to make the catch.

"Watch it!"—warn a teammate that he's coming close to an obstruction.

"Bag"—accept responsibility to cover the base.

"Cut! No play!"—cut the throw and hold the ball.

"Cut one!"—cut the throw and throw to first base.

"Cut two!"—cut the throw and throw to second base.

"Cut three!"—cut the throw and throw to third base.

"Cut four!"—cut the throw and throw to home plate.

"No play!"—there's no room to make a catch or no reasonable target is available.

"Blue"—means yes. Designate a school color or choose a hot word.

"Red"—means no. Designate a school color or choose a hot word.

If a receiver at any base does not want a throw to be cut, he gives no directions at all. Silence in general means let it be.

At the beginning of any relay throw and any bunt play, the base to which the ball should be thrown is called twice and repeated as many times as necessary, for example, "One, one!" or "Two, two!"

Verbal commands are also position specific. Here are some examples:

"In front! In front!"—the ball is in front of the catcher. The pitcher sends this message.

"Back! Back!"—the ball is behind the catcher. The pitcher is telling the catcher to turn around.

"Ball!"—the receiver calls for the ball during a rundown.

"Now!"—tells the pitcher to deliver the pitch on a special pickoff play.

Physical Communication

Nonverbal behavior is also important for delivering messages. Body language can speak volumes, but just as with words, the message must be chosen wisely and transmitted directly and absolutely clearly. Affirmation, agreement, disagreement, disappointment, confidence, uncertainty, strengths, and weaknesses can all be transmitted through body language.

Body language transmits inner feelings. All defensive players should attempt to project positive images that display confidence, enthusiasm, determination, aggressiveness, and cohesiveness. A look of determination can be a valuable tool in meeting competitive challenges. A shoulder shrug or a look of dejection builds the path to failure and fuels the opponent's competitive fires.

Players need to respond to directions, signals, and other information being conveyed to them. Their nonverbal response indicates that the message was delivered, is understood, and will be acted on. Help, gestures, commands, and directions deserve to be acknowledged in a business-like and civil manner. Credibility can be enhanced through positive body language. A particular demeanor either invites or rejects further communication.

A good deal of information on the baseball field is delivered via signals. Just as tones, inflections, and assertiveness make all the difference with verbal messages, clarity, assertiveness, and command are necessary with physical signals. Whether a player is calling a certain pitch or pointing to direct a teammate, his action should depict an assertive and positive decision. A weak or uncertain signal is confusing and often does more harm than good.

Signal systems should be clear and concise to defensive players but clever enough to make it difficult for the opposition to decipher them. The signal systems most teams employ are delivered in different ways to make it harder for the other team to pick up on them. Each could be a totally different group of signals or each set could be the same signals delivered with a hot sign or the same signals given with a pump or sequence type of delivery. Here are some common guidelines for signals:

- Make sure the signals are visible to all participants.
- Develop a timely and efficient delivery system.
- Be aware of game situations.
- Repeat signals if necessary.
- Be clear.
- Be able to adjust to different sets.

A hot sign is a designated word or a specific area on the body that alerts a player or players to an imminent signal. Most astute opposing players can decipher a steal sign within a few innings, but the difficulty increases when a hot sign is added or when the signal for the steal falls in a certain sequence.

The catcher's pitch signals to the pitcher and the infielders should be executed via three different sets. In addition, a combination of all three sets could be used to make it extremely difficult for the opposition to decipher the signals. For example, set 1 could be finger signals, set 2 could be area signals, and set 3 could be a set of signals using the mitt. An opposing team might recognize the signal for each pitch in each set, but the difficulty in knowing what pitch will be thrown is determined by which set is hot or which signal is hot.

Signs given on pickoff plays, bunt-defense coverage, or base-coverage assignments by the middle infielders should be delivered with a standard set of signals but should also have hot signs or sequence delivery methods. The shortstop and second baseman can use their gloves to cover their mouths and use a simple closed or open mouth signal. That coverage should be relayed to the pitcher via a touch system or glove signal.

Teams often make the mistake of using only the primary set of signals until the opposition has clearly deciphered the signs or until a dire situation arises. Now, the team must change to signs they rarely use. This is often in the heat of battle, when players need to concentrate on successful execution, not on seldom-used signals. If a team has more than one set of signs, has hot signs, or delivers the signs with sequences and patterns, that team should use all sets and delivery systems throughout each game.

Furthermore, signal systems should be regularly used in practice, particularly in intrasquad games. Changing from one set to another should never reduce a player's concentration from the job at hand. In a situation that requires total concentration, signals should not be the focal point.

From position to position, both verbal and physical signals must be used to communicate. On pickoff plays, signals are sent between each infielder and the pitcher. The signal may indicate the position of the infielder in relation to a base runner, the action of a particular defensive player, or a hot word for a specific signal system.

The coach sending defensive position signals should use both verbal and physical signals. He should have a delivery system to get messages to each position player, to each defensive unit, and to the defense as a whole. The coach must be able to relay a "take it off" sign in certain situations, such as a pitchout.

The signal system should include clear communication between the catcher and each infielder. Critical game situations call for the catcher to throw behind a runner. In such cases, the infielder needs to be notified. A clear set or sets of signals should be devised to let infielders know what the catcher is planning to do. Likewise, infielders should be able to signal the catcher about a pickoff play. This doesn't mean that a throw can't be made without a formal signal beforehand. The body language of the catcher or infielder is often a sufficient signal to a teammate that a throw should or will be made.

All signals should be delivered in a timely and orderly fashion. The coach or defensive player giving the signals should be clearly visible to all defensive players. He should develop a system that delivers the signal to a single player, to several players, or to the entire defensive unit. The best time to relay signals is immediately after the preceding pitch or play. Some signals require an answer and some don't. A signal should be developed that allows players to ask for a repeat of the signal. This signal is rarely used if the defensive unit is alert.

From time to time, a team's signals need to be changed, which can be done by developing a variety of sets. For example, a team might have three ways to defend a given bunt situation. In such a case, each defense should correspond to a word or to a place on the body. When the designated word is spoken or the body part touched, that particular bunt defense will be used. Develop three different words and three different areas or sequences of touches, one for each defense. This makes it more difficult for the opponent to pick up the signals. All of the sets must be used frequently in practice and in games so that they can be used in key situations.

Take nothing for granted. The simplest things are sometimes overlooked or forgotten in the heat of competition. After a close play in which the defensive unit thinks the runner is out but he has in fact been called safe, the actual number of outs may be in question before the next play. Repeat the number of outs clearly and frequently via both verbal and finger signals. Provide information to each player and repeat it often. Prior to each pitch have a plan. Pass that plan along to the defense.

Appendix

Defensive Signals System

Carroll Land

A successful team will have a defensive system it thoroughly believes in and learns to perfect. A solid defense builds confidence in both players and coaches. Confidence is the intangible that allows a coach to select the best defensive plays and alignments for the best outcomes in specific situations.

The specific game situation is probably the most important factor in a coach's decision in ordering defensive plays, alignments, and coverages. Having good information on opposing offensive players and team characteristics is also quite important. Finally, the skill level of the defensive team is of course a primary consideration.

Teamwork is key to successful defensive plays. Virtually every player needs to be informed, if not directly involved, in every defensive play. This is especially true of set plays called into action by a system of signals.

For example, consider what takes place on an attempted first-and-third steal. The catcher receives and throws the ball. The pitcher lets the ball go through to the infielder or cuts it off. The first baseman holds the runner on and yells "going!" when the runner takes off. The second baseman and shortstop agree on who will cover second and who will back up the throw. The centerfielder decides to charge the ball to reduce the distance and give himself a better chance of getting to a ball that gets by the second baseman and shortstop. The right and left fielders move in at angles toward second base in case the throw gets away and caroms in their direction. The third baseman moves to the third-base bag to influence the runner's lead. Until the throw is on its way to second base, the runner at third must be cautious. The play might have been called for the throw to be to third base or the pitcher. If the initial play is broken, defensive players have other subsequent duties, such as the pitcher moving to back up third base on a potential play.

For every play, the roles for each player must be understood by all players. When each player knows his role and the play call is communicated clearly—whether via physical sign, verbal instruction, or by-the-book baseball—confidence develops.

A runner on any base calls for a commitment of the defense to be coordinated according to predictable outcomes. This commitment and the coordination of the specific play, alignment, or coverage is determined by the coach, who initially signals his wishes in some manner so that clear communication to the team is complete and proper execution will follow.

Table A.1 lists some situations that demand defensive plays to be identified ahead of the next pitch. This is not an exhaustive list.

Other factors that affect a coach's decision when he's determining the defensive play are the shape of the field, the distances in foul territory and behind home plate, the sun or overhead lights (direction and height), wind conditions, and the way balls bounce and play in the infield and outfield and off the fences.

Table A.1 Defensive Situations That Require Prepitch Defensive Identification

Runners on base	Number of outs	Other basic factors
First base	0, 1, 2	Score, inning, runner's speed, batter's speed, outfielders' arm strength
First and second base	0, 1, 2	Hitters coming up, infielders' range, pitcher's time to home plate, catcher's time to second base, combined time to second base
First and third base	0, 1, 2	Hitters coming up, infielders' range, pitcher's time to home plate, catcher's time to second base, combined time to second base
Second and third base	0, 1, 2	Infielders move in or stay back, outfielders' arm strength
First, second, and third base	0, 1, 2	Infielders move in or stay back, outfielders' arm strength

When runners are on base, defensive decisions must be made:

- When the catcher throws to second or third base or to the pitcher, or he throws behind the runner.
- Outfielders throw to the base that the runner is approaching or to the cutoff or relay man.
- The infield aligns in, halfway, or back.
- The first baseman, third baseman, or both guard the lines.
- The outfield aligns back or in.
- The outfield shades according to the hitter's tendencies.
- For exceptional hitters, players assume unorthodox alignments, such as the Ted Williams or Barry Bonds shift.

The coach also takes into account the possibility of unusual plays, such as the suicide squeeze, safety squeeze, bunt slash, delayed or double steal, and the fake bunt and steal.

For every one of these situations, a good defensive team has a play. For these plays to be effective, they must be thoroughly understood, practiced, expected, and used. The effective coach and team take care to do this.

The defense used by a team in each of these situations is generally determined by the coach, who then gives a sign or verbal instruction to a player—usually the catcher, third baseman, or first baseman—who in turn relays the play via a visual or verbal instruction to the rest of the team. The sign may be any number of things. Touches or swipes of body parts or zones are typical. Verbal cues are also used. Signals and verbal cues must be simple enough for all players to recognize and understand. On the other hand, they must be disguised well enough to conceal them from opponents.

Disguises can be sequences, hot signs, stop or off signs, or verbal indicators such as colors, teams, nicknames, or numbers. The clever use of disguise techniques can generally prevent an offense from knowing what defensive play is coming. Multiple sets of signs and verbal cues to interchange at any time is generally successful insurance against signal theft.

The list of plays and signs that follow are simplified and generic; it's up to coaches and players to decide how much time they're going to commit to learning, practicing, adapting, and using them. Really, the signs are the easy part. Hours of practice are required to perfect many plays. Strategy development is a constant challenge because of the number of variations required to meet every situation.

Only defensive plays are identified here. Space won't permit describing the intricate patterns and timing of the numerous potential plays. Besides knowing all the plays, each player must recognize the signs and verbal cues. Each player has timing responsibilities. Angles, spatial relationships, cues from teammates and opponents, and timing are all involved in the execution of any play.

The plays, signs, and verbal cues presented in tables A.2 and A.3 represent a portion of the vast system of defensive plays. Different coaches and teams will have their own priorities in building a system that suits them.

The infielders and pitcher acknowledge each signal by touching their caps.

Table A.2 Pickoffs

	Verbal cue	Decoy
Chase and release	"C and R"	"Color-number-town"
Daylight and sprint	"D and S"	(Mix up order)
Thrust and sprint	"T and S"	"Number-team-color"
Time and trap	"T and T"	"Team-number-color"
Chase, release, trap	"CRT"	"Team-color-number"
Catcher, time, trap	"CTT"	

Table A.3 Bunt Defense

	Verbal cue	Decoy
Standard	"One"	Coach rubs once across chest; catcher repeats
Priority for out: second base	"Two"	Coach touches nose, rubs across chest; catcher repeats
Special, priority for out: third base	"Three"	Coach covers mouth; catcher repeats
Suicide squeeze, priority for out: home plate	"Four"	Coach rubs nose, squeezes hands; catcher pats chest three times, pats abdomen
Pitchout	None	Coach touches nose, mouth, nose; catcher grasps mask at release

Start Sequence

Coach's signs: Touch right ear.

Catcher's signs: Mimic coach by touching right ear.

Sequence 1

Coach's signs: Touch right ear, touch nose.

Catcher's signs: Mimic coach by touching right ear, touching nose.

Situation: Runner on first base, no outs, priority out at second base.

Defense: Hot sign (nose).

a

b

Sequence 2

Coach's signs: Touch right ear, touch chin.

Catcher's signs: Mimic coach by touching right ear, touching chin.

Situation: Runner on first, no outs, priority out at second base.

Defense: Hot sign (chin).

a

b

Sequence 3

Coach's signs: Touch right ear, touch chest.

Catcher's signs: Mimic coach by touching right ear, touching chest.

Situation: Runners on first and second base, no outs, priority out at third base.

Defense: Hot sign (chest).

a

b

Sequence 4

Coach's signs: Touch right ear, touch belt.

Catcher's signs: Mimic coach by touching right ear, touching belt.

Situation: Runner at third base, no outs or 1 out, priority out at home plate.

Defense: Hot sign (belt).

a

b

Sequence 5

Coach's signs: Touch right ear, touch back of hand.

Catcher's signs: Mimic coach by touching right ear, touching back of hand.

Situation: Runner on third base, no outs or 1 out, priority out at first base.

Defense: Infield back (back of hand).

a

b

Sequence 6

Coach's signs: Touch right ear, touch elbow.

Catcher's signs: Mimic coach by touching right ear, touching elbow.

Situation: Runners on second and third base, no outs or 1 out, priority out at home plate.

Defense: Infield halfway in (elbow).

a

b

Sequence 7

Coach's signs: Touch right ear, touch face.

Catcher's signs: Mimic coach by touching right ear, touching face.

Situation: Bases loaded, no outs, double play priority.

Defense: Chase (face).

a

b

Sequence 8

Coach's signs: Touch right ear, touch eyes.

Catcher's signs: Mimic coach by touching right ear, touching eyes.

Situation: Bases loaded, no outs, double play priority.

Defense: Daylight (eyes).

Situation: Runner at third base, no outs or 1 out, priority out at home plate.

Defense: Infield in (eyes).

Sequence 9

Coach's signs: Touch right ear, touch right cheek, touch left cheek.

Catcher's signs: Mimic coach by touching right ear, touching right cheek, touching left cheek.

Situation: Bases loaded, no outs or 1 out, cut off run or double play priority.

Defense: Fake throw to third base and throw to first base.

Situation: Runners at second and third base, no outs or 1 out, get an out or cut off the run priorities.

Defense: Fake throw to third and throw to first.

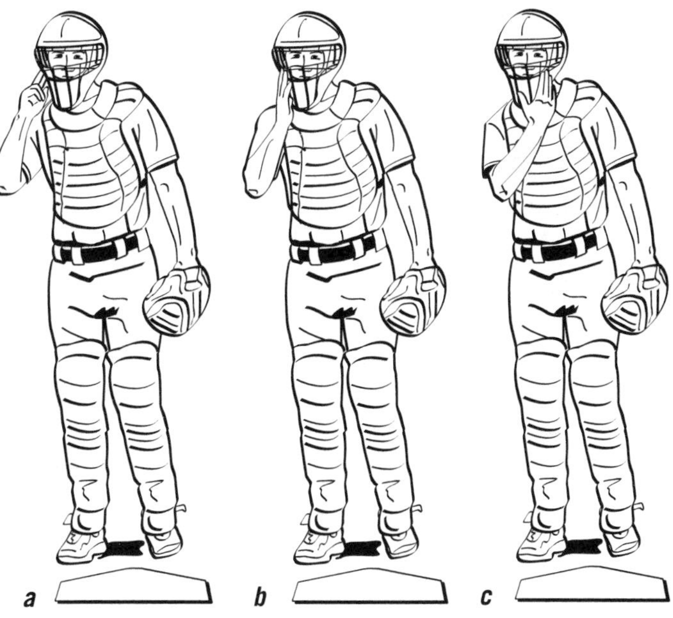

Sequence 10

Coach's signs: Touch right ear, touch tongue.

Catcher's signs: Mimic coach by touching right ear, touching tongue.

Situation: Bases loaded, no outs or 1 out, cut off run or double play priority.

Defense: Trap (tongue).

a

b

Sequence 11

Coach's signs: Touch right ear, touch straight hand.

Catcher's signs: Mimic coach by touching right ear, touching straight hand.

Situation: Bases loaded, no outs or 1 out, cut off run or double play priority.

Defense: Thrust (straight hand).

Situation: Runners on second and third base, no outs or 1 out, get an out or cut off run priorities.

Defense: Thrust (straight hand).

Situation: Bases loaded, any number of outs.

Defense: Pickoff to any base (straight hand).

a

b

Sequence 12

Coach's signs: Touch hat, touch face.

Catcher's signs: Mimic coach by touching hat, touching face.

Situation: Runners at first and third base, any number of outs.

Defense: Pickoff at first base (hat and face).

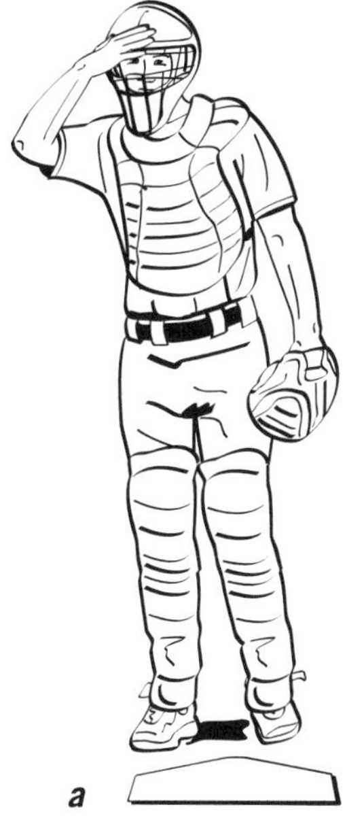

a

b

Sequence 13

Coach's signs: Touch hat, touch chin.

Catcher's signs: Mimic coach by touching hat, touching chin.

Situation: Runner at second base, any number of outs.

Defense: Pickoff at second base (hat and chin).

a

b

Sequence 14

Coach's signs: Touch hat, touch chest.

Catcher's signs: Mimic coach by touching hat, touching chest.

Situation: Runner at third base, any number of outs.

Defense: Pickoff at third base (hat and chest).

a

b

Sequence 15

Coach's signs: Touch hat, touch face, touch nose.

Catcher's signs: Mimic coach by touching hat, touching face, touching nose.

Situation: Runners at first and third base, any number of outs.

Defense: Pickoff at first base, fake (hat, face, nose).

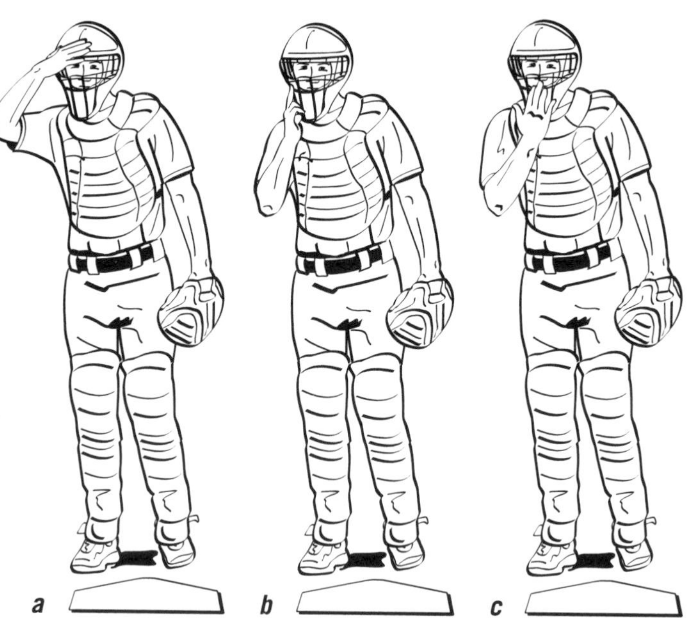

a *b* *c*

Sequence 16

Coach's signs: Touch hat.

Catcher's signs: Mimic coach by touching hat.

Situation: Runner at first base, any number of outs.

Defense: Pickoff at first base (hat).

To signal positioning for any play, the coach can use a set system of signals:

Cut off infield position: touch right ear, touch eyes.

Infield at halfway position with the outfield back: touch right ear, touch elbow.

Double-play depth, infield halfway: touch right ear, touch mouth.

Index

About the ABCA

The **American Baseball Coaches Association (ABCA)** is the largest baseball coaching organization in the world and includes hundreds of international members. The association's mission is to improve the level of baseball coaching worldwide. The ABCA assists in the promotion of baseball and acts as a sounding board and advocate on issues concerning the game. In addition, the ABCA promotes camaraderie and communication among all baseball coaches, from the amateur to professional levels. The ABCA also gives recognition to deserving players and coaches through several special sponsorship programs. It is an organization that has grown steadily in membership, prestige, and impact in recent years. The ABCA's headquarters is located in Mount Pleasant, Michigan.

About the Rawlings Gold Glove Award

Range. Arm. Agility. Serious leather. The top defensive players in baseball show these qualities every game. The Rawlings Gold Glove Award® is given to the best by those who best know how to evaluate performance. Rawlings established the Gold Glove Award to recognize the best fielders at each position. Every year managers and coaches of each Major League team select a squad of the best defensemen in their leagues, excluding their own teams.

In 2007, Rawlings will commemorate the award's 50th anniversary. The first Rawlings Gold Gloves were awarded to one player at each position across both leagues in 1957. Since 1958, the Rawlings Gold Glove Award has been presented annually to a lineup of nine players for both the American and National Leagues. Fifty years later, the Rawlings Gold Glove Award still stands for excellence. Here's to celebrating another 50 years of recognizing the "finest in the field."

About the Contributors

Charlie Greene, now retired, coached at Miami-Dade Community College from 1968 to 1997, leading the school to state championship titles in 1970, 1978, and 1981, and one NJCAA National Championship Title in 1981, for which he received the National Coach of the Year Award. In 1989, he was head coach of the U.S. national team. Greene posted a career record of 1,047-548 and is a member of the ABCA Hall of Fame.

Bob Bennett retired from coaching in 2002 with a career record of 1,302-759-4, ranking him seventh on the all-time Division I win list. In 34 years as head coach at Fresno State University, his teams had 32 winning seasons, won 17 conference championships, made 21 NCAA regional championship appearances, and played in two College World Series. Bennett was awarded 14 conference coach of the year awards and an NCAA Coach of the Year award in 1988. He coached 32 All-Americans, eight of whom were first-round draft picks. Bennett also served as head coach of the U.S. national team in 1983 and 1986.

Ed Flaherty has been head coach of the University of Southern Maine baseball program since 1986 and has established the Huskies program as one of the nation's finest with 16 post-season appearances. USM Baseball has won two national championships under Flaherty. Heading into the 2006 season, he has compiled a career record of 594-255-3 (.699 W-L pct.) Flaherty was inducted into the University of Maine Sports Hall of Fame in 1992, the State of Maine Baseball Hall of Fame in 1993, and the ABCA Hall of Fame in 2005. His instructional baseball camps are among the highest regarded in New England. Flaherty earned an undergraduate education degree with majors in history and math from the University of Maine. He holds a masters degree in administration from Southern Maine.

Davey Johnson was hired as a consultant to the team general manager of the Washington Nationals in June 2006. As the manager for Team USA baseball, Johnson led Team USA to a seventh-place finish out of an 18-team field in the 2005 Baseball World Cup, and he is also working to earn Team USA a spot in the 2008 Summer Olympics. A former second baseman and manager in Major League Baseball, Johnson played for the Baltimore Orioles, Atlanta Braves, Philadelphia Phillies, and Chicago Cubs. The four-time All Star and three time Gold Glove Award winner was also a very successful manager for the New York Mets, Cincinnati Reds, Baltimore Orioles, and Los Angeles Dodgers. Johnson was the first National League manager to win at least 90 games in each of his first five seasons, with the highlight being the World Series victory over the Boston Red Sox in 1986.

Ken Knutson became the winningest baseball coach in University of Washington history in 2004. With his 461-295-2 overall record, Knutson has a higher winning percentage (.609) than any Husky coach who headed up more than 85 games. In addition, his 13 seasons at the helm of his alma mater's baseball team have been the most successful stretch since the program's inception in 1901. During his tenure, Knutson has led the Dawgs to two Pacific-10 Conference championships, four Pac-10 Northern Division crowns, a second-place league finish, and two second-place division finishes. He has led Washington to within one game of its first College World Series appearance on three occasions. Six of Washington's eight all-time NCAA appearances have come under Knutson's watch. Knutson has been named the Pac-10 North Coach of the Year three times. He spent nine seasons with the Huskies as a player and assistant coach before taking over the duties of head coach.

Dr. Carroll Land has been the director of athletics at Point Loma Nazarene University since 1968. In 1962, he also served as the school's baseball coach after finishing an outstanding career as a pitcher for the Crusaders. His squads won back-to-back NAIA District 3 and Far West Region titles. Dr. Land is a member of the NAIA Hall of Fame, Pasadena/Point Loma Nazarene College Athletic Hall of Fame, and ABCA Hall of Fame. He received his bachelor degree from Pasadena College and went on to receive both his master's degree in education and PhD from the University of South Carolina. In 1998, the Crusader field was named Carroll B. Land Stadium by Point Loma Nazarene University.

Mike Maack was named head coach of the new Plano Blue Sox in 2006 and also serves as head varsity baseball coach for Prestonwood Christian Academy. Maack was a left-handed pitcher in the Minnesota Twins organization from 1982 to 1985 and coached in the collegiate ranks for 13 years as an assistant at Central Florida and the University of Tennessee and as the head coach at Tennessee Tech University. Since coming to Prestonwood Christian Academy in 2001, Maack's baseball teams have won a pair of District Championships and were the State Runner-Up in 2004. He was selected as the TAPPS 3A Coach of the Year in 2004.

Rich Maloney was named head baseball coach at the University of Michigan in 2002. He led the Wolverines to the Big Ten Tournament in each of his first three seasons at the helm. In his third season, Maloney also made his first appearance in the NCAA Tournament and earned his 350th career win. Maloney, who is 106-72 (.596) in three seasons at Michigan, has an overall career record of 362-216-1 (.627). His teams have won at least 30 games in each of his 10 seasons as a head coach, including all seven years at Ball State. Maloney was recognized as one of the Top Five Rising Coaches of NCAA Division I Baseball by *Baseball America* while at Ball State in 2001. A third team All-American as a senior shortstop at Western Michigan, Maloney earned two degrees at Western Michigan in communications and journalism and in English. He was named to WMU's Athletic Hall of Fame in 2004.

Jim Penders is the University of Connecticut's head baseball coach. Penders served as an assistant coach for the Huskies for seven years, during which time the Huskies posted winning seasons in each of those campaigns. As an assistant coach, Penders coordinated the Huskies recruiting of student-athletes, served as the hitting coach, and worked with the catchers. A standout on the baseball field for the Huskies during his undergraduate career, Penders was a four-year letter winner for the Huskies. He was cocaptain of the 1994 UConn squad that won the Big East Conference tournament, and the Huskies advanced to the NCAA Championship in both his junior and senior years. Penders graduated from UConn with a degree in political science and went on to earn his master's degree from the UConn School of Education.

Sam Piraro was named the San Jose State head coach in the summer of 1986 and has since become the winningest head baseball coach in San Jose State University history. Piraro is the first to guide the Spartans to multiple NCAA Tournament appearances and Western Athletic Conference pennants. As the first and only San Jose State baseball coach with more than 600 victories, his teams have an overall record of 620-469-6 in 19 seasons. He is also the only Spartan baseball coach to lead teams to seven consecutive .500-or-better seasons. In 1997, Piraro was named the Western Athletic Conference Coach of the Year and *Louisville Slugger* WAC Coach of the Year. Piraro has served as a NCAA Regional Advisor and a voting member of the *Collegiate Baseball* rankings panel and was selected to represent the West Region on the NCAA Tournament Selection Committee for the 2006 season. Piraro, an infielder on the 1971 and 1972 Spartan teams, earned his bachelor's and master's degrees from San Jose State University.

Steve Smith has been head coach of Baylor's baseball program since 1994. In his first 11 years, Smith guided the program to unprecedented heights, including the most successful eight-year run in the program's 100-year history and a College World Series appearance in 2005. He has compiled a 418-258-1 career record, all at Baylor, and holds the best winning percentage of any coach in Baylor baseball history. Smith has led Baylor to seven NCAA Regional appearances, three NCAA Super Regional appearances, one College World Series appearance, and two Big 12 Conference titles. In 2006 Smith was named Big 12 Conference coach of the year by the *Dallas Morning News, Fort Worth Star-Telegram, San Antonio Express-News,* and *Waco Tribune-Herald.* Following the 2005 season, Smith served as head coach of the USA Baseball National Team. He was named the 2000 Big 12 coach of the year after guiding the Bears to their first outright conference title in 77 years.

Scott Stricklin became the 16th head baseball coach at Kent State in 2004. In 2005, he led the Golden Flashes to a 33-win season, the second most victories by a MAC-East team. Stricklin arrived at Kent State after serving his previous three seasons as assistant coach and recruiting coordinator at Georgia Tech, where he landed a recruiting class that was ranked No. 1 in the nation by both *Baseball America* and *Collegiate Baseball* in 2002. In 2003, Stricklin helped lead the Yellow Jackets to the Atlantic Coast Conference championship in the first triple-header in ACC history. A class-A all-star in 1994, Stricklin played five seasons of minor league baseball. He played the 1994 and 1995 seasons in the Twins organization, reaching the triple-A level. Stricklin lettered three seasons as a catcher at Kent State. Stricklin graduated magna cum laude from Kent State in 1995 with a bachelor's degree in marketing.

Jerry Weinstein began his fifth year as an assistant coach at Cal Poly in charge of the pitchers and catchers in 2006. He compiled an 831-208-12 record in 23 seasons as head coach at Sacramento City College, guiding the Panthers to 16 conference championships, two co-conference titles, a state title in 1988, and a national crown in 1998. His 831 career wins is No. 1 among all California community college baseball coaches. Weinstein also has served as assistant coach for two U.S. Olympic teams (1992 and 1996) and one U.S. Pan American Games team (1987). He directed the 2005 U.S. team to a gold medal at the Maccabiah Games. Weinstein is a member of the California Community College Baseball Hall of Fame and Sacramento City College Sports Hall of Fame. He was named National Community College Baseball Coach of the Year in 1988 and 1998. Weinstein earned his bachelor's degree in history at UCLA in 1965 and earned a master's degree in physical education at UCLA in 1969.